PICASSO'S
Les Demoiselles d'Avignon

Picasso's *Les Demoiselles d'Avignon* has long been recognized as one of the most significant paintings of the twentieth century. This volume brings together essays from a variety of methodological and topical perspectives. John Golding introduces the critical history of the *Demoiselles*. Yve-Alain Bois finds in the painting the presence of trauma and opens the way to a psychoanalytical exploration. Tamar Garb asks what it could mean to women, focusing on Gertrude Stein as one of the painting's first spectators. Patricia Leighten and David Lomas explore the conjunction of prostitution and African themes from different postcolonial perspectives. Christopher Green asks what the confrontation of the European and the non-European could signify and whether this Picasso work can still be meaningfully linked to the grand narrative of modernist history. Through these various analyses, the contributors explore the power and significance of *Les Demoiselles d'Avignon*, situating the work within twentieth-century art history as a whole and debates over primitivism, sexuality, and stylistic change.

Christopher Green is Professor of the History of Art at the Courtauld Institute of Art, University of London. A fellow of the British Academy, he has served as curator for several major exhibitions, including *Juan Gris*, and is author of *Cubism and Its Enemies*, which received the Mitchell Prize in 1987.

MASTERPIECES OF WESTERN PAINTING

This series serves as a forum for the reassessment of important paintings in the Western tradition that span a period from the Renaissance to the twentieth century. Each volume focuses on a single work and includes an introduction outlining its general history, as well as a selection of essays that examine the work from a variety of methodological perspectives. Demonstrating how and why these paintings have such enduring value, the volumes also offer new insights into their meaning for contemporaries and their subsequent reception.

VOLUMES IN THE SERIES

Masaccio's "Trinity," edited by Rona Goffen, Rutgers University

Raphael's "School of Athens," edited by Marcia Hall, Temple University

Titian's "Venus of Urbino," edited by Rona Goffen, Rutgers University

Caravaggio's "Saint Paul," edited by Gail Feigenbaum, New Orleans Museum of Art

Rembrandt's "Bathsheba with David's Letter," edited by Ann Jensen Adams, University of California, Santa Barbara

David's "Marat," edited by William Vaughan, Birkbeck College, University of London, and Helen Weston, University College, London

Manet's "Le Déjeuner sur l'herbe," edited by Paul Hayes Tucker, University of Massachusetts, Boston

Picasso's "Les Demoiselles d'Avignon," edited by Christopher Green, Courtauld Institute of Art, University of London

PICASSO'S
Les Demoiselles d'Avignon

Edited by

CHRISTOPHER GREEN
Courtauld Institute of Art, University of London

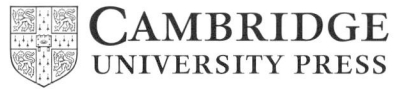

CAMBRIDGE
UNIVERSITY PRESS

PUBLISHED BY THE PRESS SYNDICATE OF THE UNIVERSITY OF CAMBRIDGE
The Pitt Building, Trumpington Street, Cambridge, United Kingdom

CAMBRIDGE UNIVERSITY PRESS
The Edinburgh Building, Cambridge CB2 2RU, UK
40 West 20th Street, New York, NY 10011–4211, USA
10 Stamford Road, Oakleigh, VIC 3166, Australia
Ruiz de Alarcón 13, 28014 Madrid, Spain
Dock House, The Waterfront, Cape Town 8001, South Africa

http://www.cambridge.org

First published 2001

Printed in the United Kingdom at the University Press, Cambridge

Typefaces Electra 10.25/13 pt. and Futura   *System* QuarkXPress® [GH]

A catalogue record for this book is available from the British Library.

Library of Congress Cataloging-in-Publication Data

Picasso's Les demoiselles d'Avignon / [edited by] Christopher Green.
    p. cm. – (Masterpieces of Western painting)
  Includes bibliographical references and index.
    ISBN 0-521-58367-5 – ISBN 0-521-58669-0 (pbk.)
    1. Picasso, Pablo, 1881-1973. Demoiselles d'Avignon. 2. Picasso, Pablo,
1881–1973 – Criticism and interpretation. 3. Cubism – France. I. Title: Demoiselles
d'Avignon. II. Picasso, Pablo, 1881–1973. III. Green, Christopher, 1943 June 11 – IV.
Series.

ND553.P5 A785 2001
759.4 – dc21

00-054702

ISBN 0 521 58367 5 hardback
ISBN 0 521 58669 0 paperback

Contents

Illustrations

Contributors

YVE-ALAIN BOIS is Joseph Pulitzer, Jr., Professor of Modern Art at Harvard University. An influential critic and essayist, he was co-founder of the French periodical *Macula*. His anthology *Painting as Model* appeared in 1990 (M.I.T. Press). In 1994–5 he co-curated the retrospective of Piet Mondrian in The Hague, Washington, D.C., and New York, contributing a major essay to the catalogue. In 1998 he curated *Matisse and Picasso* at the Kimbell Art Museum, Fort Worth, Texas, and published the accompanying book (Flamarion).

TAMAR GARB is Professor of History of Art at University College London. Publications on Berthe Morisot and women impressionists in 1986–7 established her as a major new art historian focusing on issues of gender. Her *Sisters of the Brush: Women's Artistic Culture in Late Nineteenth Century Paris* (Yale University Press) appeared in 1994. Most recently, she has published *Bodies of Modernity: Figure and Flesh in Fin-de-Siècle France* (Thames & Hudson, 1998).

JOHN GOLDING is a painter and art historian. His *Cubism. A History and an Analysis 1907–1914* (Faber & Faber), first published in 1959, remains a key text on cubism. He has been a regular contributor to the *New York Review of Books*, and in 1994 published a collection of his essays, *Visions of the Modern* (Thames & Hudson). In 1994 he co-curated the exhibition *Picasso: Sculptor/Painter* at the Tate Gallery, London. His 1998 Mellon lectures, delivered at the National Gallery of Art, Washington, D.C., have been published as *Paths to the Absolute* (Thames & Hudson, 2000).

CHRISTOPHER GREEN is Professor of the History of Art at the Courtauld Institute, University of London. His *Cubism and Its Enemies* of 1987 (Yale University Press) won the Mitchell Prize for a book on twentieth-century art. He curated the retrospective of Juan Gris held in London, Stuttgart, and Otterlo in 1992–3 and wrote the accompanying book (Gerd Hatje and Yale University Press). In 1999 he curated *Art Made Modern: Roger Fry's Vision of Art* at the Courtauld Gallery, London, editing the catalogue (Merryl-Holberton). His *Art in France, 1900–40* (Pelican History of Art, Yale University Press) appeared in 2000. He has also published a novel, *One Man Show* (Little Brown, 1995).

PATRICIA LEIGHTEN is Professor of the History of Art at Duke University. Her *Re-Ordering the Universe: Picasso and Anarchism, 1897–1914* (Princeton University Press) appeared in 1989. She has published in *The Art Bulletin*, *The Oxford Art Journal*, and *Gazette des Beaux-Arts*, among others, and edited the *Art Journal* special issue, 'Revising Cubism' (Winter 1988). She is co-author of *Cubism and Culture* (Thames & Hudson) and *A Cubism Reader* (Chicago University Press), both forthcoming. An earlier version of her essay in this book won the Arthur Kinsley Porter Prize.

DAVID LOMAS is lecturer in the Department of Art History and Archaeology at the University of Manchester. He has emerged as a specialist on surrealism and interwar art in France with essays published in a number of recent anthologies. Trained as a medical doctor, his essay in this book arises out of an interest in the interaction of art and medicine in the nineteenth and twentieth centuries. In 2000 he published *The Haunted Self. Surrealism, Psychoanalysis, Subjectivity* (Yale University Press).

PICASSO'S
Les Demoiselles d'Avignon

CHRISTOPHER GREEN

An Introduction to *Les Demoiselles d'Avignon*

THE ARTIST, THE WORK, AND THE SPECTATOR

As an artist, Pablo Picasso was well prepared for fame. There was always a spotlight on him. His stage might have been small and without glamour to begin with, but he was always aware that he had an audience. Even in the late 1890s, as an apprentice modernist in Barcelona, he was recognised to be a prodigious talent. He first showed in Paris at the age of nineteen, when he was selected for the official exhibition of Spanish art at the Universal Exhibition of 1900. Within a year, two of the new galleries showing young 'independent' painting in Paris, Berthe Weill's and Ambroise Vollard's, were buying from him. In May 1901 Vollard gave Picasso a show all to himself, a rare accolade. Between 1901 and 1904, he kept aloof from commercial success, painting underclass poverty from the vantage point of bohemian poverty mostly in Spain, but after he settled finally in Paris in April 1904, a circle of collectors and dealers keen to buy from him formed quickly enough. By 1906, among them was the American writer Gertrude Stein, whose portrait he completed that autumn (Fig. 15). Her support and that of her brothers and sister-in-law (Leo, Michael, and Sarah) gave him a position comparable to that of the older Henri Matisse, acknowledged leader of the 'Fauves', for they had been among the first buyers of Matisse's 'Fauve' work in 1905. Though still only in his mid-twenties, it was, therefore, as an emerging modernist leader – at least for a select few – that Picasso started work early in 1907 on the huge, almost square painting that would become known as *Les Demoiselles d'Avignon*[1] (Fig. 1).

By 1914, Picasso was as famous a modernist leader as Matisse, the acknowledged inventor of another major -ism, 'cubism'. It took a further twenty-five years for the *Demoiselles* to begin to emerge as one of the most important paintings not only in his oeuvre but in the early history of modernism altogether. And yet, even while he was at work on the canvas, before the summer of 1907, talk of it had reached not only Vollard, but the young German dealer Daniel-Henry Kahnweiler, newly launched in Paris, who would become Picasso's dealer, and Félix Fénéon, manager of the Galerie Bernheim-Jeune, who would become Matisse's. It may not have been exhibited at that time, but many came to see it in Picasso's Montmartre studio, artists and writers besides dealers and collectors, friends like the poet André Salmon and the painters André Derain and Georges Braque, visitors like the English painter Augustus John. As Picasso himself had, the *Demoiselles* made an impact before it became famous, and, for its small but influential audience, that impact was so great because it was so dramatically different from anything Picasso himself or any other artist working in Paris had so far painted.

There was much about the *Demoiselles* that was not different. Picasso had painted prostitutes before, and brothel subjects were a late-nineteenth-century genre. He had also taken on the theme of sexuality and danger before. His major painting of 1903, *Life*, uses allegory to do the job. And he had used expressive colour and formal distortion before too. What differentiated this picture was the way its distortions challenged the most basic assumptions about the pictorial depiction of figures and of space, and the sheer immediacy of its confrontation with so brazen a subject. The force of those differences was enhanced by the openness with which it alluded to painting from the European past: to post-Renaissance figure painting from Titian and El Greco to Ingres. It was enhanced too by the equal openness with which the picture alluded to a non-European present, what then were called the 'primitive' cultures of Africa and Oceania. The *Demoiselles* simultaneously invoked and demolished the canon celebrated in the great museums where Picasso had trained his eye, the Prado in Madrid and the Louvre in Paris.

In the mythology of modernist and postmodern art history, the status of Picasso's *Demoiselles d'Avignon* as a painting that marks a dramatic break from the past and a new twentieth century beginning is now unquestioned. Its immediacy, the directness with which the stares of each individual prostitute invite the spectator in, underlines its role in one of the central developments of art in the twentieth century: the empowering of the spectator. We, the work's spectators, are made the centre of attention.

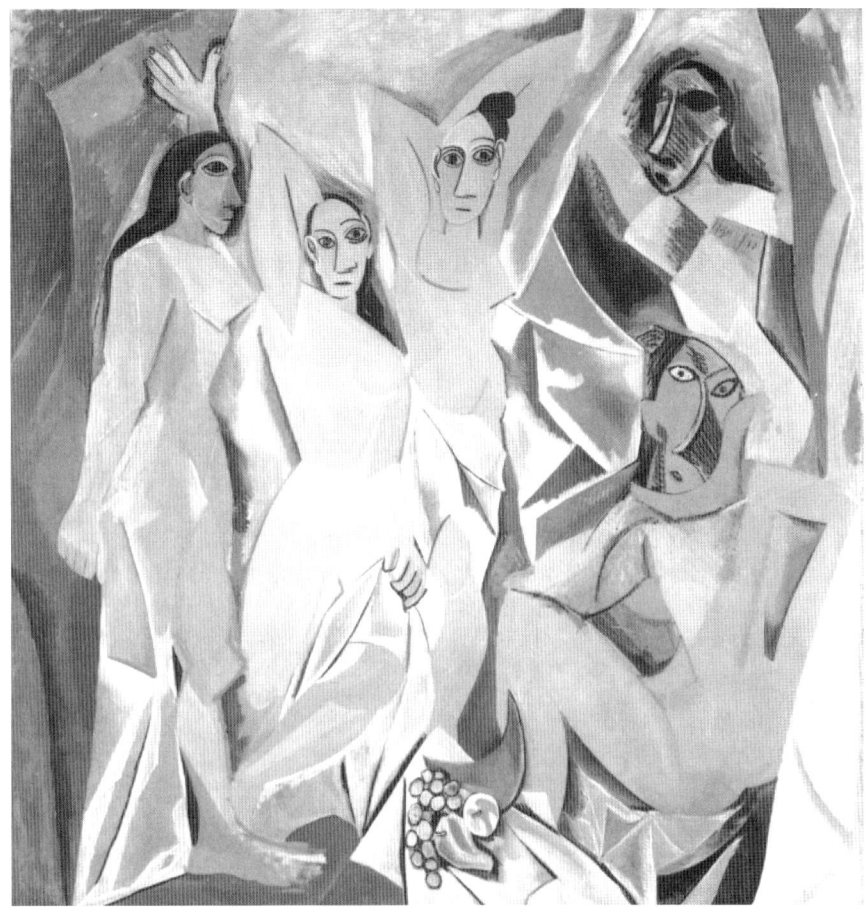

FIGURE 1. Pablo Picasso, *Les Demoiselles d'Avignon*, June/July 1907. Oil on canvas, 243.9 × 233.7 cm. Museum of Modern Art, New York. Acquired through the Lillie P. Bliss Bequest. (Photo © 1998 The Museum of Modern Art, New York.)

The work becomes not so much Picasso's statement as a challenge to us to respond and, by responding, to give it meaning. In modernism altogether, art (not merely visual art alone) has been reoriented, placing the onus on the relationship not between the artist and the work of art, but rather between the work and the spectator. Despite this crucial shift, and the role of the *Demoiselles* in marking it, writing about the picture has been as much devoted to constructing a narrative of its conception and to exploring its relationship with Picasso's biography, as to the analysis of the kind of experience it offers. Picasso and the way he produced the painting can still be made to seem more central than we – the spectator – and the way we might experience it.

THE MAKING OF *LES DEMOISELLES D'AVIGNON*

In its beginnings *Les Demoiselles d'Avignon* did not so immediately challenge the spectator, and the story of its conception and development in drawings, oil sketches, and on the canvas itself maps a long drawn-out transition from obsessive composing in self-contained frameworks, to the making of an image that is only in the end opened out to its spectators.

The main reason for the intensity with which the conception and the making of the picture has been studied is the completeness of its documentation. The sheer quantity of material related to it first became clear in 1988 with the major exhibition centred on the *Demoiselles* organised by the Musée Picasso in Paris, and shown there and in Barcelona.[2] The two-volume catalogue of this exhibition reproduced every known sketch or study then considered to be related to the work.[3]

Included were drawings from sixteen sketchbooks placed in sequence as they appear in the books along with ideas for other pictures and unrelated studies; there were also dozens of other studies and related works on canvas and wood as well as paper. Besides this mass of material, there was evidence in the form of radiographs and infrared photographs of an oil study on canvas beneath an otherwise only loosely related painting of 1907 (*Woman with a Large Ear*).[4] Much of this material could be seen in the exhibition.

Given the fundamental importance of this event in 1988, it seems right that the next two chapters in this book (by Golding and by Bois) should first have been published as reviews of the show: they represent early attempts to come to terms with the exponential growth in knowledge about the *Demoiselles* that it generated. In their immediacy, those responses make it possible actually to place the *Demoiselles* in a visual setting, surrounded, as it was, by clusters of images directly related to it, from Picasso's own sketches to major masterpieces like Ingres's *The Turkish Bath*. The work of Hélène Seckel, Judith Cousins, Brigitte Léal, Pierre Daix, and William Rubin in preparing and writing the catalogue of the 1988 exhibition has made it possible also to place the picture in a clear narrative telling the story of its making.[5] Obviously that story has to be simplified for an introduction like this, but such a narrative is the necessary preliminary to any discussion of the picture's meanings – of how its most influential spectators have interpreted it.

Picasso spent the autumn of 1906 and the winter of 1906–7 in Paris; he was working with styles and ideas he had explored during the summer of 1906, which he had spent with his partner, Fernande Olivier, in the remote Pyrenean village of Gósol in Catalonia. He was especially concerned with a reductively sculptural set of procedures for constructing the head he had adapted from ancient Iberian relief carvings excavated at Osuna in southern Spain then recently on show in the Louvre.[6] This new masklike treatment of the head, seen famously in his *Portrait of Gertrude Stein* (Fig. 15), engendered a newly massive treatment of torsos and limbs in, for example, *Two Nudes* (Fig. 7). What seems to be the first ensemble study for the *Demoiselles* appears in a sketchbook dominated by figure drawings in this primitivising 'Iberian' manner (Fig. 11); it includes sketches related to *Two Nudes*.[7] Probably jotted down late in 1906 or very early in 1907, the study presents a seven-figure composition in a horizontal format that Picasso was to develop compulsively in a series of sketchbook and loose-leaf drawings (including the much more definitive drawing heightened with pastel in Basel – Fig. 9), in a tiny oil study on wood, a lost oil study on canvas, and an oil study on canvas, discovered after the 1988 exhibition, concealed under a 1907 still life, *Jars with Lemon*.[8] The idea seems to have engaged him through to March 1907, and led to many studies of the individual figures, sometimes seen from different viewpoints, as well as of the ensemble (Figs. 12, 24, and 28).

In the seven-figure studies, five female nudes appear with two clothed male figures. Picasso later identified the clothed figure entering from the left and pulling back the curtain as a medical student and the clothed figure seated in the centre as a sailor.[9] Other sketchbook drawings show the 'medical student' with a skull (Fig. 8); in the 'first' study and the Basel drawing with pastel he carries a book. Beside the sailor, in the middle ground is a table on which is a Catalan *porón* (a drinking vessel) and a sliced melon; in the foreground of the Basel drawing is a table with a vase of flowers on it. The poses of four of the figures relate closely to their equivalents in the five-figure *Demoiselles* as it was painted: the medical student enters and raises his hand much as the nude entering from the left would; the central nude stands with her arms raised much as would the central 'demoiselle'; and the two 'demoiselles' on the right – one entering between curtains from behind, the other crouched with her legs apart to show her sex to the sailor – are posed much as they would be. In the lost oil sketch the croucher looks out at the spectator, but in the other seven-figure studies, both she and the nude entering above her seem to look across towards the medical student, who in turn seems not to look outwards at the spectator, so that the drama is to some extent contained within the curtained theatrical space. These are gazes and movements that suggest encounters between the figures: actions and interactions involving the medical student and the sailor, onto which the spectator looks.

Probably around May 1907, Picasso produced a group of sketchbook and loose-leaf ensemble studies in which he cut the number of figures to six, still within a horizontal format (Fig. 12). There remained here enough intimation of the transverse interaction between figures to suggest their own self-contained drama, but, besides the exclusion of the nude originally behind the medical student, two crucial changes occurred: first, in some of the sketches, the medical student was transformed into a female curtain-raiser and stripped, becoming another nude 'demoiselle', second, the chair in which one of the 'demoiselles' had been seated was removed, and she was placed rather ambiguously, half sitting, half reclining, in an indeterminate space beneath an arched fold in the curtain. These six-figure studies retain the sailor with the table beside him (and sometimes the melon), who is now so crammed in among the nudes that in some cases the 'seated demoiselle' seems to sit on his knee. It is with the sailor's removal and that of his melon-laden table that the five-figure ensemble of the *Demoiselles* in its large-scale painted form emerges, and it does so all at once in the oil study concealed beneath *Woman with a Large Ear* and in a quickly but confidently worked watercolour in Philadelphia (Fig. 10). These are usually dated May–June and June 1907. The Philadelphia watercolour is held together by flat linear rhythms, as had been most of the ensemble studies, and it is far from sculptural, but the styling of the figures remains Iberian. There may still be a transverse exchange of glances between the curtain puller on the left and the nude entering from the right, but the head of the croucher has now been swivelled unequivocally round so that her gaze can meet the spectator's like those of the two central 'demoiselles'. This is less obviously so in the concealed oil study, but something else of great significance to the move from a self-contained narrative to a direct confrontation between painting and spectator has happened here: the original horizontal format (a narrative format) has given way to the squarish format of the large canvas (a format Rubin has associated with the iconic).[10]

Picasso seems to have made his final moves in conceiving and making the painting in June–July 1907. They involved sketchbook and loose-leaf drawings and an oil study of the head of the croucher, but most importantly were made on the canvas itself, which was almost certainly painted in two campaigns.[11] X-rays show that Picasso first painted the work in the flattened Iberian style of the Philadelphia watercolour, leaving the two central 'demoiselles' thus. He then returned to the canvas (perhaps as much as four or five weeks later) and repainted the curtain-raiser on the left and the nude entering on the right with the croucher in front of her. This overpainting involved the heads above all, which were given an altogether different aspect, utterly unlike the oval Iberian heads of the two central nudes with their calm almond eyes. The curtain-raiser on the left was given a lidless full-face eye that looks more outwards than across, in a way that has been compared with 'Tupupau', the female ancestor spirit in Paul Gauguin's Tahitian painting of 1892, *The Spirit of the Dead Watching*, as well as with Egyptian precedents.[12] Both the nude entering on the right and the croucher now have wedge-shaped noses of snoutish ugliness, flanked by thick green hatched lines that cut across stridently contrasting reds and reddish browns. The head of the croucher has been swivelled round full face above her back and haunches, which remain facing inwards so that the head appears almost severed from the shoulders. Her nose too is twisted back to cut bladelike into her cheek as it turns towards us, a change made after brutally incisive studies of this head alone (Fig. 13). Her eyes are out of alignment and stare fixedly. Despite Picasso's later denials of any influence from "Art nègre" in the *Demoiselles*, the changes to the heads of the nudes on the right are now agreed to relate to immensely powerful but generalised recent memories of West African and Oceanic sculpture in the Musée d'Ethnographie du Trocadéro in Paris (Figs. 5 and 17), which it is assumed he first visited just before he launched into his final campaign on the canvas.[13] The immediacy of the confrontation between painting and spectator produced by his five-figure ensemble with their outgoing orientation in their almost square format was immeasurably increased by the brutal directness of the Africanized style he gave the two heads on the right.

As postscript to this account of the making of the painting, it is worth adding that the stylistic contradictions introduced by Picasso's second campaign on the canvas – especially the confrontation between the two Iberian central nudes and the two Africanized nudes on the right – has led to arguments about its status as a finished painting that will always remain unresolved.[14] Whether he regarded it as finished or not, he was happy to show it to visitors from the autumn of 1907; it was a 'complete' enough statement for him to encourage responses. When the picture was first publicly exhibited, however, which was not until 1916, it was only in rather restricted circumstances. It would not be until it was shown at the Museum of Modern Art, New York, in 1939 that it would begin to acquire the gigantic public reputation it now possesses internationally.[15] If titles are taken to complete pictures, it is significant that the painting's title – *Les Demoiselles d'Avignon* – was not attached by Picasso himself but by one of the first to write about the picture, his friend André Salmon, who attached it on the occasion of its first showing in 1916. Picasso disliked the coy prudishness of Salmon's title; he is said himself routinely to have referred to the picture simply as *'mon bordel'* (my brothel).[16]

READING THE PICTURE

Four of the *Demoiselles d'Avignon*'s most important commentators are conspicuous by their absence from this selection of essays: Daniel-Henry Kahnweiler, Alfred H. Barr, Jr., Leo Steinberg, and William Rubin. My introduction to the major differences between readings of the painting takes special account, therefore, of their contributions. A central concern is the question raised at the outset: the relationship between the artist, the work, and the spectator.

Broadly, the first serious historical assessments – Kahnweiler's in 1920 and Barr's in 1939 – constructed a passionately engaged Picasso who was ultimately concerned with finding new solutions to the problem of representing space and solid in two dimensions, solutions that shifted the emphasis from *what* was depicted to the *how* of depiction, to the making of pictorialized figures and spaces.[17] Biography was not centrally important to understanding the achievement of this artist in the *Demoiselles*; what was important were, on the one hand, the *artistic* stimuli that inspired him, hence Barr's stress on the influence of Cézanne, El Greco, and African sculpture from the Ivory Coast and the French Congo (emphatically thought of as 'art'), and, on the other hand, the ways in which the development and painting of the composition led to the flattening of space, the reductive emblematisation of figures, and their radical distortion by the (partial) shifting of viewpoints (most telling of all, the extraordinary dislocation of the frontal staring head from the rearview shoulders of the croucher).

This pictorially innovative Picasso operating most essentially in the aesthetic sphere was the Picasso of the *Demoiselles* that was far more comprehensively put together by John Golding, first of all in his article on the painting of 1958 (to the influences of El Greco, Cézanne, and 'Africa', Golding added importantly those of Derain and Iberian sculpture).[18] And it is in Golding's article along with his still fundamental 1959 study of cubism that the spectator suggested by Kahnweiler's and Barr's *Demoi-*

selles d'Avignon emerges most clearly.[19] He or she is implicitly there in the reader for whom Golding writes: this spectator is not explicitly gendered, is to be reflective as well as artistically sophisticated, and to seek not simply to experience the picture visually but to analyse particular ways of viewing it in response to its pictorial innovations. For Golding in the late 1950s as much as for Barr and Kahnweiler, the key question was the *Demoiselles*'s relationship with cubism. Kahnweiler calls it 'the beginning of cubism'; Golding sees it as in no sense a cubist picture, but as a work that opens the way to cubism by adumbrating certain of the pictorial practices we call cubist, above all the compression and flattening of space and the use of multiple viewpoints. The picture produced by this intuitive yet reflective Picasso is essentially to be viewed as opening up new possibilities. It remains a moot point whether the *Demoiselles d'Avignon* can be approached as eloquent in its own right *and* as especially significant because of its developmental relationship with cubism. In this book, Yve-Alain Bois plays down the connection; John Golding and I continue to see it as important.

The first to demand that the work be detached from evolutionary narratives of cubism was Leo Steinberg. His two-part article first published in *Art News* in 1972, and republished in revised form in *October* in 1988, literally reinvented the *Demoiselles* as the painting of a different Picasso that invited a different kind of spectatorship.[20] Steinberg asserted that for fifty years 'we have been training our eyes to ricochet off the *Demoiselles* toward cubism'. 'A more focused approach', he wrote, 'may habituate us to seeing Picasso's "naked problems" once again as nude women'.

Before Steinberg's essay, the *Demoiselles d'Avignon* was the birthplace of cubism, the marker of an epocal shift from content to form in modern painting; after Steinberg's essay, it has become the marker of an epocal shift to a new kind of engagement with sexuality, one whose immediacy was unprecedented in the history of painting. The Picasso behind such a picture is a man whose biography might be as important as his artistic influences; psychoanalysis might be as important to grasping such a picture's meanings as practical criticism. And, even more so than in the earlier writing of Barr or Golding, those meanings are to be found in the spectator as much as in Picasso, for the spectator constructed by Steinberg's essay is not merely an implied reader looking in reflectively from outside, but the one introduced at the beginning of this Introduction, the spectator as the ultimate maker of meaning – in a sense, the picture's own centre of attention.

'No modern painting engages you', Steinberg writes, 'with such brutal immediacy. . . . The unity of the picture, famous for its internal disruptions, resides above all in the startled consciousness of a viewer who sees himself seen'. If, he argues, those disruptions are resolved, they are only resolved by the engagement of the spectator, and this is made possible by the very separateness of the five figures with each of whom the spectator can engage. Instead of those transverse interrelations between figures that keep the drama within a unified narrative space in the seven- and six-figure studies, we have five figures, argues Steinberg, in their own separate spaces, and hence five outwardly projected relationships, which invite the spectator in. And just as the nudes turn back into prostitutes on hire to male clients, Steinberg's spectator is transformed from a reflective analyst into a sexual being, explicitly male. Where Barr had seen the shift from the few seven- and six-figure ensemble studies he knew to the five-figure painting as a move from an allegorical to a more immediately pictorial mode, Steinberg saw that shift as a move from the more detached representation of a sexual theme to one that urgently demanded a direct sexual involvement from the spectator.

It was Barr who discovered that Picasso originally gave the male figures in the early studies identities as a medical student and a sailor, and that the medical student carried a skull in some variants; for him, this identified the initial idea as an allegory of vice and virtue, which was effaced by the removal of both the student and the sailor. For Steinberg, the medical student represented the reflective observer and the sailor the participant, and their removal finally gave the painting over to participation: the participation of the spectator.

Far from being a probing analyst, Steinberg's spectator takes the place of the prostitute's client – the surrogate of the sailor – and the prowlike table that thrusts into the brothel from the spectator's space partakes of his phallic, penetrative energy. Figurative distortion and spatial condensation give the picture, not proto-cubist interest, but a vehemence that produces in the engaged spectator, he claims, an experience of total immersion, what he calls 'the orgiastic immersion' of 'Dionysian release'.

Since Steinberg's article appeared in 1972, writing on the *Demoiselles* has been transformed – the picture has been resexualized and the nature of its spectators has become centrally important. The essays selected for this book are all (including John Golding's) post-Steinberg pieces. At the same time, all of them, except perhaps Golding's, are indebted to and yet stand against what has been a (perhaps *the*) major presence in post-Steinberg writing, the contribution of William Rubin. Rubin's research on Picasso and the *Demoiselles* is fundamental to much that is found here, but the biographical cast he has given his interpretations is not. His achievement has been to build a wonderfully rich immediate context for the understanding of the painting in relation to Picasso, and a great deal of the material he has adduced is, in fact, relevant to an understanding of the painting in relation not only to Picasso but to its other spectators, both current and of the period before 1914. It is for this reason that, despite often profound methodological differences, Rubin's research is referenced so frequently in the pieces that follow, which tend to privilege, not the autobiographical in the picture, but its relationship with its spectators. This is mostly so too of other important recent pieces that focus on or take in the *Demoiselles*, but which are not included in this book. The contributions of Anna Chave, Hal Foster, David Fraser-Jenkins, Ron Johnson, and Michael Leja should all be mentioned; details of them are given in the bibliography.[21] John Richardson's treatment of the painting has, of course, been in the context of a biography.

A destabilized male Picasso is an important factor in both Yve-Alain Bois's and Tamar Garb's pieces, but Bois uses psychoanalytic theory to bring out the work's potential impact on all engaged spectators,[22] and Garb explores its relationship with one particular spectator, Gertrude Stein, in order to focus the unresolved problem of gender in its viewing as well as its making (what kind of a relationship can women have with a resexualized *Demoiselles* so explicitly aimed at male viewers?).[23] Picasso's psychic condition is far less a factor in Leighten's and Lomas's essays. They are concerned much more exclusively with the social, political, and ideological conditions for the making of meaning in the period, most essentially as those conditions inflect the conjunction of prostitution and 'Africa' found in the 'demoiselles'.[24] My own essay, written like Garb's specially for this book, follows on from Leighten's and Lomas's, and attempts to find a way of bringing together a discussion of its 'primitivizing' and sexual themes with a discussion of how it could be connected with cubism.[25] I have tried to remember Kahnweiler, Barr, and Golding (whose inclusion in this selection reinforces the continuing importance of his perspective) as well as to respond to Steinberg and after; and I have tried to do so without falling back on compromise. One thing will always be clear about the *Demoiselles d'Avignon*: it excludes utterly all compromise.

NOTES

1 The bohemian image of the young Picasso was most effectively disseminated early on by Fernande Olivier, his partner from 1904 to 1912. See Fernande Olivier, *Picasso et ses amis* (Paris, 1933), translated by Jane Miller as *Picasso and His Friends* (London, 1964). New light was thrown on his early career as a career, and especially on his relations with dealers and collectors, in Michael C. Fitzgerald, *Mak-*

ing Modernism. Picasso and the Creation of the Market for Twentieth-Century Modernism (Berkeley, Los Angeles, and London, 1995).

2   Paris: Musée Picasso, 26 January–18 April 1988; Barcelona: Museu Picasso, 10 May–14 July 1988.

3   Hélène Seckel (ed.), *Les Demoiselles d'Avignon.* Exhibition catalogue, 2 vols. (Paris: Musée Picasso, 1988).

4   *Woman with a Large Ear (Buste),* spring 1907. Oil on canvas, 60.5 × 59.2 cm. (Paris: Musée Picasso, MP 17).

5   Hélène Seckel and Judith Cousins provided an extensively researched chronology of the history of the painting, reports of it, reactions to it, its movements, and its early historiography. Brigitte Léal catalogued the sketchbooks and the studies comprehensively. Pierre Daix published an analysis of the picture's development in the light of the sketchbooks. William Rubin published an extensive analysis of the picture's genesis (in Picasso's experience and his psyche as well as in his drawings, etc.). Rubin's and Seckel and Cousins's texts were republished in English in revised form in Willian Rubin, Judith Cousins, and Hélène Seckel, *Les Demoiselles d'Avignon. Studies in Modern Art* 3 (New York: Museum of Modern Art, 1994).

6   These carved stone reliefs are now in the Museo Arquelogico Nacional, Madrid; they are dated between the sixth and third century B.C. They were shown in the Musée du Louvre in 1905–6.

7   This is dubbed 'carnet 2' in Seckel (1988), as in note 5.

8   The picture in question is *Jars with Lemon,* Paris, summer 1907. Oil on canvas, 55 × 46 cm. Collection Dr. Herbert Batliner, Vaduz, Liechtenstein. The discovery of the oil study beneath it is published in Hélène Seckel, 'Une Etude pour *Les Demoiselles d'Avignon*', *Poésie,* no. 60 (Paris, 1992), 121–5.

9   The identifications are reported in Alfred H. Barr, Jr., *Picasso: Forty Years of His Art* (New York: Museum of Modern Art, 1939).

10 William Rubin, 'From Narrative to 'Iconic' in Picasso: The Buried Allegory in *Bread and Fruitdish on a Table* and the Role of *Les Demoiselles d'Avignon*', *The Art Bulletin* 65, no. 4 (December 1983), 615–49.

11 Kahnweiler reported two campaigns of work on the painting. See Daniel-Henry Kahnweiler, *Der Weg zum Kubismus* (Munich, 1920). The X-ray evidence bears this report out.

12 This connection was first pointed out by Rubin in Rubin (1983), as in note 10, Appendix IX, 647.

13 It is Rubin who has most exhaustively researched the topic and argued the probability that Picasso visited the Musée d'Ethnographie at this moment; he speaks of an 'epiphany', a conjunction of factors that allowed Picasso to respond to the force of tribal sculpture in that setting. See especially, William Rubin, 'Picasso', in Rubin (ed.), '*Primitivism' in Twentieth-Century Art: Affinity of the Tribal and the Modern,* exhibition catalogue, vol. 1 (New York: Museum of Modern Art, 1984).

14 The first to state that the picture was left unfinished was Kahnweiler. He links the stylistic contradictions in the work to this contention. Golding followed Kahnweiler's analysis in the late 1950s. Rubin, however, has argued especially forcefully that the work should be considered finished. See Kahnweiler (1920), as in note 11; John Golding, *Cubism: A History and an Analysis, 1907–1914* (London, 1959); and Rubin (1983), as in note 10, Appendix XI.

15 Its first showing was as no. 129 "Les Demoiselles d'Avignon" at an exhibition organised by André Salmon, 'L'Art Moderne en France', the Salon d'Antin, 26, avenue
d'Antin, Paris, 16–31 July 1916. Its first New York showing was in the exhibition 'Art
of Our Time' at the Museum of Modern Art, 10 May–30 September 1939.

16 The best referenced discussion of the title is in Rubin et al. (1994), as in note 5,
17–19. It is Golding who recalls that Picasso often referred to the picture as '*mon
bordel*'. See p. 17, below.

17 See Kahnweiler (1920), as in note 11; and Barr (1939), as in note 9.

18 John Golding, 'The *Demoiselles d'Avignon*', *The Burlington Magazine* 100, no. 662
(London, May 1958), 155–63. Golding's reference was to André Derain's
Baigneuses, 1907. Oil on canvas, 132 × 195 cm. New York: Museum of Modern Art.
He brought together also both the relief sculpture excavated at Osuna (see note 6)
and the two heads excavated at Cerro de los Santos (Fig. 6). It was Christian Zer-
vos who, prompted by the artist, first introduced the 'Iberian influence' into the
Picasso literature. He did so in his introduction to the second volume of his oeuvre
catalogue, published by Cahiers d'art in 1942.

19 Golding (1959), as in note 14.

20 Leo Steinberg, 'The Philosophical Brothel', *Art News* 71, nos. 5 and 6 (New York,
September and October 1972), 22–9 and 38–47. Translated into French in Seckel
(1988), as in note 3. Revised in *October*, no. 44 (New York and Cambridge, Mass.,
spring 1988). As Rubin points out, quite independently of Steinberg, John Nash of
the University of Essex in the U.K. developed a very comparable approach to the
Demoiselles, which was given form earlier than Steinberg's article but without his
knowledge, in a broadcast talk on B.B.C. Radio 3, on Wednesday 24 June 1970,
titled 'Pygamalion and Medusa'. Rubin cites an elaborated typescript of this talk in
Rubin et al. (1994), as in note 5, 31.

21 Special mention should be made of David Fraser-Jenkins's contribution, which
seems to have gone unnoticed. Fraser-Jenkins has analysed the *Demoiselles* in new
and suggestive ways in relation to Cézanne's late *Bathers*, making an especially
interesting link with a photograph taken by Emile Bernard of Cézanne seated in
front of the Barnes Collection *Large Bathers*. See David Fraser-Jenkins,
'*Baigneuses* and *Demoiselles*. 'Bathers' in Cézanne, Picasso and Matisse', *Apollo*
(London, March 1997), 39–44.

22 Bois's essay is a revised version of a piece first published in 1988. See Yve-Alain
Bois, 'Painting as Trauma', *Art in America* 76, no. 6 (June 1988), 130–40, 172–3.

23 Garb's essay has been specially written for this book. Its concern with the female
spectator has been anticipated by Anna Chave, whose 1994 treatment of the topic
is highly personalized and far less concerned with the painting in its historical
moment. See Anna C. Chave, 'New Encounters with *Les Demoiselles d'Avignon*:
Gender, Race, and the Origins of Cubism', *The Art Bulletin* (December 1994),
596–611.

24 Leighten's essay is a revised version of a piece first published in 1990, Lomas's of a
piece first published in 1993. See Patricia Leighten, 'The White Peril and *L'Art
Nègre*: Picasso, Primitivism, and Anticolonialism', *The Art Bulletin* 72, no. 4
(December 1990), 609–30; and David Lomas, 'A Canon of Deformity: *Les Demoiselles d'Avignon* and Physical Anthropology', *Art History* 16, no. 3 (Oxford, U.K.,
and Cambridge, Mass., September 1993), 424–46. The first to have explored historically the theme of prostitution as it is taken up by Picasso in the *Demoiselles* was

Michael Leja. See Michael Leja, '"Le Vieux Marcheur" and "Les Deux Risques": Picasso, Prostitution, Venereal Disease, and Maternity, 1899–1907', *Art History* 8, no. 1 (March 1985), 66–81.

25 Another study exploring the relationship between the *Demoiselles* and Picasso's development between 1907 and 1910 should be mentioned. This is Neil Cox, *La Morale des lignes: Picasso 1907–10: Modernist Reception, the Subversion of Content; and the Lesson of Caricature*, thesis submitted for the degree of Ph.D. (University of Essex, 1991). Cox comes to highly suggestive conclusions as he traces Picasso's move away from an obsessive engagement with his own sexuality to aesthetic idealism.

Les Demoiselles d'Avignon and the Exhibition of 1988

It is now more than forty years since I first wrote at some length on *Les Demoiselles d'Avignon*, with the growing awareness that there could never be a definitive interpretation of this most remarkable of paintings.[1] The *Demoiselles* is one of those rare works of art that can look completely different to the same pair of eyes on each successive encounter. Individual art historians of my own generation who have written about the work more than once have done so from completely different perspectives. Younger critics, influenced by or trained in new art historical methods, have brought new insights to bear on the picture. Successive generations will continue to do so. This chapter was originally written as a review of the exhibition built up around this single painting that was shown in Barcelona and Paris in 1988. It attempts to give a brief history of the painting and of its critical fortunes.[2]

When the Museum of Modern Art mounted its huge Picasso exhibition in New York in 1980, it obtained the full support of the Picasso museums in Paris and Barcelona on condition that the great work, in a sense the cornerstone of New York's collection, might be allowed to cross the Atlantic once more. The New York exhibition was a triumph – the greatest Picasso exhibition there has ever been or will be, even though the late work was inadequately represented. Many of the works assembled will never be reunited: *Guernica,* for example, was afterwards restored to Spain, according to the artist's ultimate wish, and is now after an interval when it was shown in a dependency of the Prado under grotesque conditions, reigning supreme in the Reina Sofia, Madrid's own new museum of modern art. The relatively small *Demoiselles* exhibition was a triumph too, but of a different nature. It was accompanied by a two-volume catalogue, which makes the *Demoiselles*,[3] together with *Guernica*, one of the two most extensively documented twentieth-century paintings.[4] In the catalogue, William Rubin wrote at length about the picture with his customary thoroughness and incisiveness. It is now a moot point whether *Guernica* or the *Demoiselles* is the most famous image of the art of the twentieth century. *Guernica* has engaged the attention of specialists and commentators of every persuasion and has driven several of them insane. The *Demoiselles* remains more central to concepts of modernism and is ultimately the more important work – one of those rare individual works of art that have changed the course of visual history.

The *Demoiselles* was conceived and executed in a small filthy studio in a ramshackle wooden building known as the Bâteau-Lavoir, perched on the slopes of Montmartre. The picture can't have been seen by all that many people in the years after it was painted, and, with one exception, almost nothing was written about it at the time, or even subsequently, by the people who must have seen it in its original studio setting while it was being painted or immediately afterwards. Fernande Olivier, who was living with Picasso at the time, does not mention it in either of her memoirs.[5] Neither does Apollinaire, although he had written so poignantly on Picasso's earlier work and was already doing more than anyone else to bring Picasso to early fame.

Max Jacob, who in the early years of the century shared with Picasso his top hat, his bed (they slept in it separately in relays), and indeed his very existence, and who at the time of the *Demoiselles* remained in many respects his alter ego, referred to the great painting only once, years later, and then casually, almost in passing.[6] Another of Picasso's writer friends, the poet, critic, and journalist André Salmon, did however discuss the picture at some length in his *La Jeune peinture française*, which appeared in the autumn of 1912, and it was he who set the tone and formalistic approach in which the work was to be discussed for some fifty years to come.

Less surprisingly, we know about the reactions of Picasso's painter friends only through their work, or at secondhand, through hearsay. Derain, probably with Balzac's Frenhofer in mind, predicted that one day Picasso would be found hanged behind the painting.[7] In the event it was the picture that to a certain extent hanged Derain. An artist of great intelligence and enormous natural gifts, he now produced a large, lifeless answer to the *Demoiselles*, a three-figure piece called *La Toilette*, which he subsequently destroyed; he recovered his balance, but the direction of his art had been permanently altered.

Matisse was made angry by the *Demoiselles* and seems to have thought it something of a bad joke,[8] although he reacted to it indirectly when in 1908 he produced his great *Bathers with a Turtle,* now in the St. Louis Art Museum. Braque, too, initially disliked the *Demoiselles,*[9] but he studied it harder than any other artist, and indeed his subsequent friendship and collaboration with Picasso led to the cubist revolution. Critics and collectors were similarly baffled. Gertrude Stein tells us that Shchukin, who was becoming a patron of Picasso's, said, 'What a loss for French art'.[10] Leo Stein was derisive.[11] Vollard, always taciturn, said nothing.[12] Kahnweiler, who was soon to become Picasso's dealer, subsequently became obsessed by the picture; but he was also made uneasy by it right until the end of his days.[13]

The *Demoiselles* was first shown publicly at the Salon d'Antin in 1916, an exhibition organised by André Salmon. The picture, Picasso's only entry, became the centrepiece of the exhibition, which was extended by a couple of weeks – cultural events of a comparable importance (literary and musical sessions accompanied the show) were rare in wartime Paris. It was here that the painting, originally known to Picasso's intimates as 'Le Bordel philosophique', acquired its present title. Picasso must surely have agreed to the way Salmon listed the work, but he came to dislike the title intensely, presumably because it seemed evasive and genteel; and he most often referred to the painting simply as *'mon bordel'.* Although the Avignon of the title has been associated with a brothel in Barcelona's *carrer d'Avinyo,* near where Picasso's family lived, William Rubin is probably right in suggesting that Salmon chose the title because since the time of the papacy Avignon had carried overtones of sensuality and vice; the Abbé de Sade, Rubin reminds us, who was uncle and tutor of the divine marquis himself, quoted Petrarch on the subject.[14]

The *Demoiselles* was almost certainly seen at the Salon d'Antin by the great couturier and Maecenas Jacques Doucet, who was subsequently to acquire it. But it was André Breton, acting as Doucet's literary and artistic advisor, who urged his patron to make the purchase in a series of letters of such eloquence that we can only regret he never wrote about the painting at greater length and independently, so to speak (what a marvellous companion piece it would have made to that small masterpiece, 'Phare de la Mariée', his essay on Duchamp's *Large Glass*). In November 1923, when Doucet appears to have been still wavering, we find Breton writing, 'It is a work which for me goes beyond painting, it is the theatre of everything that has happened over the past fifty years, it is the wall before which have passed Rimbaud, Lautréamont, Jarry, Apollinaire, and all those whom we continue to love'.[15] A year later, after the sale had been completed, we find him still reassuring Doucet: 'Here is the painting which one would parade, as was Cimabue's *Virgin*, through the streets of our capital'.[16]

Doucet paid 25,000 francs for the work, an astonishingly small sum even at that time, and Picasso probably agreed to the sale because Doucet had promised to bequeath it to the Louvre (it never got there, but Doucet had almost certainly not acted in bad faith, and it is very likely that the French state would have verbally rejected the offer of such a controversial work). Picasso never forgave Doucet for having got the work out of him so cheaply, and he refused to come and see it when it was finally installed in the luxuriously appointed studio house in Neuilly into which Doucet moved in 1928. There it was given pride of place on the landing of an extraordinary staircase (the steps were of silver and red enamel under the heavy glass, and the newel posts took the form of exotic birds), conceived by Doucet himself and executed by the sculptor Csaky. Opposite the *Demoiselles* stood enormous double doors by Lalique (rescued from an earlier dwelling) that led into the 'studio' and beyond into the room where oriental antiques were displayed. The picture itself was encased in a forged metal frame especially designed for it by Pierre Legrain, who had originally achieved fame as a bookbinder but had also become recognised as one of the greatest French craftsmen of his time. The Bâteau-Lavoir was a world away.

In August 1929 A. Conger Goodyear, who was president of the trustees of New York's Museum of Modern Art, was taken to see the Doucet collection, and he was bowled over by it and its setting. Alfred Barr, then the museum's director, starred the *Demoiselles* in the list of paintings he wanted to put together for a Picasso show that was originally to have taken place in 1931, but for various reasons was not mounted until 1939. In the meantime Doucet had died, the house had been demolished, and Madame Doucet had sold the collection of eleven Picassos (the eleventh turned out to be in fact by Braque) to the Seligmann Gallery, which had branches in Paris and New York. The *Demoiselles* was sold for six times what Picasso had received for it.

The picture sailed for New York in October 1937 on the *Normandie*, the Legrain frame travelling separately. In November it went on show at the Seligmann premises on East Fifty-first Street to the accompaniment of considerable publicity. On 9 November Barr, who now described the picture as 'the most important painting of the twentieth century', urged the advisory committee to propose the picture to the museum's trustees.[17] In December the sale went through (things moved fast in those days). The picture went on view in May 1939 in an exhibition entitled 'Art of Our Time', which was designed to commemorate the tenth anniversary of the museum and its reopening in its present premises. The fate of the Legrain frame remains a mystery. It is unclear (to me at least) whether the canvas was shown framed at the Seligmann Gallery, but the gallery must surely have received the frame. The Museum of Modern Art appears to have no records of it.

The *Demoiselles* exhibition of 1988 consisted of the great canvas itself, a handful of paintings that led up to it, and some dozen oil paintings, water-colours, and drawings that relate directly to it; equally revealing and excit-ing were the sixteen sketchbooks that recorded the processes of Picasso's mind and eye at work over a period of some nine months from the autumn of 1906 through to the high summer of 1907. These he kept him-self until his death, and until recently they were relatively unknown. The problems of sequence and date surrounding the sketchbooks and the indi-vidual leaves within them have not been completely sorted out; and given Picasso's unmethodical working processes they probably never will be. But the sketchbooks make it immediately obvious that this was by far the most elaborately plotted of all Picasso's masterpieces. Finally, there was what amounted to a small exhibition within an exhibition – a group of 'things seen'. Many people expressed reservations about this section of the exhibi-tion and saw it as extraneous or didactic. I myself found it fascinating, demonstrating as it did that working from photographs and reproductions, the actual feel of works of art, the presence with which they confront us, becomes so completely lost.

The relevance of a particular El Greco, *The Vision of Saint John* (now in the Metropolitan Museum, New York, Fig. 2), known until recently as *The Seventh Seal* (and to Picasso himself probably and most importantly, as *Pro-fane Love*) was first pointed out by Ron Johnson in 1980 and then elabo-rated on, at the same time and entirely independently by Rolf Laessoe and, in even greater depth, by John Richardson.[18] The affinities between this El Greco and the *Demoiselles* are so striking, not only at a multiplicity of visual levels, but also spiritually and psychologically, that it is hard not to believe that Picasso began the actual execution of the *Demoiselles* under its direct stimulus. Picasso had known and consulted El Greco's work for some time past, and he had almost certainly often seen this particular work, which belonged to the Spanish painter Zuloaga, then resident in Paris. But as so often with Picasso, revelation seems to have struck at precisely the

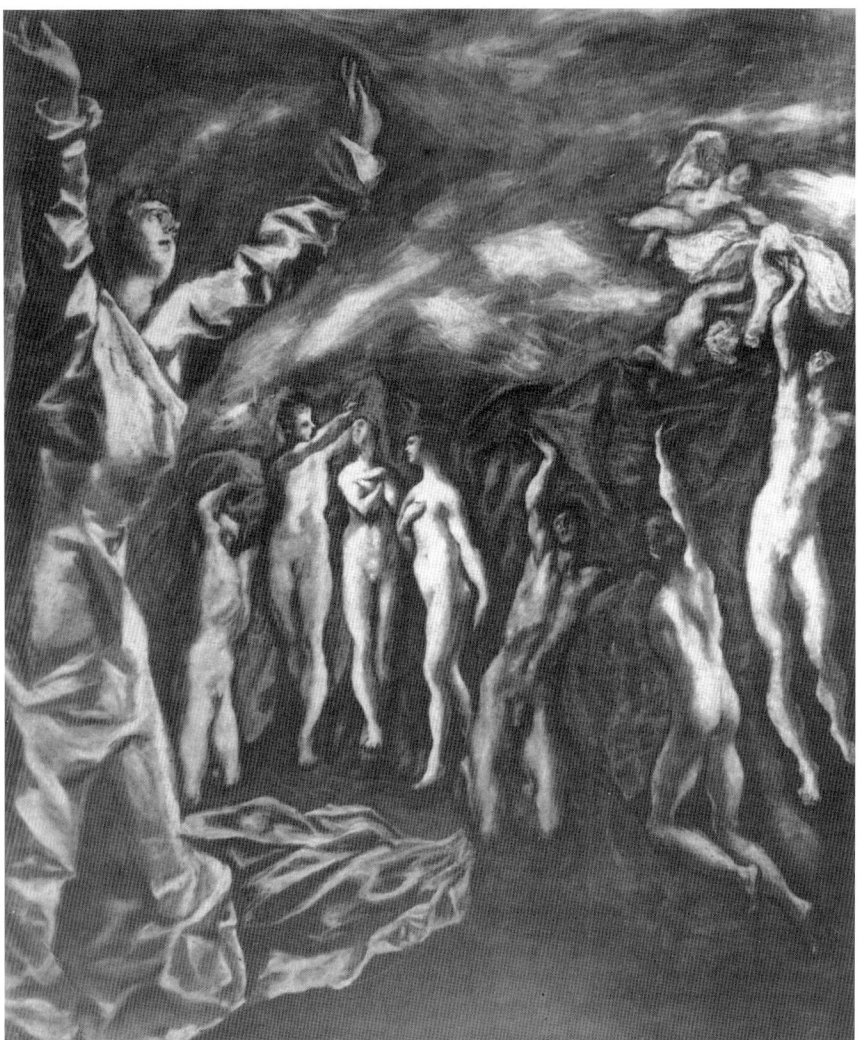

FIGURE 2. El Greco, *The Vision of St. John*, 1608–14. Oil on canvas, 225 × 193 cm. The Metropolitan Museum of Art, New York.

appropriate moment; and maybe this faculty is one of the attributes of true genius. It is hard to see much of El Greco in any of the surrounding studies. The presence of this singularly apocalyptic El Greco behind the *Demoiselles* helps to explain why Breton, for one, viewed the painting of the interior of a whorehouse as a mystical experience.

Picasso must have seen Ingres's *The Turkish Bath* (Fig. 3) in the great

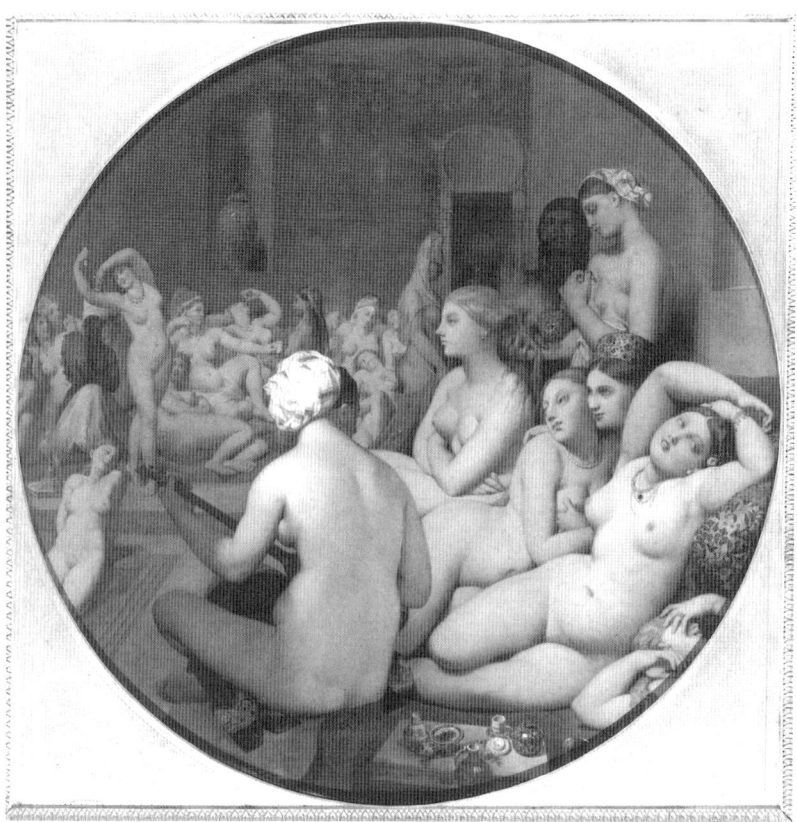

FIGURE 3. Jean-Auguste-Dominique Ingres, *The Turkish Bath*, 1859–63. Oil on canvas (tondo), diameter 108 cm. Musée du Louvre, Paris. (© Réunion des musées nationaux – Louvre.)

Ingres retrospective at the Salon d'Automne of 1905. He certainly admired it and it was to obsess him in old age. It stands behind the *Demoiselles*, but at a distance. Cézanne's *Five Bathers* (Fig. 4), like the El Greco, strikes an instant chord of psychological rightness in relationship to the *Demoiselles*, and its sublimated but still uneasy sensuality seems infinitely closer to it than does the melting eroticism of the Ingres. Gauguin's *Oviri* (Musée d'Orsay) makes the point that for Picasso Gauguin's sculpture was more important than his painting. Matisse's *Blue Nude* (Baltimore Museum of Art) and Derain's *Bathers* (Museum of Modern Art, New York), both seen at the Salon des Indépendants of 1907 (it opened in March), are in different ways relevant to the *Demoiselles*, although they seem to exist in very different worlds from it; and great paintings though they are, the

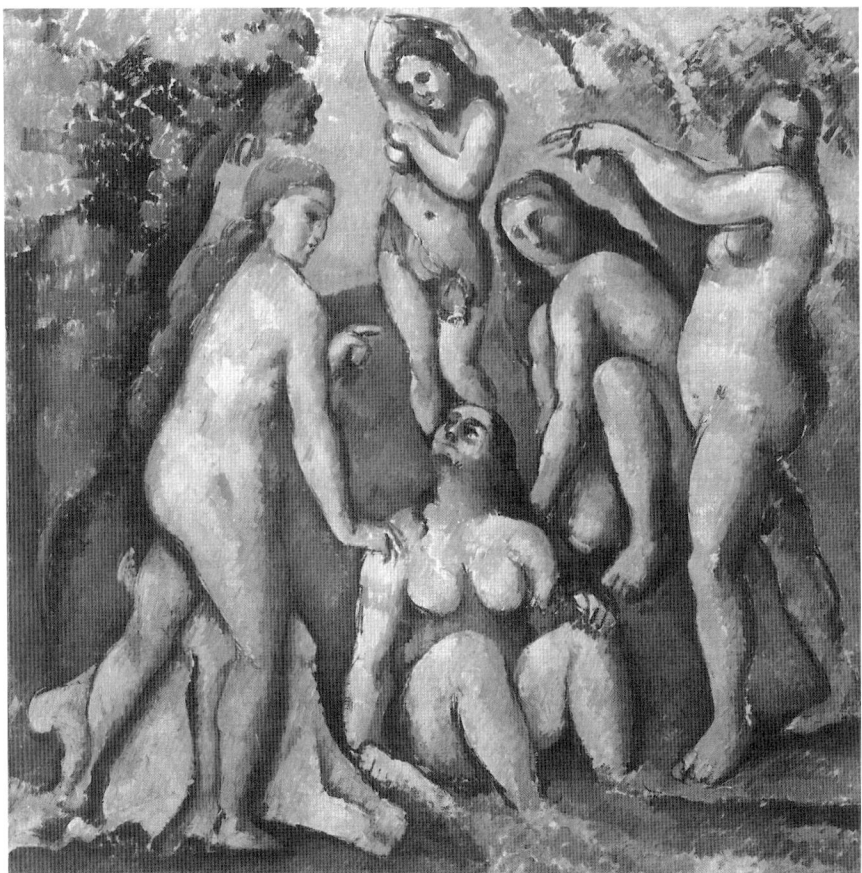

FIGURE 4. Paul Cézanne, *Five Bathers*, 1885–7. Oil on canvas, 65.5 × 65.5 cm. Öffentliche Kunstsammlung Basel, Kunstmuseum.

Demoiselles dominated and tamed them. The tribal art from Africa and the New Hebrides in the exhibition (Figs. 5 and 17) simply served to confirm what so many of us have always maintained: that while he was actually at work on the *Demoiselles* Picasso experienced its impact. As in the case of El Greco, Picasso had already been aware of tribal art – his friends and colleagues had been talking about it and collecting it for at least a year – but it was at this moment that its implications struck home in the violence of the two 'demoiselles' at the right-hand side of the composition.

Complementing the tribal art, and anticipating its impact on the *Demoiselles*, was a life-size stone Iberian head of a man, dating from

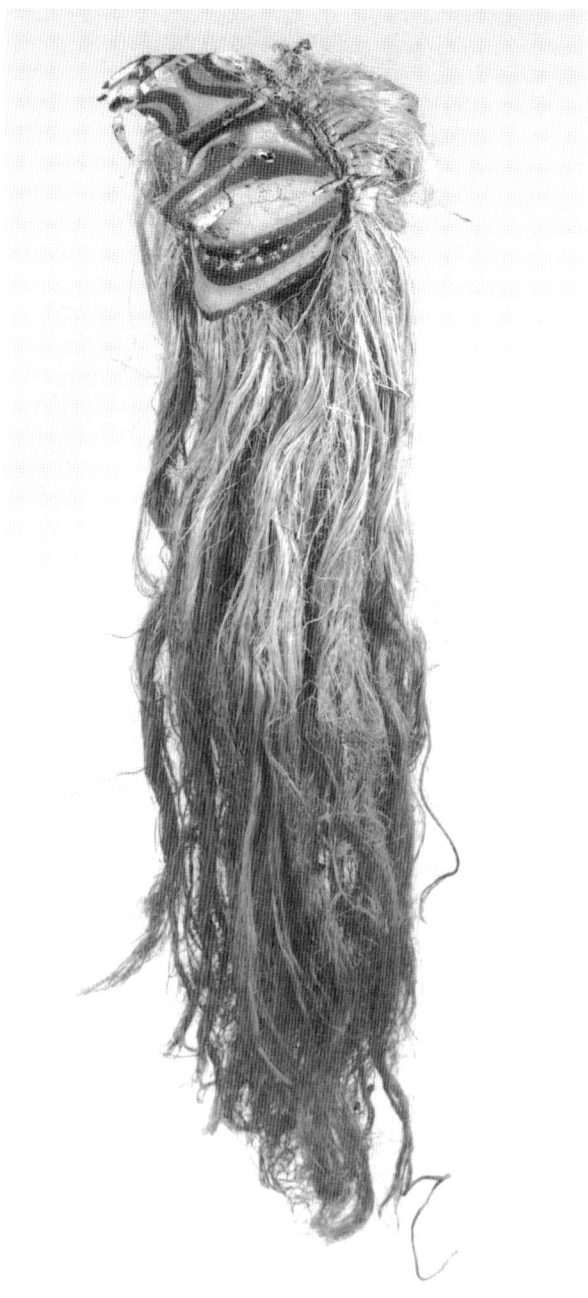

FIGURE 5. Mask Malekula, Vanuatu. Painted palmwood, 63.5 cm. high. Musée de l'Homme, Paris. (© Musée de l'Homme, Paris, photograph M. Delaplanche.)

between the fifth and third centuries B.C., and hence to a primitive period of the peninsula's indigenous art (Fig. 6). This had been stolen from the Louvre in March 1907 and almost immediately entered Picasso's possession. An object of very little obvious aesthetic worth, it nevertheless has extraordinary presence. Half the head has been virtually obliterated by erosion; the other half displays an enormous scroll-shaped ear, a sharp wedge-shaped nose, and a great bulging eye. These features are echoed in the heads of the two central 'demoiselles', and, as X-rays and preparatory studies show, underlie the heads of their companions.

Here we are confronted for the first time with one of the rawest and most profound aspects of Picasso's genius – his ability to take something that in itself comes pretty close to being nothing, and to transform it into great and meaningful art. In his catalogue essay for *Le Dernier Picasso* exhibition, which happened to coincide in Paris with that of the *Demoiselles*, John Richardson wrote evocatively of how the Andalusian grasps a person or an object by his stare or steady gaze, possesses it, rapes it.[19] But if traditionally the *mirada fuerte* is a male prerogative, here it is given to the five naked women. The two outer figures stare past and through each other. The other three transfix us completely with their gaze, and it is only subsequently that we become aware of them as bodies. Eventually the painting stares us down.

Even before the richness of the sketchbooks had been revealed to us, the basic iconography of the picture had been frequently rehearsed in the phase of the literature on the painting initiated by Alfred Barr in his *Picasso: Forty Years of His Art*, which accompanied the Museum of Modern Art's 1939 exhibition. Two men were to have been included in the composition: a sailor seated among the women and a figure (later identified by Picasso as a medical student) who entered the composition from the left; he holds either a skull (Fig. 8) or a book, and on one occasion both. As the sketches evolved, the first to go was the medical student. Ultimately, the sailor himself disappears. We, the spectators, are now seated at the inner table of the brothel (originally there had been two tables), opposite the 'demoiselles', and we have by implication become their clients. The watercolour sketch from the Gallatin Collection in Philadelphia (Fig. 10), which corresponds most closely to the *Demoiselles*, is, I suspect, not a final preparatory study for the painting but a subsequent footnote to it, a record of what the picture looked like before Picasso went back into it after his traumatic encounters with the tribal art displayed in the Trocadéro (now the Musée de l'Homme). Thirty years later, recalling this revelation, Picasso spoke to Malraux of the *Demoiselles* as his first 'exorcism'

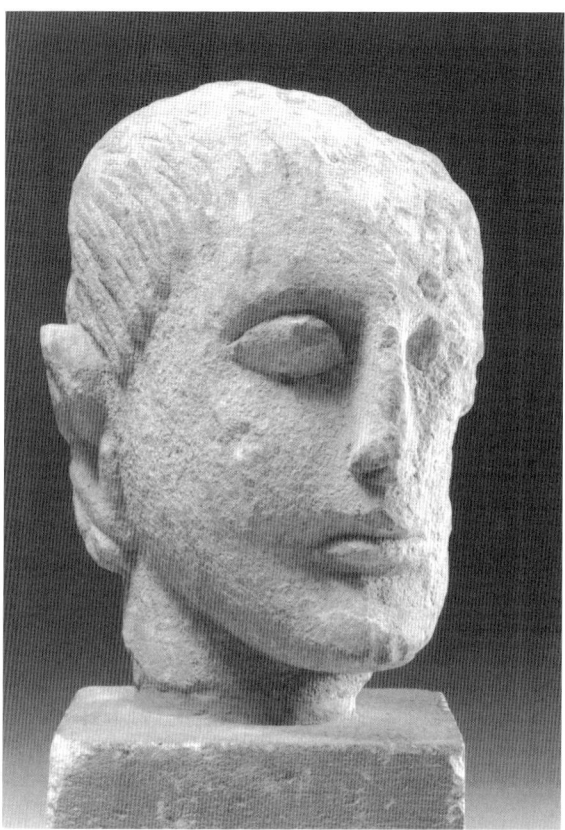

FIGURE 6. *Head of a Man*. Iberian; Cerro de los Santos, fifth–third century BCE. Lime-stone, 46 × 27 × 17 cm. Musée des antiquités nationales, Saint-Germain-en-Laye. (© Réunion des musées nationaux – Saint-Germain-en-Laye.)

picture: 'For me the masks were not simply sculptures, they were magical objects. They were weapons to keep people from being ruled by spirits, to help free themselves'.[20]

Leo Steinberg's essay of 1972, included in the 1988 catalogue, reads as persuasively as ever;[21] and it now seems strange that for fifty years writers, like myself, should have written about the painting in almost entirely for-malistic terms, and put to one side its erotic implications and thus denied the painting some of its supreme physicality. Rubin has frequently expressed his debt to Steinberg. He now reaffirms it but wonders if Stein-berg did not indeed go far enough in his 'psycho-sexual' analysis. Rubin can find no direct link between the head of the squatting 'demoiselle' (the most apocalyptic of all) and any tribal masks that Picasso might have seen. He now suggests that Picasso's imagination was fuelled by memories of the syphilitic patients he saw when he visited the hospital prison of St-Lazare (and its morgue) in 1901; its female inmates were prostitutes contaminated by venereal diseases.

In this connection Rubin reproduces some truly horrifying photographs from the turn of the century showing the heads of women suffering from tertiary syphilis.[22] Picasso may well have been haunted by such nightmares; but the head of this 'demoiselle' and the study for it have about them a hypnotic and barbaric beauty as well as an overpowering and corrosive vitality that makes the confrontation with the photographic images of pustular decay oddly gratuitous. These heads of Picasso still look deeply tribal and atavistic to me, and since he was ultimately interested simultaneously in the spirit that lay behind tribal art and in the formal visual principles that made that spirit manifest rather than in any particular example, I see no reason why he should not have manipulated these to his own psychological and expressive purposes. The squatting figure in the *Demoiselles* was the last to be executed, and she remains the most enigmatic.

For that matter, and despite the wealth of research that has now been placed at our disposal, the picture itself remains something of an enigma. That Picasso should have felt compelled to make a major effort and statement at this point in his career was only to be expected. He undoubtedly saw himself in rivalry with Matisse, and Matisse's *Le Bonheur de vivre*, shown at the Salon des Indépendants in 1906 (Fig. 29), had set the seal on his reputation as leader of advanced young French painting. In acknowledged and friendly rivalry Matisse and Derain had at the Indépendants of 1907 shown their two large 'blue' paintings. Prostitution and its dangerous consequences had been a major theme in Picasso's work in the early years of the century. But why should he have returned to the subject at this particular moment in his life, and why should he have chosen it to effect a major stylistic revolution? Although Picasso was still experiencing financial hardship, his work had begun to sell well to important dealers and collectors. The paintings done at Gósol in the summer of 1906, which in a sense represent him at his first full maturity, are classicizing and breathe an air of deep calm and contentment. Fernande Olivier had come to live with Picasso towards the end of 1905, and for the first time in his life he appeared to be enjoying a stable relationship with a beautiful woman whose physicality matched his own.

The choice of subject matter for his great new canvas may in part have been a deliberate and defiant answer to the hedonism of the work of

Matisse and his fellow Fauves. Apollinaire with his insatiable appetite for erotica may well have been an influence; the original manuscript of his *Les Onze milles verges*, bearing the date of 1907, was one of Picasso's most treasured possessions. It is an erotic tour de force, and one of its set pieces is an orgy in a brothel. Rubin is almost certainly right in suggesting that it was Apollinaire who gave the painting its original title, *Le Bordel philosophique*. Several authors have suggested that Picasso himself had been attacked by venereal disease, and given his early way of life this is at least likely; if so, something may have happened to remind him of the episode. The years between 1898 and 1902 had seen the climax of the battle between those who wanted to abolish government control of prostitutes and those who wanted to regulate their activities, and the subject was still very much in the air.[23]

The second volume of Fernande Olivier's memoirs, which was posthumously published, makes it clear that when she met Picasso she was leading a promiscuous life, and this may account for some of the excessive possessiveness he showed towards her. Their 'adoption' of a thirteen-year-old orphan, Raymonde, seems to have introduced further complication into their communal life. In August 1907 Fernande wrote to Gertrude Stein in distress, saying that she and Picasso were separating. By the end of the first week of September she had left. She was soon to return; but during the first half of 1907 there were tensions in the studios at the Bateau-Lavoir and these must have found their way into the general atmosphere of the building and into the *Demoiselles* itself.

But it is to the works of the autumn of 1906 that we must turn for premonitions of what was to come, and the tensions here are, or so it seems to me, purely visual and pictorial (Fig. 7). They show massive female nudes whose girth is so distended that one can only convey an impression of them in words by describing them as pneumatic lay figures, pressed up against a glass support and pumped fuller and fuller of air, so that they become increasingly swollen and monumental in appearance while simultaneously flattening up against and across the surface that is immediately in front of them. An explosion was inevitable, and this explosion was the *Demoiselles*.

The nudes that precede it, unique in the history of art for their distention, have themselves been discussed in psychosexual terms; but just as many of the figures of Cézanne's maturity assume the quality of still lifes, so these creations of Picasso seem to me to be pregnant with purely formal and visual possibilities. The erotic implications of the *Demoiselles* are married to its formal innovations and are conveyed by them as Leo Steinberg

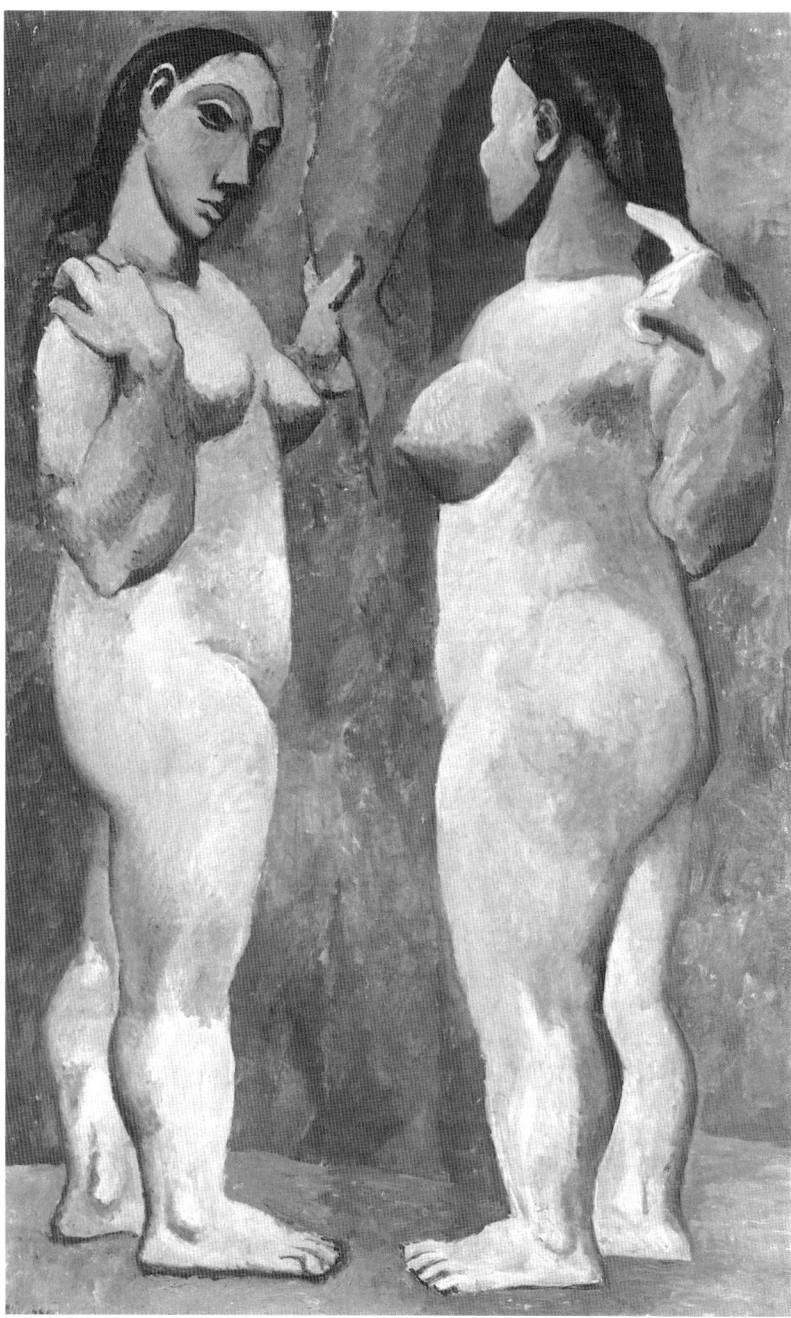

FIGURE 7. Pablo Picasso, *Two Nudes*, 1906. Oil on canvas, 151.3 × 93 cm. Museum of Modern Art, New York. Gift of G. David Thompson in honour of Alfred H. Barr, Jr. (Photo © 1998 The Museum of Modern Art, New York.)

has so convincingly demonstrated. But apart from a couple of expressionistic footnotes to the painting, it was succeeded, as it had been preceded, by what was on the whole a period of calm, of pictorial experiment and analysis. In the *Demoiselles* Picasso began to shatter the human figure and the pictorial conventions for rendering it. He spent the rest of his artistic life dissecting, reassembling, and reinventing it.

Seen within the context of this particular exhibition, the *Demoiselles* looked, if certainly not benign at least calmer and more self-contained than ever before; it was as if history had at last reached out and enfolded it. Two years later in New York it was used as a screen, almost as a barrier, to introduce the Museum of Modern Art's exhibition *Picasso and Braque: Pioneering Cubism*. Seen in this context it had regained all its old ferocity, its power to disorient and disturb. And it served as a reminder of the fact that although *Les Demoiselles d'Avignon* is not a cubist painting, more than any other single work it helped to provoke the cubist revolution.

NOTES

1   John Golding, 'The *Demoiselles d'Avignon*', *Burlington Magazine* 100, no. 662 (May 1958), 155–63.
2   This chapter first appeared in *The New York Review of Books* (21 July 1988), and then with revisions in John Golding, *Visions of the Modern* (London, 1994). A few further revisions have been made here.
3   Edited by Hélène Seckel, it contains essays by Leo Steinberg, William Rubin, Pierre Daix, and a chronology by Seckel and Judith Cousins.
4   For a discussion of the literature on *Guernica*, see Ellen C. Oppler (ed.), *Picasso's Guernica* (Norton, 1987), and Herschel B. Chipp, *Picasso's Guernica* (University of California Press, 1989).
5   Fernande Olivier, *Picasso et ses amis* (Paris, 1933); Fernande Olivier, *Souvenirs intimes. Ecrits pour Picasso* (Paris, 1988).
6   See catalogue of the exhibition under discussion, Vol. 2, 471, note 36.
7   As in note 6, 654.
8   As in note 6.
9   As in note 6, 670.
10 As in note 6, 650.
11 Gertrude Stein, *Picasso* (Paris, 1938), 18.
12 See catalogue, vol. 2, 685–6.
13 As in note 12, 658–68. In the years between 1955, when I first went to see him and his death in 1979, Kahnweiler often talked to me about the *Demoiselles*.
14 As in note 13, 376–8.
15 As in note 12, 585.
16 As in note 12, 590.
17 As in note 12, 614. The Advisory Committee of the Museum of Modern Art is clearly echoing Barr's views.

18   Ron Johnson, 'Picasso's *Demoiselles d'Avignon* and the Theater of the Absurd', *Arts Magazine* 55, no. 2 (October 1980); Rolf Laessoe, 'A Source for Picasso's *Les Demoiselles d'Avignon*', *Gazette des Beaux-Arts* 110 (October 1987); John Richardson, 'Picasso's Apocalyptic Whorehouse', *The New York Review* (23 April 1987).

19   John Richardson, 'L'époque Jacqueline', in *Le dernier Picasso* (Paris: Centre Georges Pompidou, 1988), 55–75.

20   André Malraux, *La Tête d'obsidienne* (Paris, 1974), 18–19.

21   Leo Steinberg's 'The Philosophical Brothel' was first published in two parts in *Art News* 71, nos. 5 and 6 (September and October 1972), 22–9 and 38–47. It appears translated into French in Catalogue, vol. 2. It has also been republished in English with revisions in *October*, no. 44 (New York and Cambridge, Mass., spring 1988).

22   The photographs published in Catalogue, Vol. 2 do not actually show the effects of tertiary syphilis, as David Lomas pointed out in 'A Canon of Deformity: *Les Demoiselles d'Avignon* and Physical Anthropology', *Art History* 16, no. 3 (Oxford, September 1993), the publication on which his chapter in this volume is based. Rubin published photographs of deformations caused by congenital syphilis in his revised version of the catalogue essay in William Rubin, Judith Cousins, and Hélène Seckel, *Les Demoiselles d'Avignon. Studies in Modern Art* 3 (New York: Museum of Modern Art, 1994) 131–2, note 170.

23   See Michael Leja, '"Le Vieux Marcheur" and "Les Deux risques": Picasso, Prostitution, Venereal Disease, and Maternity, 1899–1907', *Art History* 1 (1985).

3

YVE-ALAIN BOIS

Painting as Trauma

S ince the 1970s, our understanding of Picasso has been made more complex by various art historical studies. Central to the reassessment of Picasso and his position in modernism has obviously been his great work, the *Demoiselles d'Avignon*. Even in the most revisionist approaches to Picasso's art, this picture remains a key monument of this century's culture. The exhibition organized by Hélène Seckel around the *Demoiselles* (the first grand-scale show put on by the Musée Picasso) gives us the opportunity to check and reevaluate the foundational status of this work in the history of early modernism.[1] As a small exhibition centered around a precise question, it is a model of its kind. It offers us as complete a documentation as possible on the great bordello picture, including all the major studies, sketchbooks, sources, and, of course, the painting itself. Moreover, it is accompanied by a massive two-volume catalogue that will certainly become a landmark in the field. In other words, for once we have an exhibition that conceives of museological activity as an intellectual pursuit, not merely as pure spectacle.

From the outset, the thesis of this exhibition is clear: the *Demoiselles* is a manifesto, the elaboration of which involved a vast construction site into which Picasso threw everything – all his ideas, all his sources, all his energy. Thus the sheer quantity of works assembled for this exhibition: 9 sketchbooks (out of 16) concerning the *Demoiselles* (unfortunately only one of them is displayed page by page – the others are merely open at a double page); some 60 studies and sketches for the picture (mostly in oil); and 20 or so peripheral works, either from Picasso's own earlier work or from other artists. Yet, despite the size and complexity of the exhibition, its remarkable clear layout gives one the impression of turning the pages of a book, clarifying all the hazards encountered in the course of the work's elaboration, without becoming overtly didactic.

Indeed, standing alongside and paralleling the exhibition is its catalogue, in which all the research and documentation for the exhibition is set forth.[2] The catalogue comprises altogether over 700 pages, with approximately 1,300 illustrations. The first volume, which contains pictures with brief commentaries, consists of reproductions of all the works in the exhibition, plus every page of each of the sketchbooks connected with the *Demoiselles* (except for the sixteenth sketchbook, in which only the first half is relevant to the *Demoiselles*, the rest having been filled up later). Many of these sketches have already been reproduced in Zervos's catalogue of Picasso's works, but there they were presented in a haphazard and incomplete way, out of chronological or thematic sequence (one wonders on what scheme Zervos ordered and selected Picasso's works). Needless to say, this new and exhaustive presentation represents a valuable addition to Picasso studies.

The second volume of the catalogue contains critical analyses and art historical documentation. It begins with Leo Steinberg's ground-breaking article, 'The Philosophical Brothel', written over fifteen years ago (first published in *Art News* in 1972).[3] Aside from remaining the best piece written about the picture, it can also be said that the essay itself governs the layout of the present exhibition. Moreover, Steinberg has now added to it a postscript that speaks ironically of the anti-Picasso context in which the original essay was written and goes on to note the grotesque effects it has subsequently had (biographism and psychologism running amok, wild searches for sources). Steinberg's piece is followed by an incredibly long article by William Rubin entitled 'The Genesis of *Les Demoiselles d'Avignon*', in which he recapitulates his more recent articles on the picture[4] and fully describes the critical fortunes of the painting since the first discussion of it by Picasso's dealer, Daniel-Henry Kahnweiler. (We might note in passing that the puzzle of the title, which was given to the painting by André Salmon, has not been made any clearer by Rubin; he assures us that there was never a bordello in Barcelona in the Carre d'Avinyo.[5]) Next, Pierre Daix's 'History of *Les Demoiselles d'Avignon* in Light of Picasso's Notebooks' helps us understand the odd combination of speed, obsessiveness, and multifariousness that shaped Picasso's thought when elaborating the composition of his large canvas.[6] His essay is followed by a fascinating, though unpretentious, contribution to the catalogue, the extensive chronology of the *Demoiselles* prepared by Hélène Seckel and Judith Cousins.[7] This section chronicles the early history of the painting from the time of its first appearance to its entry into MOMA in 1939: who saw it? when? how? We learn, among other things, that before its acquisition by MOMA the picture was displayed publicly in Paris only for fifteen days, in a semiprivate salon put together by Salmon.[8] And, with the exception of Gelett Burgess's remarkable article in the *Architectural Record* in May 1910 ('The Wild Men of Paris'), we also learn that the *Demoiselles* was not published until 1925 – and then in *La Révolution surréaliste*. The first monograph to reproduce it was Gertrude Stein's in 1938! Thus the key painting of the century was virtually unknown prior to its departure for New York. Even more extraordinary, we learn that Jacques Doucet, who bought the painting from Picasso for a song in 1924,[9] tried to give the picture to the Louvre, which apparently rejected it!

Rounding out the catalogue, Seckel provides a critical anthology of the writings about the painting by various 'witnesses', as well as Picasso's own remarks about his work. Alleviating the frustration caused by the silence or quasisilence of many important witnesses (Picasso's painter colleagues, his mistress Fernande Olivier, Max Jacob, Apollinaire, Gertrude Stein), Seckel thoroughly examines all of the extant reminiscences, comparing one to another. When several different sources all simultaneously point to the same thing, this tends to confirm the veracity of the fact in question; inversely, one-person reports may be unreliable. Simultaneous or unique recollections are both, unfortunately, rare, and the great utility of this philological examination lies in its demonstration that many clichés about the work are the result of a cumulative series of successive remarks. This painstaking analysis, never previously attempted, will henceforth be indispensable to anyone who wishes to get a historical fix, free from all the distortions that are present even in the earliest commentaries, on the ever-fresh force of the painting's impact.[10]

The exhibition is divided into three sections: sketches and studies; *prodromes*, or works by Picasso prior to the *Demoiselles*; and *choses vues*, contingent borrowings from art historical tradition and so-called primitive art. To this plan might have been added a section of 'postscripts', because for at least two years after the *Demoiselles* was painted – say, up until the work done at Horta de Ebro in 1909 – we are dealing with Picasso's own interrogation of his great work. But then we would have to ask, did that interrogation ever cease? It may seem curious to some that the exhibition stops short of a consideration of Picasso's cubist works. But here, as elsewhere, the means available dictated the selection of the best possible scenario, in this case the particular version of the painting's evolution put forward by Steinberg and later confirmed by Rubin's erudition. Their scenario needs no postscript because it deals exclusively with the genesis of the *Demoiselles* and with the painting's thematic structure.

Both Steinberg and Rubin vehemently protest the long-held definition of the canvas as 'the first cubist picture', and their arguments are totally convincing. Such a definition, which leads to a whole series of completely outmoded associations with 'the abandonment of subject-matter' for the sake of 'form', long prevented any rigorous commentary on the picture. It was read more for what it 'presaged' than for what it accomplished (thus one of Steinberg's major interpretive moves was to dissociate the picture from cubism, slightly exaggerating the 'stylistic coherence' of the canonical cubist works in contrast to the 'lack of unity' in the *Demoiselles*[11]). Of course, no one denies that cubism itself would not have been possible without the breach this great picture (and all the labor that accompanied its creation) opened in the Western pictorial tradition. It is just that the effect was not as immediate as was once believed. It was obviously traumatic, meaning that it arose out of what Freud called 'deferred action', and we could even say that, in a certain sense, the entire cubist adventure was an attempt to understand and to comment on the import of this traumatic breach. But this would (and should) be the subject of another exhibition.

In this exhibition, then, we have a restricted corpus, one that focuses solely on the prolonged gestation of the *Demoiselles*. But even given this specific concentration, the first of the exhibition's organizational categories – sketches and studies – is both vast and difficult to take in (we are dealing with the 'most worked on' picture in the history of art). Rubin expresses this when he writes that 'it is not possible to specify the precise number of studies Picasso made for the *Demoiselles*, due to the way in which his various projects grow into and out of one another'.[12] Similarly, Daix demonstrates that the sketches in the notebooks evolved through 'graphic contamination', one configuration suggesting a digression that refers in turn to another work in progress or already completed. Thus it is impossible to dissociate, for example, work on the *Demoiselles* from work on *Nude with Drapery*, which broke into the train of concentration on the larger work and was itself only to be completed later (and there were many other such digressions). In the exhibition, we are given only the preparatory works 'directly' related to the *Demoiselles*. These still make up a considerable number: Rubin notes that some 400 or 500 can be listed, in every technique. Yet even this count – a quantitative leap over what had been available to Steinberg – seems modest to me.

With the *prodromes* and the *choses vues* there is a similar problem in controlling the sheer quantity of relevant material. Keenly aware that he was creating a major work (he had the canvas elaborately relined before even beginning work on it, making it a model of solidity[13]), Picasso allowed his visual memory free play. Like Manet with *Déjeuner sur l'herbe* (which Picasso also had in mind, according to André Suarès[14]), Picasso meant to take on the whole history of painting while recapitulating his own work, hoping thereby to open up a radically new era. Here, too, the exhibition is controlled by a decision to limit these investigations to the essential.

The room devoted to *prodromes* opens the exhibition and shows the importance of the work alone at Gósol during the summer of 1906 and in Paris during the fall, for the prehistory of the *Demoiselles* (i.e., invention of the facial 'mask', the theme of a group of nude figures). Here we find, inter alia (and including many drawings combining these various compositions): the large gouache *Three Nude Figures* (two women and an adolescent with an erection who is holding the phallic form of a *porrón*); the work called *The Harem*; the large Prague *Seated Nude*; and the *Two Nudes* from MOMA (Fig. 7) – all painted in 1906. The connections between these works and the 1907 picture have already been pointed out by Steinberg.

The room containing the *choses vues* is almost at the end of the exhibition, just before the room containing the *Demoiselles* itself and a dozen or so oil sketches of faces and torsos. It is an anthology of the things that have often been associated with the picture. But by being placed where it is, almost at the end of the exhibition, it serves to echo what has preceded it rather than as a display of source material. We see two *Bathers* by Cézanne (Fig. 4) (one that belonged to Matisse); Ingres's *The Turkish Bath* (Fig. 3) (whose colors seem surprisingly subdued when juxtaposed to the *Demoiselles*); Matisse's *Blue Nude*; and Derain's *Bathers* (a parallel that seems increasingly less convincing). There are some sculptures: Gauguin's *Oviri* (c. 1891–3), shown at the 1906 Salon d'Automne, whose pose recalls that of Michelangelo's *Dying Slave* in the Louvre; one of the two Iberian heads stolen from the Louvre by Apollinaire's secretary, which haunted Picasso's search for a physical type for the 'medical student' in the early version of the picture, and, finally, two African pieces (one of them a Fang mask from Derain's collection) and an Oceanic mask (Fig. 5). In short, we are shown things that Picasso must certainly have seen, but without any

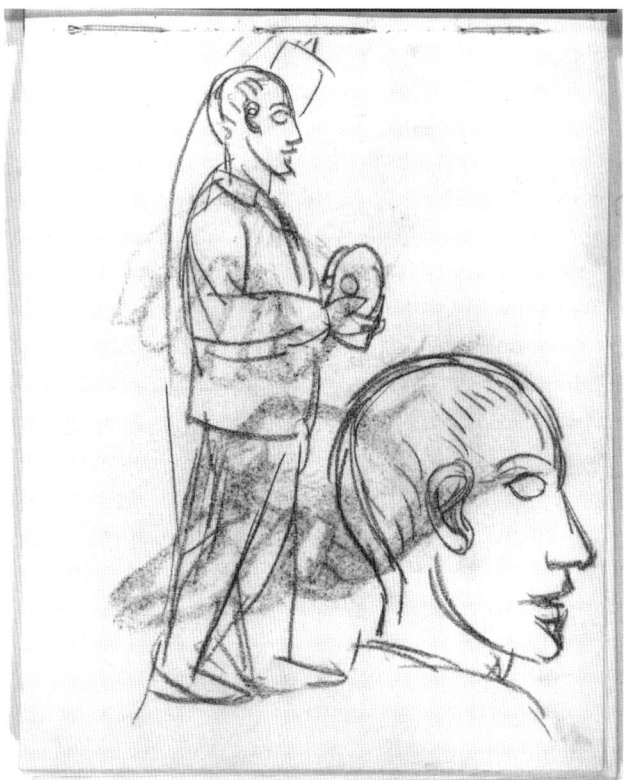

FIGURE 8. Pablo Picasso, *Studies for the Medical Student*. Carnet 3, 37V. March 1907. Pencil on beige paper, 19.3 × 24.2 cm. Musée Picasso, Paris (MP 1861). (© Réunion des musées nationaux – Picasso.)

undue emphasis being put on them and with great discretion. 'Sources' are not paraded before us with sworn-to pedigrees; rather we are shown parts of the past we can choose to consider, or not, when engaging in one of the countless possible historical readings of the *Demoiselles*.

Between those two limits – *prodromes* and *choses vues* – comes the exhibition itself, which fully succeeds in giving us an impression of a mind in action. Slightly unfaithful to Picasso's own working method (his concept of the entire picture emerged simultaneously with his working out of his characters' poses), the first room contains the elements of the picture's mise-en-scène, as established by Steinberg. This develops first from a series of sketches (Figs. 8, 11, and 12) leading to a highly theatrical (Steinberg calls it 'baroque', Rubin calls it 'narrative') overall sketch, containing seven figures (Basel Museum) (Fig. 9): a clothed sailor seated among five prosti-

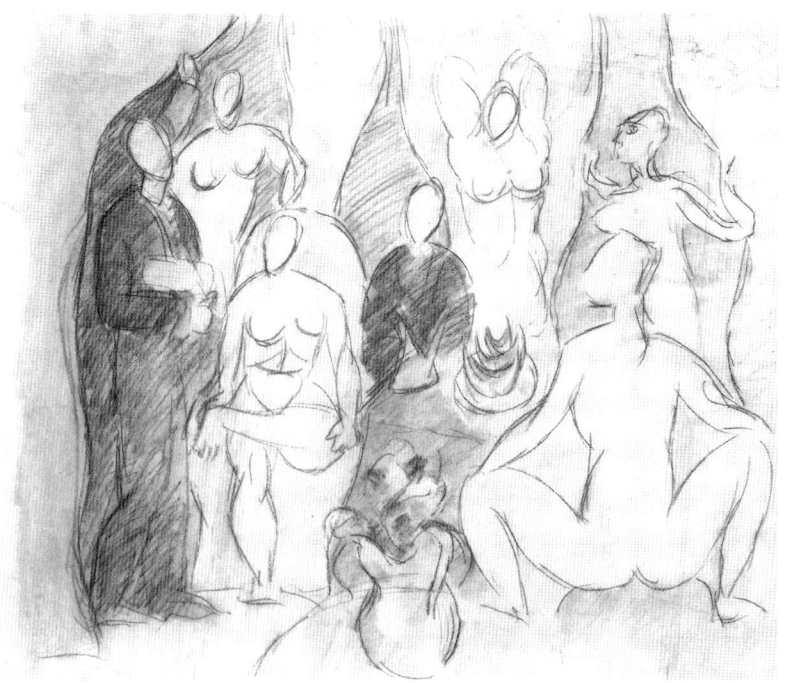

FIGURE 9. Pablo Picasso, *Study with Seven Figures for 'Les Demoiselles d'Avignon'*. March–April 1907. Pencil and pastel on paper, 47.7 × 63.5 cm. Öffentliche Kunstmuseum Basel, Kupferstichkabinett.

tutes, each of whom is turning her head towards the intruder, a medical student entering at the left holding a book in his hand (he too is clothed). Picasso worked on this overall composition for several months, studying in his notebooks the pose of each of the characters (a process superbly delineated in the next room, which is devoted to these variations). Although Picasso attempted to accentuate the interrelationship of these figures, in the end he was obviously not satisfied. First, he did away with one of the standing 'demoiselles' (there are many compositional sketches at this point). Then, in a brutal change, he transformed the student into a female figure. Finally, he eliminated the sailor. All these changes made it gradually more difficult to immediately place the scene narratively as the entrance of someone into a bordello.

From this point forward, the work was conceived as a group of five figures; this was the definitive solution retained in the final canvas. But it wasn't all that simple. The only comprehensive study with five figures is the watercolour in the Philadelphia Museum of Art (Fig. 10). In some

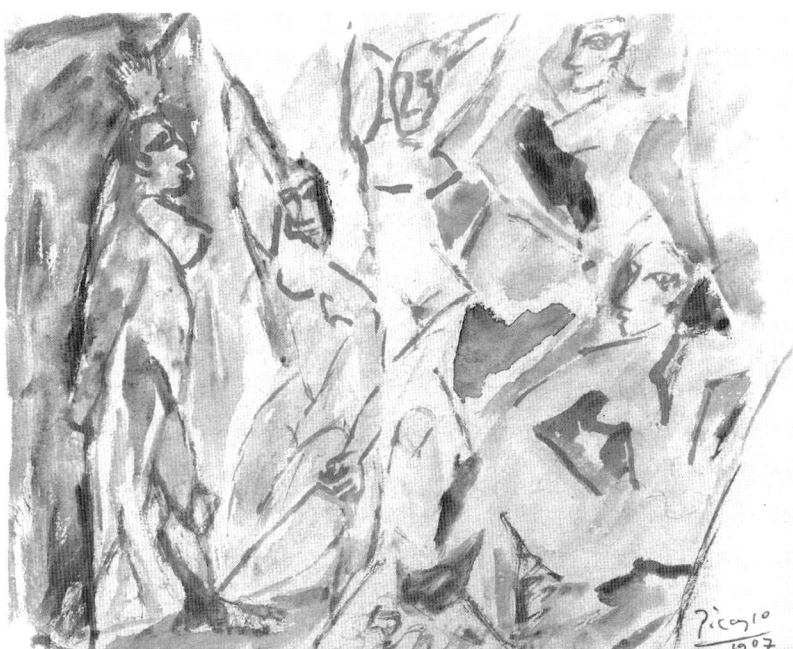

FIGURE 10. Pablo Picasso, *Study with Five Figures for 'Les Demoiselles d'Avignon'*, June 1907. Watercolour on paper, 17.4 × 22.5 cm. Philadelphia Museum of Art, A.E. Gallatin Collection.

respects this study is very close to the final picture, but it lacks the essential stylistic disjunction between the right half of the picture (the 'African' viragoes) and the left (with its 'Iberian' inspiration). A great deal of ink has been expended on the issue of this disjunction, particularly because it opens up the complex question of Picasso's relationship to African art (this stylistic disjunction was also the basis for Kahnweiler's notion that the painting is unfinished). *There is no overall drawing* that reflects the stylistic discontinuity; the final transformation seems to have occurred on the canvas itself. Moreover, there is another disparity between this study and the final painting. Whereas the Philadelphia watercolour (like most of the previous sketches) has a horizontal format, the finished picture is an almost square, vertical rectangle. But the fact is that these two late formal decisions – stylistic disjunction and squarish format – are linked to an earlier decision to eliminate the two male figures, the medical student and the sailor.

We must ask then, what is the story of this male duo? Picasso told Alfred Barr that the man entering from the left had once been carrying a skull (this is confirmed in the many sketches now known) (Fig. 8). Barr thus interpreted this earlier version as 'a kind of *memento mori*', or as 'an allegory or charade on the wages of sin', with the male pair signifying the contrast between virtue and vice. Rejecting this moralistic interpretation, Steinberg posited a Nietzschean allegory about cool, detached learning versus the demands of sex. In the notebooks, the man on the left, identified as 'a medical student', is holding either a skull or a book, sometimes both (Figs. 8 and 11). He is *the one who does not participate*; he doesn't even look at the 'demoiselles'. As for the timid sailor, he is there to be initiated by fearsome females, the Africanisms of certain of them deliberately emphasizing, according to a cliché of the time, their 'animality'.[15]

Taking up Steinberg's essay, Rubin further posits an interpretation of the male pair as a cryptic double self-portrait, revealing the profound ambiguity of Picasso's attitude towards women. It is interesting to note that whereas Steinberg associated the figure of the student, later to become a woman, with the character of Max Jacob – 'a man morally drawn to, but repelled by, the love of woman, fluctuating between what he called his

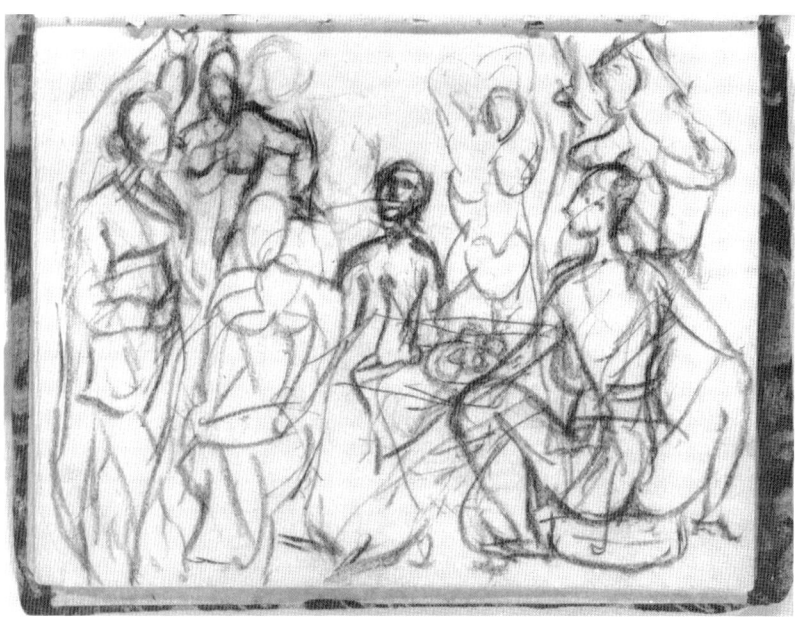

FIGURE 11. Pablo Picasso, *Study with Seven Figures for 'Les Demoiselles d'Avignon'*. Carnet 2, 32R. Winter 1906–7. Pencil on beige paper, 14.7 × 10.6 cm. Musée Picasso, Paris (MP 1859). (© Réunion des musées nationaux – Picasso.)

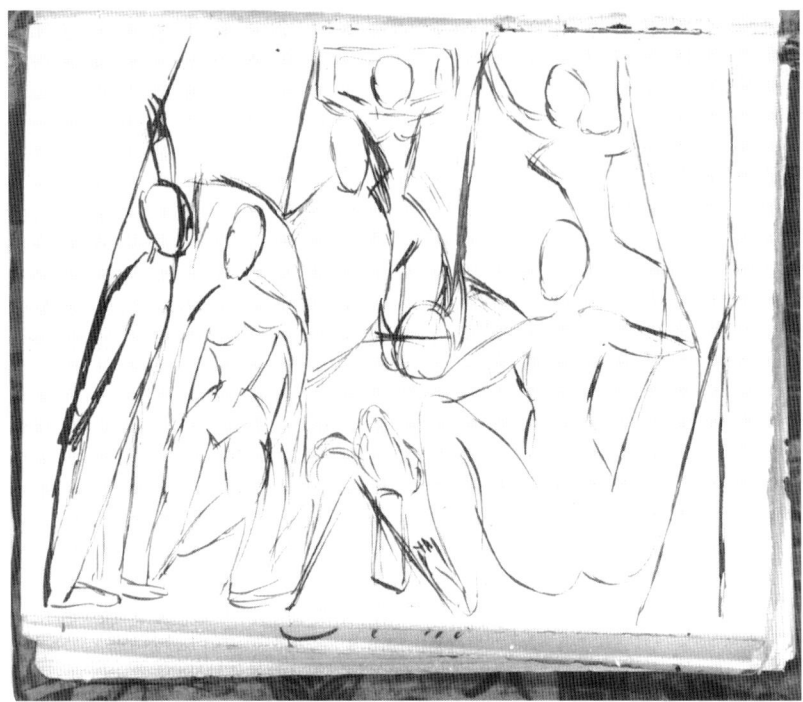

FIGURE 12. Pablo Picasso, *First Study with Six Figures for 'Les Demoiselles d'Avignon'*. Carnet 6, 1R. May 1907. Pen and india ink on beige paper, 10.5 × 13.6 cm. Musée Picasso, Paris (MP 1862). (© Réunion des musées nationaux – Picasso.)

"*amours d'enfer*"' and contrition[16] – Rubin views the sailor as a portrait of Max Jacob grafted onto a self-portrait. And yet Steinberg did note the enigmatic pose of the sailor, whose timidity and evident androgyny in some sketches and drawings contrasts with the phallic attribute – the *porrón* – on the table.[17] What does this mean? Is it not odd that, basing their readings on certain facial traits found in the notebooks and on a certain lack of assurance as to sexual identity, both Steinberg and Rubin should have identified one or another of these male figures with Max Jacob?

Such iconological ambiguities are not, in my opinion, merely coincidental. Indeed, they are entirely determined by what was gradually to become the picture's thematic content: the primordial question of sexual difference. And in this connection we should also note that the bodies of certain of the 'demoiselles' were masculine in many of the drawings and sketches (Fig. 28). This is particularly true of the one known as the 'seated demoiselle' because such was her position in many preliminary sketches.

It is perhaps not by chance if this figure took on so much importance in Steinberg's interpretation: he was the first to make use of Günter Band-mann's observation according to which this 'demoiselle', who seems to be standing in the painting is in fact not even seated but lying down, like a *gisant* seen from above. Changing both sex and position, the figure func-tions like a marker of the countless shifts occurring on the canvas, all con-verging towards an effect of disunity.

The strength of Steinberg's interpretation resides in his managing to demonstrate the causative link between the total isolation of the five pros-titutes vis-à-vis one another in the final picture and the suppression of the initial version's allegory. Whereas in the first scenario the characters react to the student's entrance and the spectator looks on from outside, 'in the *Demoiselles* painting', according to Steinberg, 'this rule of traditional nar-rative art yields to an anti-narrative counter-principle: neighboring figures share neither a common space nor a common action, do not communi-cate or interact, but relate singly, directly, to the spectator. . . . The event, the epiphany, the sudden entrance, is still the theme – but rotated through 90 degrees towards the viewer conceived as the picture's opposite pole'.[18] Thus the stylistic disjunctions and spatial imbalances noted by Steinberg. In order to enable the picture's unity to engulf the spectator (which, according to Steinberg, it does more brutally than any painting since Velázquez's *Las Meninas*), and in order for that unity to reside 'above all in the startled consciousness of a viewer who sees himself seen', a way had to be found to forestall the constitution of any narrative that would neces-sarily have distanced the viewer. And yet, in characterizing this picture, can we not speak of a radical exclusion of the spectator? As Steinberg views the picture, it is self-referential, even onanistic; it impales itself like a *machine célibataire* on the corner of the assaultive table. This initiates contradictory movements of visual protention/retention as a metaphor for coition.[19] Further, the frightful warning stare of the 'demoiselles' seems to declare figuratively the exclusion of the spectator. Doesn't their shattering gaze rid us of any desire to enter the picture's space?

Steinberg had already noted in 1972 that the suppression of the allegory accompanied the exchange of a horizontal format and the adoption of a square, and, in 1983, Rubin was to reverse the terms of Sixten Ringbom's celebrated book and emphasize the passage from a narrative to an 'iconic' space during the picture's creation ('iconic' is not to be read here in the sense it has in Peirce's semiotic terminology. Ringbom, whom Rubin does not mention, refers explicitly to the hieratic organization of devotional paintings prior to the fifteenth century, by opposition to the narrative structure of religious pictures in the Renaissance).[20] Like Steinberg, Rubin noted that the suppression of the allegorical element had unleashed a violence of figuration in Picasso that owed nothing to the traditional symbolist code to which he had hitherto been attached. Addressing Steinberg's idea of pansexualism, Rubin gave it a new twist by emphasizing the theme of death in the first version, which Steinberg had been too quick to set aside,[21] and linked this to Picasso's morbid fascination with the syphilitic prostitutes in the Saint-Lazare hospital. Rubin concluded,

> The final painting no longer contains a specific narrative reference to Picasso's dread of disease and death. There, this dread is subsumed in a broader, more universal fear of mortality that is communicated through more direct pictorial means. We sense the thanatophobia in the primordial horror evoked by the monstrously distorted heads of the two whores on the right of the picture, so opposite to those of the comparatively gracious 'Iberian' courtesans in the center.[22]

I have always been surprised, when reading Steinberg's essay and Rubin's subsequent texts, at the lack of any reference to the major Freudian notion of the 'castration complex'. If only on the metaphoric level, the sexually indeterminate nature of many of the figures in the sketches for the picture and the phallic uprightness or 'erection' of Steinberg's 'gisant' are prime indicators of this. Another indicator is Picasso's own death anxiety, revealed in the early version of the composition in which the medical student carries a skull, an object read by Rubin as a sign of Picasso's mortal fear of syphilis. More importantly, the stunning of the spectator (as described by Steinberg) and the interruption of the narrative by the iconic representation (as set forth by Rubin) seem to me to refer directly to scenarios rehearsed by psychoanalysis. One thinks, here, either of the dream of Freud's most famous patient – in which he found himself standing petrified at his window, being stared at by *motionless* wolves (the dream being the aftereffect of the shock of the primal scene) – or of Freud's short text on the head of the Medusa, with all its multitude of meanings (these include, we will recall, the notion that the Medusa's head is the female sex organ – the sight of which arouses castration anxiety in the young male; the image of castration itself [decapitation-castration]; and the denial of castration, on the one hand by a multiplication of penises [her hair consists of snakes] and, on the other, by its power to turn the spectator to stone, in other words, into an erect, albeit dead, phallus).[23]

In fact, in his catalogue essay for the present exhibition, Rubin makes an oblique reference to Freud's Medusa text when he mentions a lecture given by John Nash in 1970 for the BBC in which the same parallel was drawn.[24] This is one of the new elements in Rubin's interpretation of the picture. Unfortunately, although Rubin maintains a slight distance from the vast outpourings of recent biographical information on Picasso,[25] he does not, I feel, pursue *this* suspicion as far as he might have. Instead he confines himself to the anecdotal and iconological. He enlarges on his 1983 supposition that Picasso may have been gripped by fear of venereal disease and reiterates his 1985 musings on semantic-formal 'affinities' between the features of the crouching 'demoiselles' and certain African sickness masks (which, as Rubin insists, Picasso did not see), designed to ward off syphilis by depicting its ravages. But he goes even further: he includes four photographs of women with faces hideously deformed by *osteosyphilitis* (this making for very *entartete kunst* indeed) and suggests that the horror of similar sights might be the unconscious source of the 'African' features of the crouching woman.[26] I find this argument unfortunate for two reasons. First, founded on a hypothesis whose usefulness I fail to grasp (Picasso's so-called panic fear of syphilis), this theory diminishes the painter's considerable plastic inventiveness, reducing it to a kind of documentary seismography (the work merely documenting either something he has seen or some purported factor in his private life). But second, and more importantly, it undermines the sophisticated conceptualization attained by Rubin's own analysis (from 'narrative' to 'iconic'). Elaboration of the Medusa text, on the other hand, would have enabled him both to consolidate his earlier theories and to reactualize Steinberg's reading.

The Medusa (castration) metaphor is, in fact, the one that, in the evolution of the *Demoiselles*, best accounts for the suppression of allegory, on the one hand, and, on the other, the apotropaic brutality of the finished picture. As already established by Louis Marin, in his remarkable analysis of Caravaggio's *Medusa* in the Uffizi, the Medusa is a cipher of antihistory. A word on the opposition around which Marin's book is structured: Poussin, whose pictures participate in the repression of the act of enunciating proper to any historic discourse, could not abide Caravaggio and said that he had been born to *destroy painting* (Félibien). Caravaggio's inability to 'compose a real story' (Badaglione), along with his rejection of perspective, led him to realism (understood as an attempt to address the spectator 'directly'; to go from the 'once-upon-a-time' aspect of Poussin's pictures to 'Look at me, I'm watching you!').[27] The same reproach (realism as a consequence of the incapacity to narrate) would later be used by contemporary critics of Courbet and, to a lesser extent, Manet. This passage from 'historical' *énoncé* (the impersonal statement of fact) to 'realist' *énonciation* (the act of stating, which presupposes a locutor) is the same shift that

Steinberg is describing when he speaks of a 90-degree rotation of the plane of action and what Rubin means when he analyzes the structural transformation from 'narrative' to 'iconic'. Thus the Medusa myth (as set forth in Caravaggio's painting in the Uffizi) functions as a 'return of the repressed'. It thematizes the spectator's petrification (the theoretical basis of Renaissance monocular perspective), and it makes the female sex organ (the Medusa's head) the essential interrupter of narrative, the icon that challenges the (male) spectator by signifying to him that his comfortable position, outside the narrative scene, is not as secure as he might think.[28]

Further (and this is only a hypothesis that should be worked out at greater length), because castration anxiety is linked to the patricidal fantasy, this metaphor itself, if taken far enough, may enable us to understand the fury with which, Fernande Olivier tells us, Matisse was seized when he saw the picture, or the horrified stupefaction of Braque or Derain; they thought, as Poussin did of Caravaggio, that Picasso 'was out to destroy painting'. In fact, can we not suppose that, in the *Demoiselles*, Picasso was saying aloud what they did not even dare to think themselves, namely, 'If we have the courage to kill the father (tradition, law) symbolically, this is what we will get, this thing so monumentally terrifying in both its freedom and its constraint'? Not that Picasso would have been the first to defy tradition, but he might have been the first to perceive the libidinal foundation of such a combat.

In developing the hypothesis further, we would have to, first, rigorously compare the *Demoiselles* with *Las Meninas* (as Steinberg has suggested), particularly in light of Michel Foucault's contention that the elision of the spectator in Velázquez's canvas epitomizes the fundamental conditions for representation in the classic era. Further, we would want to return to Michael Fried's broader consideration of the opposition between theatricality and absorption as a constituent of modernism.[29] But for the present, I would prefer to conclude this digression with an elipsis. The *Demoiselles* creates a fundamental break with the symbolist tradition, and that break may be linked to an investigation into what Lacanian psychoanalysis calls the symbolic (i.e., the order of the law – governing the Oedipus complex and its correlative, the castration complex – that structures our personality and gives access to every construction of opposition, be it language, society, or, even, art). Such an investigation could not be made in an allegorical (symbolist) way, but had to be transferred by Picasso to the level of pictorial codes, with which he worked on the definitive version of the *Demoiselles* (hence the use of stylistic disjunction to depict the structure of opposition per se). At least that is the light in which I read Steinberg's words: 'As the action turns through ninety degrees to confront the viewer, the picture ceases to be the representation of an adventure enjoyed by one or two men and becomes instead an experience of ours, an experience, that is, of the painting'.[30]

In the section of the exhibition devoted to the evolution of the seven characters over the course of the picture's development, we have a horizontal showcase in which many of the notebooks are displayed. Here we see all the actors, in an order following, from left to right, the composition itself in its various stages. We find the face of the medical student (whose features are borrowed from the previously mentioned Iberian sculpture); the profile of the 'demoiselle' who replaces him, to the left of the painting, and whose improbable hand accentuates one of the most important spatial discontinuities in the *Demoiselles*; the extraordinary work on the muscular composition of the 'demoiselle' who was later eliminated (her posture in the early sketches does not correspond to her position in any overall composition studies where she is still present); the seated 'demoiselle', at first strikingly masculine (Fig. 28), who will turn into Steinberg's 'gisant' after having undergone the 'graphic contamination' of the angular linearity of the *Nude with Drapery*; the torso and face of the sailor, sometimes wearing a beret and pea jacket, sometimes with his hair in a chignon; the still life, carefully worked out in the studies (the flowers and *porrón* eliminated in favor of slices of watermelon, which has less directly sexual connotations); the 'demoiselle' with her lifted arms, who undergoes the most drastic transformations (from hefty caryatid to 'Black-Deco' statuette, symmetrical, geometrical, clasped arms making a horizontal line behind her head, different from the solution finally adopted); the standing 'demoiselle' on the right, who will turn into one of the 'African' whores and the subject of the most oil 'sketches' and the most *post-scriptums*; lastly, the crouching 'demoiselle', in whom all of Picasso's graphic and coloristic violence seems to be concentrated and whose improbable position (we see her body from the back but she is facing towards us) sums up on the figurative level the symbolic movement of protention/retention that apes the sexual relationship and regulates the entire spectator–picture relationship.[31]

Steinberg's – and then Rubin's – elaborate and detailed interpretations have made us familiar with these various characters. Therefore it is not surprising that we find no major revelations in this room. Still, there are some surprises in this presentation of characters, which is much less schoolmarmish than my description makes it seem (bear in mind the constant need to move from the sketches on the wall to those in the notebooks). The greatest surprise is created by one of the two sketches of the face of the crouching 'demoiselle' (Fig. 13). Whereas the first is very close to the final version, the other one manages to achieve an even more daring 'deformation'. Looking at this gouache, which I consider one of the high points of the show, a head of a woman with chin resting on her hand (a kind of transformation of torso into face[32]), we realize how much the relation of cubism to the work on the *Demoiselles* is like that of an after-effect to its trauma. Indeed, because Picasso rejected the insane amorphism of this face, we can measure the distance he still had to travel – through analytic cubism and all its researches – in order to arrive at the radical semiological rupture that was to be synthetic cubism.[33] Indeed, not until the spring of 1913, with his series of *papiers collés* that analyse the minimal possible number of signs needed to denote a guitar or a face, would Picasso understand just what was at stake in the new economy of signs he first brought into play in this study.

A second surprise afforded by the exhibition is somewhat understated (it is found in a passageway leading to the room containing *choses vues*). We already know about what I would call Picasso's 'art-deco' interest in African art. This interest is manifested in the sketches with symmetrical cross-hatching on a vertical axis to represent a back or those transforming the 'demoiselle' with raised arms into a geometrical figure, her arms forming a circle around her body, and so on. But here we have studies of proportions in the strictest Renaissance tradition (Fig. 24) (we are reminded of Dürer or Luca Pacioli). These studies, directly related to the *Woman with Clasped Hands* (in the exhibition, painted on a canvas already covered with oil sketches for the 'demoiselle' with raised arms), are of two kinds. Sometimes horizontal lines pass through the principal joints of the body (in which case they are given letters, as in a treatise on proportions, although of course here we do not know what the letters refer to); at other times the entire body is drawn inside a series of equal and intersecting lozenges. In both instances, the body of the frontal figure, its arms slightly bent, hands joined at the crotch, is divided into equal parts, idealized according to a previously chosen module. And this is the surprising thing. For what could be further from Picasso's final version than this delectable little bit of geometry? I would even go so far as to say that the purging of such almost academic procedures was a necessary step toward, achieving the disruptive character of the *Demoiselles* (which, needless to say, contains no reference to them whatsoever). This type of 'studio recipe' was later the very stuff on which minor cubists fed (we recall their fascination with the golden section and other similar nonsense).

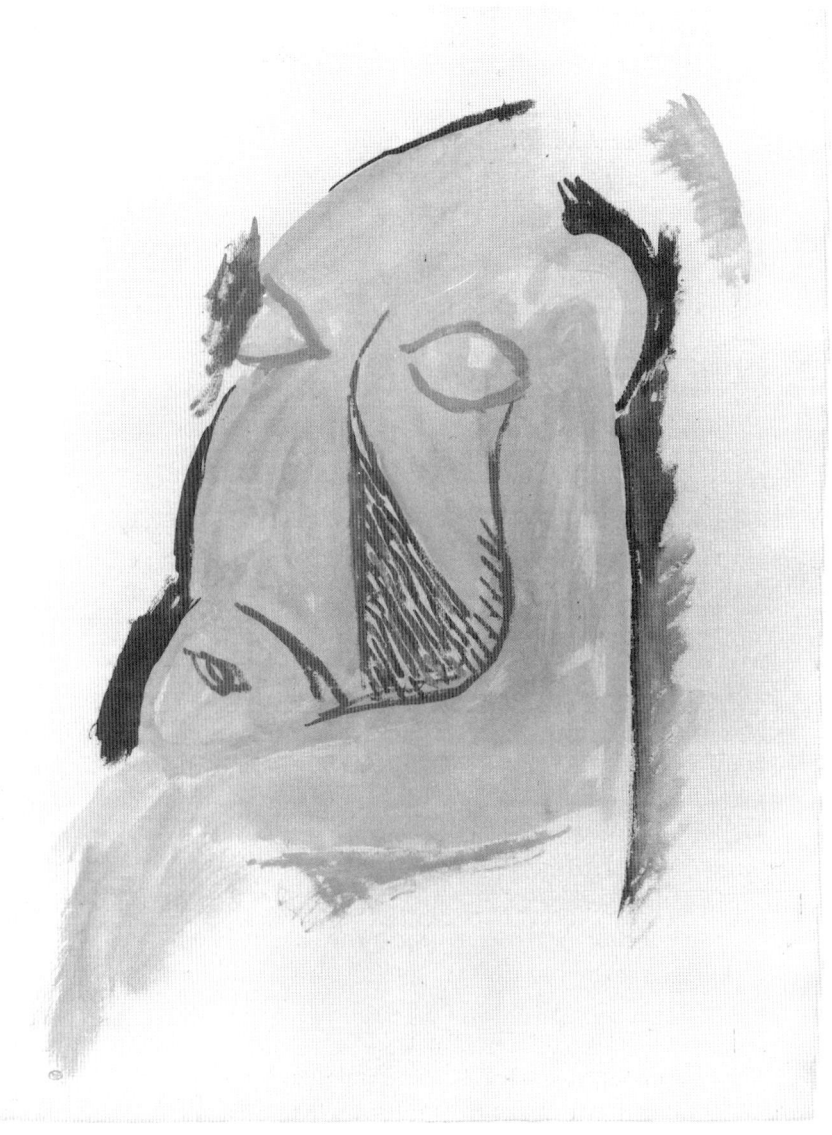

FIGURE 13. Pablo Picasso, *Head Study for the Crouching "Demoiselle"*, June–July 1907. Gouache on paper, 63 × 48 cm. Musée Picasso, Paris (MP 539). (© Réunion des musées nationaux – Picasso.)

Just as Picasso shed allegory in order to give full play on a truly symbolic level to the erotic and morbid theme of the *Demoiselles*, he also abandoned the symbolist idealism of these geometric stylizations. Nothing is more precious than evidence of that rejection, and Daix's examination of the sketchbooks is highly useful here. In particular, it enables us to conclude that although there were indeed two working 'campaigns' on the *Demoiselles*, the hiatus between them was short and consisted, first, of a provisional detour by way of the *Nude with Drapery* (very *art nègre*), and, second, of a return to one of his favourite characters from his stay in Gósol: Josep Fontdevila, whose angular features were reactivated in Picasso's memory by his work on an ink drawing based on a charcoal portrait of Salmon. Daix notes the extent to which Gósol studies represented for Picasso an occasion for inventing the facial 'mask', which enabled him shortly afterwards to solve the problem of the *Portrait of Gertrude Stein* (Fig. 15). It is as if, with the return to the Fontdevila facial type, a return contemporary with work on the *Nude with Drapery*, we can see a conflict between two concepts of the African art Picasso had just discovered: African art as pure geometrical design (what I call the 'Black-Deco' version) and African art as apotropaic savagery (the 'Medusa' effect). A sketch page for the Salmon portrait (whose importance to the *Demoiselles* has already been noted by Rubin) shows this conflict taking place, because both versions of 'Africa' appear on it together.[34] Examination of the notebooks confirms that a conflict did indeed occur just prior to the dramatic move from the sketches to the canvas itself. Now we have good reason to believe it was the resolution of that conflict (with the triumph of 'savagery') which enabled Picasso to start painting. Thus his 'interruption' of work on the *Demoiselles* – or the supposed gap between two campaigns – turns out to have been no interruption at all.

At last we come to the great picture itself. Its stature is all the greater now that we have witnessed the complexity, the length, and the compulsive nature of its gestation. The painful reduction of seven figures to five (countless notebook pages attest to the difficult resolution of this process of elimination) is seen to have been worth it. The Flaubertian adage according to which the most important thing is to know how to omit has never seemed so true. The *Demoiselles* is surrounded by studies of torsos and faces (not, in the strict sense, really studies for the picture at all) that form a constellation around it (and once again we notice the passage from 'Iberian' to 'African' types). The exhibition eloquently shows us that Picasso never undertook a major work without examining every possibility, without setting up a dialogue between the picture on which he was toiling and all the marginalia that, without having seemed to, enabled him to solve its problems.

One of the last works in the show is the unique study of a face truly in profile with one eye full front. It is the perfect example of an independent study – the positioning of the face is unlike anything in the *Demoiselles*, and yet it is clear that Picasso was thinking of the 'demoiselle' on the left and that he cleverly rejected for her this overly simple solution of complete profile (we can see the edge of her other eye in the large picture, which, as Rubin notes, immediately gives volume to her flattened profile). Nothing could conclude the exhibition better than the revelation of this detail, because – and this is the great lesson we are being taught – with Picasso what is rejected is always highly significant. The setting aside of this formulaic Egyptian manner demonstrates one last time that with this painter nothing was ever taken for granted, no stylistic decision was ever made just because of some preordained rule.

Steinberg has already noted that the abolition of the principle of internal coherence in the *Demoiselles* was one of Picasso's most telling blows against Western pictorial tradition. Everything in this exhibition displays the ferocious energy with which he constantly refused to make his painting conform with regard to the unity of theme (allegory), of geometry (proportions), of style (Iberian or African), or of medium (flatness). The fact that he managed to build this masterpiece on the destruction of preceding representational conventions, while working in virtual isolation, is the amazing act on which all the art of our century is built.

NOTES

1 This chapter was originally written as a review of the exhibition. Though account is taken (especially in the notes) of subsequent publications, it has been left close to the form in which it was first published, preserving the sense of direct response to what was an exceptional event, in which the *Demoiselles* was shown together with much of the visual material in one way or another connected with it. The original review appeared with the same title in *Art in America* 76, no. 6 (June 1988), 130–40, 172–3. It was translated from French by Richard Miller.

2 Hélène Seckel (ed.), *Les Demoiselles d'Avignon* (Paris: Musée Picasso, 1988), 2 vols.

3 Leo Steinberg, 'Le Bordel philosophique', as in note 2, vol. 2, 320–64. Originally published as 'The Philosophical Brothel', Parts 1 and 2, *Art News* 71, nos. 5 and 6 (September and October 1972). Republished with revisions in *October*, no. 44 (New York and Cambridge, Mass., spring 1988). I shall henceforth refer to this publication.

4 William Rubin, 'La genèse des *Demoiselles d'Avignon*', in *Demoiselles* (1988) vol. 2,

368–487. A revised version of this essay is published in *Studies in Modern Art*, no. 3 (New York: Museum of Modern Art, 1994), 13–144. I shall henceforth quote from this publication, referring to it as 'Genesis'. Rubin's earlier essays include 'From Narrative to "Iconic" in Picasso: The Buried Allegory in *Bread and Fruitdish on a Table* and the Role of *Les Demoiselles d'Avignon*', *Art Bulletin* 65, no. 4 (December 1983), 615–49, and 'Picasso' in *"Primitivism" in 20th Century Art* (New York: Museum of Modern Art, 1984), vol. 1, 240–343.

5   The first title Salmon mentions for the picture is *Le B . . . Philosophique*, perhaps from Apollinaire (Rubin detects a reference to *La philosophie dans le boudoir*, Apollinaire having been a great fan of Sade), but it was also referred to as *Le bordel d'Avignon* by Picasso's close friends at the time (*demoiselles* was chosen by Salmon when he showed the picture in public in 1916, probably to avoid scandal). Picasso first associated the name 'Avignon' ('a very familiar name, connected to my life') with Barcelona ('I was living around the corner from Avignon Street. It is there that I bought my paper, my watercolour supplies') and later with the city of that name and a bordello there (Max Jacob's grandmother was from Avignon). Zervos would seem to have been the first to report Picasso as having said that the bordello in question was in the Carre Avignon, and Barr repeated the statement, which thus took on quasi-official status. On all this, see Rubin, 'Genesis', 17–19.

6   Pierre Daix, 'L'histoire des *Demoiselles d'Avignon* révisée à l'aide des carnets de Picasso', in *Demoiselles* (1988), vol. 2, 490–545.

7   Hélène Seckel and Judith Cousins, 'Chronologie', in *Demoiselles*, vol. 2, 558–623. This has been translated in *Studies in Modern Art*, as in note 4, 145–205. I shall henceforth refer to this publication as Seckel-Cousins.

8   Since the publication of this review, evidence has surfaced indicating that the painting might have been displayed in 1918, at the joint Matisse-Picasso exhibition organized by Paul Guillaume (and prefaced by Apollinaire). See Etienne-Alain Hubert, 'Appendix to the Chronologie', in *Studies in Modern Art*, as in note 4, 206–12.

9   Strange twist of fate: at the time he wrote to Suarès. Speaking of his collection and in particular of the *Demoiselles* and the *Red Fish* of Matisse (also at MOMA), Doucet remarked, 'Now I'm ready and can wait; the Americans won't get them'. Quoted in Seckel-Cousins, 179.

10 Seckel, 'Anthologie', *Demoiselles*, vol. 2, 627–88. This anthology is translated in *Studies of Modern Art*, as in note 4, 213–56. I shall henceforth quote from this publication, referring to it as Seckel. This synoptic presentation of an infinitely more complete body of texts than is generally available deserves detailed examination (many of the interpretations put forward for the picture are shot down). I shall mention only the case of Kahnweiler because his critical history of cubism remains one of the most credible, and intelligent, of all the 'early witnesses'. Thus Kahnweiler's notion that the picture is unfinished, one taken up by every critic until Steinberg's denunciation of it as foolish and Rubin's marshalling of supporting evidence gradually took shape in various articles by the German critic/dealer: first as hypothesis, then as certainty, and, finally, supported by Picasso's own word. Comparison of Kahnweiler's various versions of his first encounter with the picture, in all its implacable rigor, is the best way to refute his famous contention.

11 Steinberg, 'Philosophical Brothel', 61. Elsewhere Rubin points out the link, in

Kahnweiler's writing, between the so-called unfinished state of the picture and the fact that it marked the beginning of cubism. Because, on the one hand, this paradigm change concerns only the right ('African') side of the *Demoiselles* and, because, on the other hand, Kahnweiler's neo-Kantian aesthetics demanded that a work of art have internal stylistic coherence, he was forced to suppose that, had he been able to, Picasso would have painted the entire picture in 'African' style (yet nowhere does Kahnweiler provide any explanation for this so-called interruption, and today, after the fact, it seems surprising that his theory remained valid for so long). See Rubin, 'Genesis', 119, note 6.

12 Rubin, 'Genesis', 22–3.

13 It is because of its fragility that the picture has travelled so infrequently since its acquisition by MOMA.

14 Letter from Suarès to Jacques Doucet, 10 March 1924: 'The *Demoiselles* are Picasso's *Déjeuner sur l'herbe*. In fact, he secretly thought of it'. Cited in Seckel-Cousins, 179.

15 Steinberg gave Picasso's symbolist 'thought about woman as the image of animal destiny' – a very common fin de siècle theme for which Picasso uses the signifier of 'African' form – a Nietzschean interpretation (Steinberg, 48). Rubin was to explore in detail the period's linkage of 'Africa' and 'animality' in his article for the *'Primitivism'* catalogue, 'Picasso', 258 ff.

16 Steinberg, 'Philosophical Brothel', 41. The text reads: 'As Picasso's former roommate, literary mentor and most intimate friend of those years, [Jacob] must have caused the artist to ponder that mysterious housing of sexuality which is a man's body; and to brood over the differences between possessing and being possessed by, one's sex'.

17 The sailor is one of the most enigmatic figures and, as demonstrated in the room in the exhibition devoted to the different characters, he underwent the greatest number of transformations: first highly personalized in some sketches – he is sporting a moustache and examining the cigarette he is rolling – he next becomes a mere asexual cipher, wearing a beret/chignon in some of the oil sketches. Note also the fact that at least two physiognomical 'types' are envisaged for the sailor, either 'African' or 'Iberian', indicating that Picasso only eliminated the character at the very end, once he had found a somewhat less allegorical way to transmit something of his secret.

18 Steinberg, 'Philosophical Brothel', 13.

19 Rubin explores further this metaphor, more literally, in a memo written while Steinberg was working on 'The Philosophical Brothel', and which he paraphrases in his catalogue essay, speaking of the space in the *Demoiselles* (curtains and pink membranes) as a vaginal space and referring to certain notebook sketches as endowing 'the curtains anthropomorphically with contours that suggest feminine torsos, towards which the "arrow" of the penetrating table seems directed'. Rubin, 'Genesis', 127, note 105.

20 Cf. Sixten Ringbom, *Icon to Narrative: The Rise of the Dramatic Close-Up in Fifteenth-Century Devotional Painting* (1965). For an interesting comment on Steinberg's text, the problem it considers and nineteenth-century pictorial tradition, see Werner Hofmann, 'Réflexions sur "l'Iconisation" à propos des *Demoiselles d'Avignon*', *Revue de l'Art*, no. 71 (Paris, 1986), 33–42. Rubin remarks that, framing the

period of work on the *Demoiselles* are three other large canvases by Picasso, which underwent the same type of transformation during their creation: *Family of Saltimbanques* (1904–5), *Three Women* (1908–9), and *Bread and Fruitdish* (1908–9). Thus we are dealing with a general tendency in Picasso's art during those years. See Rubin, 'From Narrative to 'Iconic', 626.

21 Steinberg: 'Why a medical student? . . . And why the skull as his symbol? . . . Perhaps because a medical student is the one member of human society who can, and who does, look at a skull with thoughts other than thoughts of death – i.e., looks at it as an object of scientific enquiry'. 'Philosophical Brothel', 40–1.

22 Rubin, 'From Narrative to "Iconic"', 630. This passage is repeated verbatim in his 'Picasso', 254.

23 The account of the psychoanalysis of the Wolf Man appeared in German in 1918. The text on the head of the Medusa, 'Das medusenhaupt', written in 1922, was published posthumously in 1940 and translated into English in 1941. It appears in *The Standard Edition of the Complete Psychological Works of Sigmund Freud*, James Strachey (ed.) (London, 1955), vol. 18, 273–4. At the time this review was written, I was not aware of the fact that Richard Wolheim had already made the connection between the *Demoiselles* and the Wolf Man's dream. However, Wolheim extends this one connection to Picasso's entire oeuvre, which I would *not* do. See Wolheim, *Painting as Art* (Princeton, 1987), 286 ff.

24 This broadcast lecture, 'Pygmalion and Medusa', has hitherto been overlooked in the critical literature on the *Demoiselles* and thanks are owing to Rubin for having rescued it from oblivion. However, in order for it to become part of the actual 'documentation' it should, obviously, be published.

25 Cf. Mary Matthews Gedo, *Picasso: Art as Autobiography* (Chicago, 1980), in which the author goes so far as to state that the painter had contracted a venereal disease, about which Rubin voices only timid doubt (true, later in his own text Rubin characterizes Picasso as the 'most autobiographical of painters', 'Genesis', 59. Steinberg's irony, in the postscript to his text, is sharper: 'But if this were indeed the rock-bottom truth about a picture still acclaimed as "the first modern painting," would this tell us something we perhaps ought to know about being modern?' 'The Philosophical Brothel', 71. Such are the limits of all biographism: holding the biographical to be the essential Cause (whereas it is at best merely one of many elements playing a part in the semantic stratification of a given work), it ends up in what Roland Barthes has called *asymbolia*, that is, the blockage of the infinite circuit of interpretation. For a vehement attack against the 'biographical reduction' to which Picasso's work is today being subjected, see Rosalind Krauss, 'In the Name of Picasso', in *The Originality of the Avant-Garde and Other Modernist Myths* (Cambridge, Mass.: MIT Press, 1985), 23–40.

26 The four photographs published by Rubin in the catalogue *Demoiselles* (1988) are not, in fact, of syphilitic deformations, as David Lomas pointed out in 'A Canon of Deformity: *Les Demoiselles d'Avignon* and Physical Anthropology', *Art History* 16, no. 3 (Oxford, September 1993), the publication on which his chapter in this volume is based. Rubin publishes six further photographs, which are of deformations caused by congenital syphilis, in his revised version of the catalogue essay in *Studies in Modern Art*, no. 3, 131 and 132, note 170.

27 See Louis Marin, *Détruire la peinture* (Paris: Editions Galilée, 1977), passim. Of

course, Caravaggio is not the first to be addressing the beholder in this 'realist' fashion: one can find scores of donors and saints directly summoning the spectator in devotional painting (Flemish in particular), and in Italian mannerist paintings, many 'parergonal' characters point the attention of the beholder to this or that element of the scene. But in these cases this mode of address is functional: in devotional painting, it is a matter of underlining the act of faith or the donor or the saint as an example to follow; in mannerist painting, the goal is to blur the limit between the imaginary space (that of the painting) and the real space (that of the beholder), by playing on the topical ambiguity of the frame. Caravaggio is the first to ignore these justifications. I thank Charles Dempsey for his precisions concerning this historical question.

On Courbet and the Medusa, see Neil Hertz, 'Medusa's Head; Male Hysteria under Political Pressure', first published in *Representations*, no. 4 (Fall 1983) and reprinted in Hertz, *The End of the Line* (New York: Columbia University Press, 1985), 161–215. However, Hertz agrees with Michael Fried, for whom Courbet's art 'avoids anxiety' (see Fried, 'Courbet's Feminity', first published in *Gustave Courbet* [Brooklyn Museum, 1988] reprinted in Fried, *Courbet's Realism* [Chicago: Chicago University Press, 1990], 189–222 and 339, note 32).

Manet's situation is ever more complex and deserves greater consideration here. We note that, according to Fried, what differentiates his art from that of the Le Nain brothers or Velázquez is that 'there is not a single large multi-figure painting in Manet's *oeuvre* in which more than one of those figures looks at us', which also distinguishes his work from the *Demoiselles*. Indeed, compare what Steinberg has to say about the manner in which the 'demoiselles' are isolated from each other and address the spectator directly, with Fried's statement: 'I believe that Manet seems consciously or otherwise to have felt that to have *more* than a single figure look directly at the beholder would in effect be to establish a number of individual and, so to speak merely psychological, relationships between the beholder on the one hand and the figures in question on the other. Whereas Manet seems to have wanted to establish a particular kind of relationship between the beholder and the painting as a *whole*, in its essential unity as a *painting*': Michael Fried, 'Manet's Sources', *Artforum* (March 1969), reprinted in *Manet's Modernism or, The Face of Painting in the 1860s* (Chicago: Chicago University Press, 1996), 469, note 26. It may be precisely this type of ontological unity Picasso is basically criticizing in the *Demoiselles*, which seems to be Steinberg's opinion. Finally, the last item in the dossier: the Medusa myth itself seems to have a direct link to the invention of the mask as indicator of metamorphosis; see David Napper, 'Perseus and the Gorgon Head', in *Masks, Transformations and Paradox* (Berkeley: University of California Press, 1986), 83–134.

28 The notion of the 'female body' as a diagetic 'switch' has been analyzed by feminist criticism, particularly in connection with cinema. The first important text on the question is Laura Mulvey, 'Visual Pleasure and Narrative Cinema', *Screen* 16, no. 3 (Autumn 1975), 6–18.

29 Here too it is a question of following a Steinberg intuition that sends us to Riegl's book on the Dutch group portrait to clarify his '90-degree turn' statement. Riegl's opposition between two types of pictorial coherence corresponds to two types of 'attention' (internal coherence of the picture based on the 'attention' of the

depicted figures; external coherence based on the appeal to the spectator and his 'attention') and does not differ fundamentally from the structure set up by Fried. On certain links between seventeenth-century Dutch art, Caravaggio, and the problem raised by Fried vis-à-vis Courbet and Manet, see Svetlana Alpers, 'Describe or Narrate? A Problem in Realistic Representation', *New Literary History* 8, no. 1 (Autumn 1976), 15–41.

30 Steinberg, 'Philosophical Brothel', 45–6.

31 Steinberg has devoted a lengthy discussion to this character in 'The Philosophical Brothel' and analyzed this motif of the front/back view as a constant in Picasso's art and as the expression of a desire for radical possession (see his 'The Algerian Women and Picasso at Large', *Other Criteria* [Oxford: Oxford University Press, 1972], 125–234, passim). If we pursue the castration metaphor, it is interesting to refer to the 'anal coitus' theory invented by the 'Wolf Man' to alleviate his castration anxiety, and to Freud's lengthy treatment, at the end of his analysis of that case, of the links between the eroticism and the castration complex. Further, we recall that Steinberg views the large picture, *Three Women*, which follows the *Demoiselles* in Picasso's career, as a mythic scene of creation, exploring sexual difference ('Resisting Cézanne: Picasso's "Three Women"', *Art in America* [November–December 1978], 114–33, passim).

32 According to Rubin, John Nash was the first to identify this figure, a sketch of which appears twice in Picasso's notebooks, with the features of the crouching woman. Nash was also the one who mentions a torso transformed into a face. See Rubin, 'Genesis', 113 and 115.

33 Here I would refer to my essay on the relationship between synthetic cubism and African art, 'Kahnweiler's Lesson', *Representations* (Spring 1987), reprinted in Bois, *Painting as Model* (Cambridge, Mass.: MIT Press, 1990), 65–97. Picasso's rediscovery of African art in 1912 must have reactivated many of the ideas he had conceived and then abandoned during his work on the *Demoiselles*, particularly that of the arbitrary nature of the sign. This supports what I have written about the traumatic effect of the picture (and its functioning as 'retrospective translation').

34 See Daix, 'L'histoire', 514–8; also Rubin, 'Picasso', 284–5, and 'Genesis', 109 ff.

4

TAMAR GARB

'To Kill the Nineteenth Century'

SEX AND SPECTATORSHIP WITH GERTRUDE AND PABLO

The *Demoiselles d'Avignon* has spawned many spectators. From the privileged coterie in the Bâteau-Lavoir to the generations of experts, witnesses, detractors, and defenders who have speculated about its origin, meaning, genesis, and significance, it has generated an unprecedented amount of dispute and debate. But about one thing there is universal agreement, expressed either tacitly or explicitly in all the written accounts of the picture: the *Demoiselles d'Avignon* was intended to be viewed by men – virile, heterosexual men of European origin, not unlike the painter himself. The fact of the matter is, however, that most of the men who first looked at the painting in the privileged conditions of Picasso's studio could not recognise themselves as its addressees. They could not fathom its formal disjunctions, its incoherence, its peculiar iconic hybridity. Neither did it appear to speak to their sexual fantasies, their dreams of dominance or fears of castration.[1] They could not 'penetrate' the painted surface or experience themselves as subjects interpolated by the picture in highly sexualised terms as Leo Steinberg, Robert Rosenblum, and William Rubin were later able to do.[2] Illegible as art, the *Demoiselles d'Avignon* could not function as a screen for the projection of desire. As such it was a 'failure',[3] a 'horrible mess',[4] 'something mad and monstrous',[5] a 'tragedy'.[6] Only much later, when its pictorial transgressions had been tamed by formalist teleologies and its secret history had been revealed by careful tracking of studies and sketches, could this picture provide the narrative spur to scintillating tales of sex and seduction in which the five angular, masked figural hybrids it represented would be animated into lascivious 'whores' whose rampantly sexual 'nature' was to be controlled and consumed by the hungry gaze of expert, virile viewers.

Feminist scholars have been right to point out the patriarchal interests served by latter-day interpretations of the painting and curatorial initiatives surrounding its display. As Carol Duncan astutely argues, the position that the *Demoiselles d'Avignon* occupies in the dominant modernist narrative of modern art has helped to construct a mode of viewing and producing modern art that is exclusive of women as agents, as producers and active participants in the elaboration of high culture.[7] In this narrative and in the institutionalised hierarchies set up by the ritualised procession through the development of modern art that the picture's placement in the Museum of Modern Art, New York, invited until recently, male masters experiment with form and meaning through the image of the sexualised female. Her body, as Anna Chave has demonstrated, functions as the matter that is manipulated in the interests of modernist progression.[8] For such scholars the *Demoiselles d'Avignon*, with its distorted rendering of five female figures incarcerated in an enclosed interior space, has come to epitomise the misogynist core of modernist experimentation. There is nothing for women in this game. The picture both misrepresents the women it 'depicts' and excludes actual women from constituting its audience or participating in its radical project. Chave's response to this closed circuit, this exclusively male symbolic system, is to perform the curiously anachronistic act of identification with the depicted 'women', as if real sex workers rather than phantasmatic phantoms were on view here, thus colluding, to my mind, with the literalist readings of the picture to which she so vehemently objects.[9] Neither Duncan nor Chave spend much time considering the fact that one of the first appreciative responses to this picture came from a woman, an extraordinary, unconventional, bold, and defiant woman it must be said, but a woman nevertheless.

Gertrude Stein, expatriate American writer and close friend of Picasso, was one of the *Demoiselles*'s first viewers. She and her brother Leo had befriended Picasso the year before he finished the picture when they had begun to buy his work through the dealer Clovis Sagot.[10] Leo had only recently initiated Gertrude into the rarefied world of collecting and appreciating art objects, especially the work of Paul Cézanne to which she was to remain devoted for the rest of her life. It was the encounter with this artist that was to affect her own work profoundly. Stein's developing empathy with Cézanne's compositional strategies (as a model for her own modernist reconceptualisation of the nature of writing) was to make her receptive to Picasso's refusal of traditional modes of representing objects and figures in space. Through Cézanne, Stein was to claim, she had learned to take the 'realism of the composition' as seriously as the 'realism of characters'. It was through his example that she learned to mistrust the transparent illusionism of nineteenth-century modes of realism, to discard the mendacious catharsis of linear narrative structures, and to explore the egalitarian possibilities of regarding all objects or characters as equally deserving of attention, creating a nonhierarchical all-overness in her prose, which was, in her view, the verbal equivalent to Cézanne's spread-out, decentred surfaces.

Stein claimed to have written *Three Lives*, first published in the summer of 1909, seated in front of Cézanne's *Portrait of Mme Cézanne*, which she and Leo had bought in 1904.[11] Although she and Leo shared a passion for Cézanne at this point, they understood him entirely differently. Where Leo located Cézanne as the culminating point of a venerable tradition that emanated from the Renaissance, Gertrude saw in his compositional strategies a fundamental break from the past.[12] They licenced her own radical inquiry into the mechanics of her medium. It was Leo's lack of comprehension of her project and his scornful denigration of her abilities as a writer that were to contribute greatly to the unbreachable break in her relationship with her brother. And when, to her dismay, her brother insisted on keeping the small Cézanne still life of apples they owned when they split the collection between them, it was Picasso who sought to console her by painting her a small watercolour of an apple that he assured her would represent the quintessential 'Cézanne' apple.

Stein's literary explorations, her self-conscious investigation of the tools of writing, the armature of language, and her bold eschewal of the conventional use of grammar, syntax, and structure produced a prose that, in Leo's view, was nothing short of nonsensical. Indeed the terms within which he dismissed her writing were not dissimilar from his disparaging remarks about Picasso and the 'cubist-funny business' that he grew to detest. Neither of them, he claimed, understood their medium. As a result what they produced was 'Godalmighty rubbish'.[13] By the time Gertrude and Leo came to view Picasso's large experimental canvas, therefore, their taste and sensibilities had already begun to diverge, and where Leo, in keeping with most of Picasso's friends and aquaintances, found the picture indecipherable, Gertrude felt an intuitive sympathy for the struggle that had produced it despite, or maybe because of, its 'awful' power.[14] As a writer, she identified with the enormous exertion the picture evi-

denced. Years later, she was to comment on her encounter with this extraordinary painting:

> He who created a thing is forced to make it ugly. In the effort to create the
> intensity and the struggle to create this intensity, the result always produces a
> certain ugliness. Those who follow can make of this thing a beautiful thing,
> because they know what they are doing, the thing having already been
> invented, but the inventor, because he does not know what he is going to
> invent, inevitably the thing he makes must have its ugliness'.[15]

Stein was struck by the painting's rejection of traditional aesthetic principles. She knew that it could not be understood in terms of conventional
notions of beauty. Indeed its very 'ugliness', its 'brutality', rather than
being negative properties of the work, testified to the struggle its production had involved. It was this struggle that was thematised in the work's raw
incoherence, its openly exploratory amalgam of styles and references, its
lack of resolution or 'finish'. Works of art functioned, in her words, as
'chronological testimonials to the "struggle" to realize the artist's vision'.[16]
A work's 'ugliness' was a necessary corollary to its innovativeness. Indeed
Stein liked to refer to her own work of this period in just these terms. To
talk of art that was 'ugly' or 'brutal' was, in her view, to praise its innovative
power. She liked to refer to the 'ugly giants' then being created by Matisse,
Picasso, and herself. In the words of Leon Katz, 'The "brutality" of each of
their works was the outcome of the process that created them – the successive shuckings off of old habits of seeing and rendering, and the ultimate
emergence of a new art'.[17]

Stein was at this time struggling with her own monumental novel *The
Making of Americans*, which, like the *Demoiselles d'Avignon*, functioned
for her as a laboratory work in which different styles and forms of expression coexist in a state of tension and conflict, the traces of which are left
unresolved in the final work. It was a testing ground, not a resolved artistic
statement, and it was its very exploratory rawness that, in Stein's terms,
constituted its significance. Anything, Stein held, that was truly new could
not be understood by existing aesthetic criteria. As such, it could not
immediately register as beautiful. Only its eventual absorption into tradition could make of it an object familiar enough to be called beautiful.
The fact that it was perceived as unbeautiful was the mark of its iconoclastic grandeur, its rich facilitating power.

Stein, the modernist writer, prided herself on understanding Picasso,
the vanguard artist, when few others in the inner circle did. She alone, she
felt, comprehended the radicalness of his project.[18] It was one with which

she felt total sympathy and with which she completely identified. To Stein, she and Picasso were united in a desperate struggle against the stultifying conventions of previous art. Their project was radically iconoclastic, violent, even murderous. They had set out 'to kill the nineteenth century' and they would be ruthless in the process.[19] Stein recognised, therefore, the patricidal power of *Les Demoiselles*, but unlike her contemporaries, she was not daunted by it.[20] She was to remain irreverent about fathers and male authority figures throughout her life. In her last years she was to write scathingly of them:

> [F]ather Mussolini and father Hitler and father Roosevelt and father Stalin and father Lewis and father Blum and father france. . . . There is too much fathering going on just now and there is no doubt about it fathers are depressing.[21]

By 1907 Stein was herself fatherless and was arrogantly dismissive of her literary forbears. Her task was to take literature forward by annihilating her predecessors. It was the *Demoiselles*'s assault on tradition that parallelled her own rejection of traditional narrative and linguistic models, and it was with Picasso as a radical artist rather than the 'demoiselles' as victimised 'women' that she was willing to empathize. It was this masculine identification that was facilitating for Stein. She seems not to have been upset by the caricatural and primitivising rendering of the female figures in Picasso's painting. What the painting represented to her was an attack on a genre, not an attack on women. She identified with the artistic agency thematised in it, rather than the image of femininity brutalised by it.[22] Indeed when Stein was later to describe her encounter with the painting in her elaborately staged autobiography, she attributed to her lover, Alice B. Toklas, the feelings of fear and bewilderment that characterised so many of the first viewers of the picture, and thereby distanced herself from such views:

> Against the wall was an enormous picture, a strange picture of light and dark colours, that is all I can say, of a group, an enormous group and next to it another in a sort of red brown, of three women, square and posturing, all of it rather frightening. Picasso and Gertrude Stein stood together talking. I stood back and looked. I cannot say I realised anything but I felt that there was something painful and beautiful there and oppressive but imprisoned.
>
> I heard Gertrude Stein say, and mine. Picasso thereupon brought out a smaller picture, a rather unfinished thing that could not finish, very pale almost white, two figures they were all there but very unfinished and not finishable.
>
> Picasso said, but he will never accept it. Yes, I know, answered Gertrude Stein. But just the same it is the only one in which it is all there. Yes, I know, he replied and they fell silent.[23]

Stein represents herself as united in creative empathy with Picasso, contending with an impressionable 'wife' and a hostile community of connoisseurs and amateurs represented by her brother, the 'he' of the passage. It was most likely Leo's hostility that prevented the Steins from acquiring the picture, although he consented to buying some related preparatory sketches and drawings from the period.[24] In the passage from *The Autobiography of Alice B. Toklas*, Leo is positioned as the uncomprehending outsider of whom Gertrude and Pablo speak. They are locked in a conspiratorial alliance, two artists who collude in constructing their own isolation and concomitant 'genius'.

Stein knew that 'genius' was a quality exclusively reserved for men, but this did not deter her from embracing it.[25] Indeed it might have been its very 'masculinity' that made it desirable to her. In a characteristically self-aggrandising way she scrawled in her notebook, 'Pablo & Matisse have a maleness that belongs to genius. *Moi aussi* perhaps'.[26] Stein did not feel herself circumscribed by the cultural constraints of 'femininity'. She was an admirer of the Viennese psychologist Otto Weiniger, a rabid anti-Semite and antifeminist, and the author of *Sex and Character*, a curious study of human sexuality based on the claim that all human beings are fundamentally bisexual while asserting the ineluctable difference between the sexes: men exclusively are capable of genius and women (like Jews) are doomed to live out their destinies as sexual beings, reproductive animals incapable of higher thoughts or reflexive self-knowledge. Ambivalent both about her femininity and her Jewishness, Stein internalized the negative associations with both these terms while never actually denying them as part of herself.[27]

The 'masculine Gertrude Stein' has been the subject of much discussion. The phrase draws its meaning from the essentialist vocabulary of early twentieth-century sexology and is built on the gender ideologies of late nineteenth-century medicine, psychology, and social theory. As an intellectual woman who was childless, Stein risked being categorised as an unnatural creature whose 'ovaries, robbed of energy rightfully theirs, would atrophy, her menses become irregular, sterility and cancer ensue. No longer reproductive, she would begin to look like a man. Her breasts would shrivel, facial hair develop'.[28] Stein occupied the liminal social and sexual space of the 'new woman'. Different from most women because of her intellectual aspirations and artistic ambitions, she was also regarded as deviant because of her sexual preferences and unorthodox domestic arrangements. Eschewing fashion, corsetry, and the fineries of feminine self-adornment, Stein came, in the terms of her contemporaries, to epitomise the 'mannish lesbian',[29] or in Havelock Ellis's language, the 'sexual invert'. He conceived of the 'true invert' as 'neither man nor woman, a "third sex" or trapped soul'.[30] In the Paris of the 'belle époque', Stein's foreignness, her Americanness, would have compounded her ambivalent gender status. The progressive politics and independent lifestyles of so many expatriate American women in Europe made them appear entirely different from the adored 'Parisiennes', deemed to possess all the allure and charm of a sexualised femininity. Picasso, himself, was struck by the indeterminate gender identities of the assertive women and effete young men he met in the Stein household. '*Ils sont pas des hommes, ils sont pas des femmes, ils sont des américains*', he is reported to have said.[31]

Stein's masculine identification has been the subject of much feminist discussion.[32] The mimicry of conventional marital hierarchies in her relationship with Toklas as well as her avoidance of Parisian lesbian subcultures and embracing of masculine models of mastery and agency have made her an unlikely feminist heroine, but her importance in modernist literary history, her use of literature as a forum for the exploration and exploitation of gender positions, her forthright independence and unique way of negotiating her identity as writer, collector, woman, and lesbian have made her the object of tireless fascination. Stein's sexuality, her elaboration of a coded lesbian erotica in her writing, and the deliberate sartorial ambiguities she evoked in her costume (neither obviously feminine nor masculine in its address), as well as her huge appetite and unashamed love for food and fleshly pleasures, made of her a figure who seems to have lived in the body as much as in the mind.[33] As such Stein's transgressions of the boundaries of appropriate 'feminine' behaviour were so radical that they exploded the very boundaries of normative gender and sex roles. Images of her from the period help to construct the image of a femininity unfettered by conventional models and norms. Félix Vallotton's portrait of 1907 shows a monumental shrouded figure, dressed in an indeterminate gown covering an ample body (Fig. 14). A contemporary photograph shows Stein covered in loose garments, large pendulous breasts hanging freely over her ample belly, legs crossed and feet bare, more reminiscent of an archaic fertility goddess or Buddha figure than a turn-of-the-century woman. Represented here is a body free from social restraint, a powerfully womanly body but one that concedes nothing to reigning constructions of femininity.

Stein's struggle to come to terms with her sexual orientation and her negotiation of conventional gender roles paralleled her encounter with language and literature. Language, like living, was hard won for Stein. It was neither to be taken for granted nor was it easily absorbed and deployed. From a radical modernist perspective, nineteenth-century realist modes reproduced conventional social models even as they held them up for scrutiny. A departure from the truisms that fuelled the romantic plots of realist fiction entailed an interrogation of its forms as much as its mythologies. Neither sex nor style could be taken for granted, and the interrogation of the one was intimately connected with the interrogation of the other.

When Stein assessed the painterly prowess of her friend Picasso, therefore, she understood that sexuality and style were both at stake here, but she felt such a sympathy with the interrogative power of the attack on convention and the exploratory sexuality of the man who had mounted it, that she seems not to have minded that the vehicle of the attack was via the image of a body not unlike her own. Perhaps Stein was too sophisticated a modernist to mistake the image for the real thing. Perhaps she was so identified with masculine models of agency that she failed to notice the potential for her own symbolic objectification here. Perhaps the raw sexuality conferred on the bodies in the *Demoiselles* appealed to her erotic tastes. What must have been apparent to her was that what Picasso had destroyed was an ideal of femininity that had offered her no more comfort (nor opportunities for identification) than did the curious confections which were the product of his iconoclastic fervour.

What is clear is that Stein did not separate sexual energy from creative endeavour. Nor did she see sexuality as an altogether wholesome and comfortable affair, something that could be taken for granted and lived out unproblematically. For one thing, it was necessarily separated from reproduction in her experience of it, and therefore functioned as a form of being that escaped the instrumental codes of bourgeois sociability. What was more, she was able to settle in to her own identity as a writer only when she came to accept her sexuality as both different and necessary. Sex, like art, challenged the social order. Indeed, like many turn-of-the-century intellectuals, Stein understood the one as a powerful component of the other, but rather than conceiving of sex as productively sublimated into art in the Freudian sense, she saw it as a necessary physical and earthbound corrective to an overmystical conception of art.[34]

A sexually active woman herself, Stein was highly conscious of Picasso's sexual exploits and needs. He was, she alleged in her notebooks, 'dirtier' than other men, but, she asserted, such *sale sexualité* could be, in an artist, an important means of countering other worldly and transcendent notions of aesthetic experience.[35]

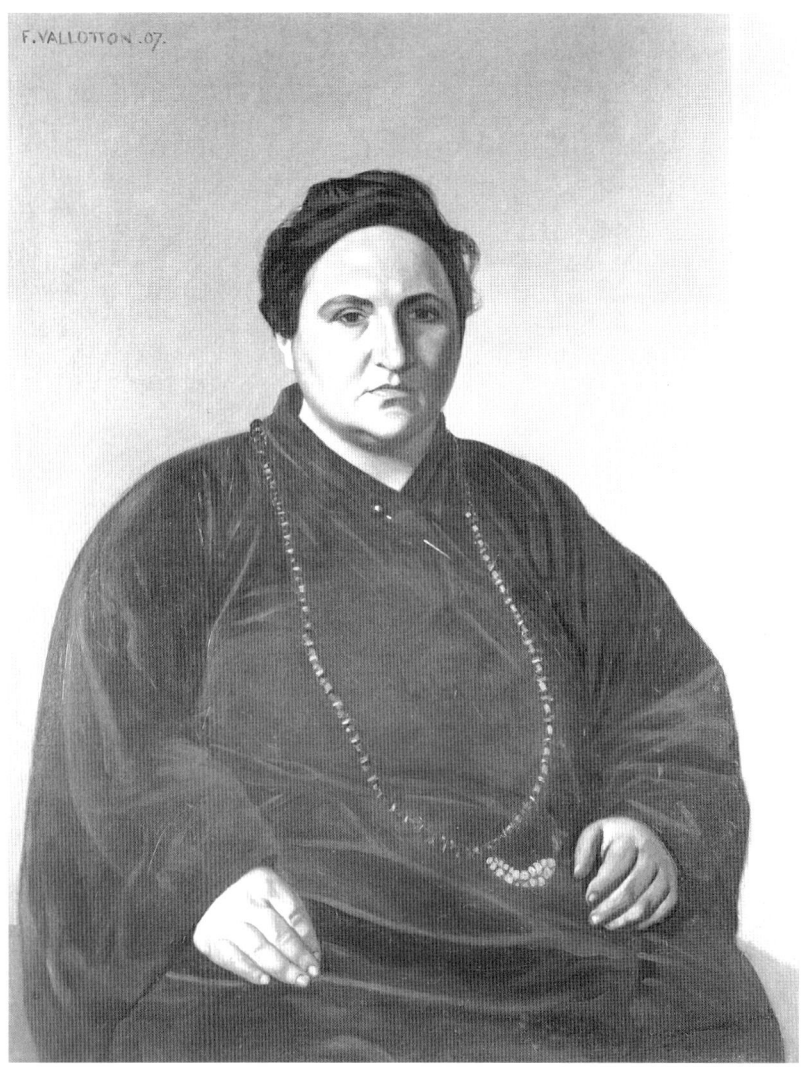

FIGURE 14. Félix Vallotton, *Portrait of Gertrude Stein*, 1907. Oil on canvas, 100.3 × 81.3 cm. The Baltimore Museum of Art: The Cone Collection, formed by Dr. Claribel Cone and Miss Etta Cone of Baltimore, Maryland, BMA 1950.300.

Stein was not frightened by Picasso's sexuality or physicality. Maurice Sterne recalled an incident when he and Stein went to call on Picasso but found that he was not at home. Pinned to the door they saw a drawing 'showing a man with a marked resemblance to the painter sitting on the toilet'. Sterne, unlike the amused Stein, thought this 'highly improper'. She, he reports, chortled, 'Isn't he cute?'[36] Picasso's fleshly needs were not incompatible with his extraordinary talent. Indeed for Stein, they helped to constitute it. It was his physicality that saved him, like her, from an overmystical approach to art. It was with pride that she described herself as an 'earthy boy'.[37] Stein referred to Picasso and his lover Fernande as the 'Picassos' and relegated Alice to look after the 'wife' while she consorted with the 'genius'.[38] And as Fernande serviced Picasso's needs, so Alice serviced hers. It is possible, therefore, that Gertrude's identification with Pablo included her identification with his 'dirty', but artistically 'necessary', sexuality.

In a culture in which the received lexicon of lesbian eroticism had largely been expressed in pornography aimed at the titillation of men, it would have been surprising if the residual associations of lesbianism with *'sale sexualité'* did not rub off onto Gertrude's own self-image, whether consciously or not. And as she relished her newfound pleasures, writing copiously in her unpublished manuscripts of the richness of her erotic life with 'pussy', one of the many pet names with which she referred to Toklas, she must have known the guilt and secrecy, as well as the pleasures, that come from forbidden love.[39]

For Picasso, the confrontation with Stein's sexuality and liminal gender identity seems to have precipitated a productive aporia.[40] The painterly investigations for the *Demoiselles d'Avignon* took place just after the hard-won resolution of the troublesome and portentious *Portrait of Gertrude Stein* that Picasso had put aside after months of struggle, only to complete afer his summer vacation in Gósol in 1906 (Fig. 15). The solution to Picasso's legendary 'inability to see' Stein after the eighty or so sittings he had demanded led him to adopt a mask based on Iberian prototypes to both substitute for and represent 'her'. But Picasso's painterly encounter with his female friend and patron did not end with the portrait. About a year after completing the *Demoiselles*, Picasso was to pay tribute to his friend and patron by means of a curious little Cézannesque ceiling painting that addressed her libidinal as well as her literary proclivities. In his *Homage a Gertrude (sic)* a group of six sexualised naked female angels bear gifts of fruit and music for the woman whose name is emblazoned on a curiously anthropomorphic scroll supported by two of the nudes in what appears to be a heavenly bedchamber (Fig. 16). The *Demoiselles d'Avignon,* with its representation of deviant sexualised women, 'masculine' in their refusal to represent normative 'feminine' modesty and decorum, is situated therefore between a portrait of another kind of 'masculine' woman and a phantasmatic figure painting that is a tribute both to her 'manly' creativity and subversive sexuality.

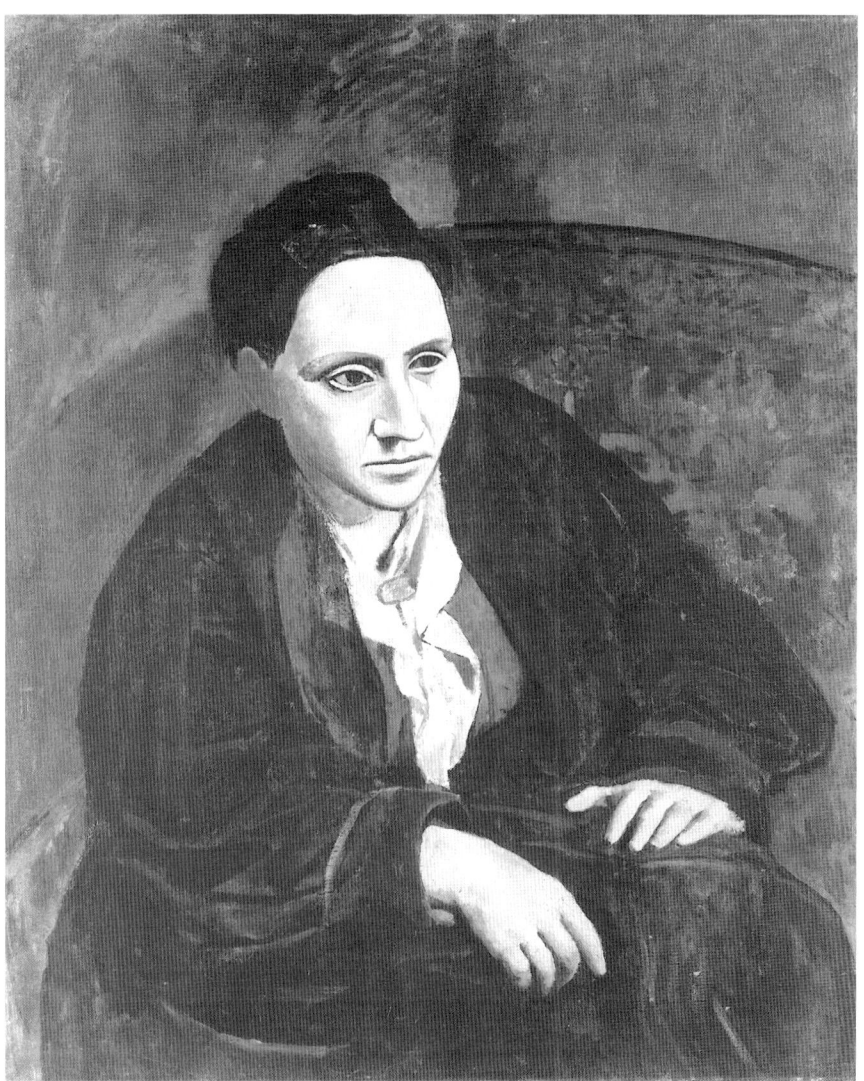

FIGURE 15. Pablo Picasso, *Portrait of Gertrude Stein*, winter 1905–6 and autumn 1906. Oil on canvas, 99.6 × 81.3 cm. Metropolitan Museum of Art, New York, Bequest of Gertrude Stein, 1946.

Robert Lubar has convincingly argued that Picasso's 'difficulties' with the *Portrait of Gertrude Stein* stemmed from the complex negotiation of sexualities and subjectivities that the encounter with his sitter entailed.[41] Far from being merely a stylistic gesture, the renowned erasure of the head and subsequent masking of Gertrude's features functions in this reading as the result of a (productive) failure to contain Stein within familiar social and psychic categories and accepted conventions of (female) portraiture. Her imposing physical presence and liminal sexual identity exceeded the boundaries of representability. Only with the model absent could Picasso resolve the problem of representing her, and then she is reinstated as a monumental but masked presence, secret, defended, and private. Her 'masculine' pose (hunched shoulders, ample lap with heavy unadorned hands resting assertively on thigh and knee), voluminous physicality (her portly presence occupies three quarters of the picture space), and austere physiognomy (her piercing stare and determined mouth, her handsome and finely delineated face) make no concessions to accepted ideals of fashionable femininity. Stein is here enshrined as an impressive figure, statuesque and imposing rather than stereotypically seductive or charming.

A number of illuminating precedents for Picasso's portrait have been sought. Most famous of these is the link to Ingres's *Portrait of Monsieur Bertin* where the transposition from portly male subject to female figure is highly suggestive in terms of gendered conventions of portraiture. There is also a significant similarity between Picasso's portrait and Degas's *Portrait of Mary Cassatt*, another unconventional image of an independent American woman in which stance, deportment, and demeanour are drawn from accepted modes of representing male rather than female figures. Cassatt, positioned in the same three-quarter view as Stein, sits eagerly forward in her chair, legs open, hands playing nervously with what appear to be *cartes de visite*, knees apart. But perhaps the most significant precedent in terms of Stein and Picasso's relationship was the *Portrait of Hortense Fiquet* (Mme Cézanne) that the Steins had bought in 1904 and was to hang in a room in the rue de Fleurus together with the *Portrait of Gertrude Stein* for many years.

The androgyny of Cézanne's figures (particularly his bathers, an example of which the Steins owned and that hung in the rue de Fleurus in 1906) has long been noticed.[42] But in his portraits, too, Cézanne had deployed few of the conventional signifiers of sexual difference. Both his male and female portraits have an equivalent statuesque quality in which the sitters seem to retain a dignified self-referentiality that makes no gratuitous or inviting gesture towards a putative spectator. The female sitters remain as remote and impassive as their male counterparts. Cézanne shows no interest in the portrayal of personality or the fleeting expressions of the moment. He subjects his sitters to the same rigorous scrutiny as he

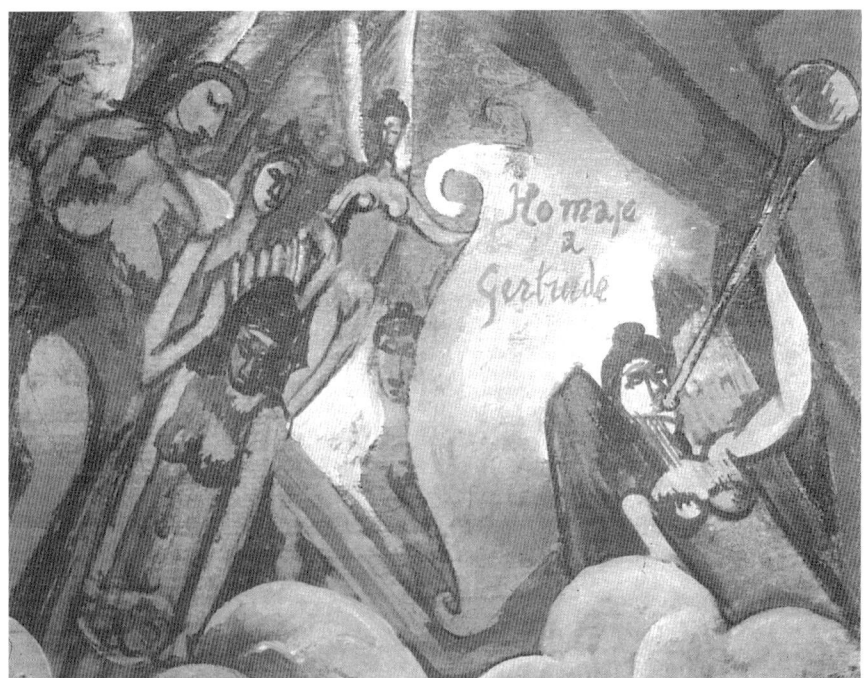

FIGURE 16. Pablo Picasso, '*Homage a Gertrude*' (*sic*), 1909. Tempera on wood, 26 × 21 cm. Private Collection, New York.

does any object, and the result is the creation of a masklike impassivity that may invoke a generic melancholy but never a transient emotion. The outer packaging of gendered subjectivity is hardly invoked here. This probably explains his dealer Vollard's assertion that 'ordinarily a portrait of a woman always is more expensive than a portrait of a man' . . . but that 'with Cézanne it does not make any difference'.[43] What better model for the picturing of a 'masculine woman', therefore, than the much admired androgynous countenance of Mme Cézanne.[44]

The 'sexuality' at stake in the *Portrait of Gertrude Stein* is of a different order than that of the *Demoiselles d'Avignon*. The first picture negotiated portrait precedents in order to construct the subjectivity of a sexually liminal figure, who, for the purposes of this chapter, becomes the historical spectator of the second. The second, in tackling the image of the prostitute, dealt with the image of a socially marginal figure, one whose femininity was perceived to be at risk, not because of her rejection of men as sexual partners but because of her excessive embrace of them and her eschewal of the normative female roles of wife and mother. It is no coincidence that Picasso chose the current image of a deviant femininity through which to articulate his disaffection from classical conceptions of composition, space, and spectatorship. As David Lomas has convincingly argued, the body of the prostitute itself came to represent 'the very antithesis of classical beauty and Picasso was able to exploit this signification in order to effect a stylistic revolution which sought to overturn a classical order of representation'.[45] Not only was the prostitute regarded as potentially masculine, but she was also regarded as potentially lesbian and therefore represented a terrible threat to the social order.[46] Unlike the lesbian, however, for whom patriarchal institutions could find no use (they were superfluous), the well-regulated prostitute served men well and was tolerated and feared simultaneously. And the particular lesbian activities in which prostitutes were thought to engage could be controlled by being constructed as erotic spectacle for heterosexual men.

We have no record of Stein's response to the subject matter of the *Demoiselles d'Avignon*. Whether she even 'recognised' the figures as representing prostitutes is impossible to tell. Recent research has revealed that she was probably aware of her brother's sexual exploits with prostitutes and that like many nineteenth-century predecessors she divided women into two classes, the mother and the whore, one 'consumed by the object of sex, the other with the sex act itself'.[47] Indeed Stein elaborated her own taxonomy of types in which people were described as epitomising the 'maternal', 'spinster', 'prostitute', 'servant', and so on. But whether any of these types were associated in her mind with the figures in Picasso's *'grande machine'* is impossible to determine. Certainly she would have noticed that these were not 'classical nudes', that everything about the way these figures were conceived and constructed challenged the conventions by which such figures had previously been known. And although we do not know what she made of the subject matter of the picture, we do know that it did not stand in the way of her appreciation of its significance. Nor was it likely that it offended her. Stein had long admired Cézanne's *Bathers* whose transgressive androgyny was equally baffling to many contemporary viewers. Her exposure to his highly sexualised and tempestuous early work at the 1907 retrospective (which included paintings like the *Temptation of St. Anthony* and *The Eternal Feminine*, both profoundly misogynistic allegorisations of women's destructive sexuality) had not altered her admiration for him. The *Demoiselles* could be read as a large-scale elaboration of sentiments already deeply embedded in traditions of figure painting, as exemplified by early Cézanne, rather than as offering something altogether new on the menu of misogyny.

It is not surprising that when Picasso chose to honour Stein sometime late in 1908 or early in 1909, he did so in profoundly Cézannesque terms, evoking the early canopied composition of *The Eternal Feminine* at the same time as calling to mind the *Demoiselles d'Avignon*, with all its formal radicalism and explosive sexual power. Stein, after all, had been one of the few viewers who had shied away from neither.[48] Picasso's *Homage a Gertrude (sic)* (1909) was intended for a female spectator but does not defer to contemporary conceptions of 'feminine' discretion and modesty. In fact, its full frontal address to the spectator and its staging of a framed and draped interior space mirrors that of *The Eternal Feminine* and *Les Demoiselles* quite closely. In all three pictures, the erotic is staged in a triangular, curtained space, but whereas *The Eternal Feminine* situates Woman as a reclining, wounded, blind goddess surrounded by her trumpeting male supplicants, *Homage a Gertrude (sic)* defers to a female deity that is beyond the picture space, potentially pleasured by the sight of her adoring angels.[49] In this respect it is reminiscent of the *Demoiselles* where the figures are arranged to address a spectator who surveys them from beyond the picture space. When Edouard Manet had painted his own homage to a contemporary female artist, Berthe Morisot, nearly fifty years earlier, he had paid tribute to her 'femininity' by staging a still life of appropriately female accoutrements: violets, fan, and letter, all metonymically associated with Woman. The writing 'A Mlle Berthe Morisot' on the letter invokes the conventional amorous tribute of the '*billet doux*', with Manet as the devoted suitor, the love-struck admirer.[50] In his homage Pablo addresses Gertrude as a peer rather than a paramour. If anything, she is constructed by the scene and the inscription as 'one of the boys' with whom it is appropriate to share a joke, the recipient of amorous attention and admiration from a bevy of busty supplicants.

Homage a Gertrude (sic) was intended to be tacked onto the ceiling above Stein's bed and to be viewed from below.[51] Its miniature scale, though, amounts to a bathetic parody of a grandiose baroque ceiling painting (it measures all of 8 ¼ × 10 ¾ inches) confirming its status as a playful private joke between friends.[52] But its placement, however funny, indicates that it was intended to address Stein's sexuality, with the scale and raunchiness of an early Cézanne, in the intimacy of her bedchamber.

In the painting Picasso arranged a chorus of six naked angels, bearing fruits and blasting forth their praise in a faceted and curtained heaven that seems like a celestial equivalent to the brothel of Avignon. The picture is bordered on the left by a heavy-breasted giantess who frames the scene in a manner reminiscent of the left-hand figure in the *Demoiselles*. In front of her is a figure who carries her platter of round succulent fruits at pelvic level in an obviously sexual gesture while behind her a half-hidden creature plays an accordian. The figure on the right blasts forth her praise on an elongated tubular instrument that stretches like a long, lascivious tongue up the right-hand section of the picture. The angels are simultaneously other worldly (they are undressed and sport huge peaked wings) and earthbound. Their hairstyles are markedly contemporary, carefully coiffured on the top of their heads in typical fin de siècle fashion, and their heavy breasts and contours are crudely and suggestively painted in dark outlines. Mounted above billowing breastlike clouds, the highly sexualised bodies of the curvaceous chorus address the viewer frontally, trumpeting forth her grandeur as they present her with a voluptuous, centrally placed scroll, swollen like a ripe female body emerging full of sexual promise from the inner recesses of the picture. On this anthropomorphised offering is inscribed the message 'Homage a Gertrude'.

Besides being the address of one artist to another and one sexual being to another, this tribute is also directed from one foreigner to another, the word 'homage' being written in the English manner without the two 'm's' of the French spelling. Also missing is the accent on the 'a', making the inscription stand for an illiterate and failed attempt at assimilating into the host culture. This provides one of the crucial sites of Pablo and Gertrude's encounter, their distance linguistically and culturally from their chosen place of residence. In their broken French and foreign accents, they were rank outsiders in their adopted country. Together they must have spoken a hybrid of English, French, and Spanish, misunderstanding one another constantly and yet empathetically united in their 'difference'. The clumsy inscription, with its abuse of the laws of grammar and 'misspelling' of the crucial word at the heart of the picture, is a telling indication of the solace that these two outsiders must have found in one another. If for Gertrude this oversexed, irreverent little Spaniard offered a model of artistic agency in an unintelligible, even hostile social context, then for Pablo this extraordinary American writer who was neither a 'woman' nor a 'man', neither a competitor nor a disciple, provided the ideal if unlikely viewer for one of the most irreverent pictures that had ever been created.

Whether Picasso had known that this would be the case in advance or not, his experience of the almost universal hostility which greeted his '*grande machine*' must have made Stein's appreciation of this work appear all the more remarkable. And so this typically sexist fin de siècle Spaniard found an unlikely ally in a lesbian, Jewish, American writer on whose support, both emotional and financial, he came to depend. The nature of his painted homage is a testimony to the intimacy that this unlikely pair shared. In being addressed as both a creative and carnal being, Stein was being attributed with a fuller subjectivity than that allowed most turn-of-the-century women. For whereas Picasso's embrace of a '*sale sexualité*' was de rigueur for the triumphalist expression of vanguard masculinity, for Stein it was more risky. Not only did she have to bear the consequences of her denial of the cultural construction of the 'feminine' in her person and profession, but she also risked colluding, unknowingly perhaps, with an oppressive metaphorics of the feminine in her embrace of vanguard culture and the models of artistic subjectivity it endorsed. It was, after all, Stein's own arrogant assumption of masculine models of mastery and creativity, as exemplified by her friend Picasso, which enabled her to write with an energy and an arrogance that was profoundly 'unfeminine'.

In the year that Picasso painted the 'homage', Stein would write adoringly of him:

> This one always had been working. This one was always having something that was coming out of this one that was a solid thing, a charming thing, a lovely thing, a perplexing thing, a disconcerting thing, a simple thing, a clear thing, a complicated thing, an interesting thing, a disturbing thing, a repellant thing, a very pretty thing. This one was one certainly being one having something coming out of him. This one was one whom some were following. This one was one who was working.[53]

For Stein, it was Picasso's energy that was paramount. The adjectives used to describe the 'thing' that he produced were contradictory: 'disturbing', 'pretty', 'repellent'. It was the indefatigable industry and creativity of the man 'whom some were certainly following', and who 'was always having something come out of him something having meaning', whatever that meaning might be, that impressed and inspired his friend.

In his 'homage', a tiny, little noticed picture that the Picasso literature has all but passed over, Picasso acknowledged in retrospect that his friend had understood and accepted him. Picasso's *Homage a Gertrude (sic)*, then, pays tribute to a woman who, while understanding the *Demoiselles d'Avignon*'s formal brutality as the product of a redemptively 'dirty sexuality', was capable of encountering it without flinching. In addressing a female spectator in terms reminiscent of early Cézanne, this tiny picture provides a challenge to our received understanding of the monumental *Les Demoiselles d'Avignon*, a picture whose profoundly earthbound carnality seems to take on, in this context, the aura of an other worldly, celestial salutation in which angels with clipped wings hail their audience, male and female, with a double-edged offering of fruit and profane love.

NOTES

I am grateful to my M.A. students at University College London for their discussion of issues raised by this topic. Thanks too to the members of research seminars at the Courtauld Institute, the University of Chicago, and the Center for Literary and Cultural Studies, Harvard University, for their searching questions. I am particularly grateful to Caroline Arscott, Briony Fer, Christopher Green, Robert Lubar, Rasaad Jamie, and David Solkin for their generosity.

1   On the castration hypothesis, see Yve-Alain Bois, 'Painting as Trauma', *Art in America* (June 1988), 131–41 and 172–3. Reprinted here in revised form, pp 24–42.

2   See L. Steinberg, 'The Philosophical Brothel, Parts 1 and 2', *Art News* 71, no. 5 (September 1972), 20–41 and no. 6 (October 1972), 38–47; W. Rubin, 'La genèse des *Demoiselles d'Avignon*, in H. Seckel (ed.), *Les Demoiselles d'Avignon* (Paris: Musée Picasso, 1987), 2 vols. Translated into English and revised in *Studies in Modern Art*, no. 3 (New York: Museum of Modern Art, 1994); R. Rosenblum, 'The Demoiselles Sketchbook No. 42, 1907', in A. Glimcher and M. Glimcher (eds.), *Je Suis le Cahier: The Sketchbooks of Picasso* (London: Thames & Hudson, 1986), 53–75.

3   The assessment of Daniel Henri Kahnweiler as related by John Richardson, *A Life of Picasso: 1907–1917*, vol. 2 (London, 1996), 34.

4   In the words of Leo Stein, from his *Appreciation: Painting, Poetry and Prose* (1947), quoted in Pierre Daix, *Picasso: Life and Art* (New York, 1993), 79.

5   Kahnweiler as quoted in Daix, as in note 4, 81.

6   On Picasso's isolation after completion of the *Demoiselles*, see J. Richardson, 45. On the response of the Russian collector Shchukin, who proclaimed 'what a loss for French art', see G. Stein, 'Picasso' (1938) in E. Burns (ed.), *Gertrude Stein on Picasso* (New York, 1970), 27. Interestingly Stein's own writing was also greeted as fearsome by some of its first readers. See for example the response of the American poet Donald Evans to *Tender Buttons* in 1914: 'The last shackle is struck from context and collocation, each unit of the sentence stands independent and has no commerce with its fellows. The effect produced on the first reading is something like terror'. Quoted in D. Souhami, *Gertrude and Alice* (London, 1991), 170.

7   See C. Duncan, 'The MOMA's Hot Mamas', *Art Journal* 48, no. 2 (Summer 1989), 171–178. Reprinted in Carol Duncan, *The Aesthetics of Power. Essays in Critical Art History* (Cambridge and New York, 1993), 189–207.

8   See A. Chave, 'New Encounters with *Les Demoiselles d'Avignon*: Gender, Race, and the Origins of Cubism', *The Art Bulletin* 76, no. 4 (December 1994), 587–611. Here Chave builds on an earlier argument that Carol Duncan made in her influential and important 'Virility and Domination in Early Twentieth Century Vangarde Painting' reprinted in Broude and Garrard, *Feminism and Art History, Questioning the Litany* (New York, 1982), 292–313.

9   The effort such an identification entails is hardly credible. Chave's attempts to universalise women's experience of their own sexual exploitation involves creating artificial equivalences between her experience of being sexually surveyed, despite the protection of her own avowedly privileged subject position, that of New York sex workers and the 'prostitutes' who allegedly provided the models for Picasso's figures. Chave thus confers subjectivity on the five 'demoiselles' and thereby mistakes them as real rather than as the psychically charged products of Picasso's febrile imagination.

10 For an excellent account of the Stein/Picasso relationship, see Leon Katz, 'Matisse, Picasso and Gertrude Stein' in *Four Americans in Paris* (New York: Museum of Modern Art, 1970), 51–64.

11 For a discussion of Gertrude Stein's involvement with Cézanne, see L. Katz (1970), 52–4. For an in-depth discussion of the aesthetic links between Stein and Cézanne, see J.L. Walker, 'The "Reality" of Cézanne and Caliban', in *The Making of a Modernist: Gertrude Stein* (Amherst: University of Massachusetts Press, 1984), 1–18.

12 On the importance of Cézanne's 'decentralized composition' for Stein, see R. Dubnick, *The Structure of Obscurity: Gertrude Stein, Language and Cubism* (Urbana and Chicago: University of Illinois Press, 1984), 18.

13 See L. Katz and E. Burns, "They Walk in the Light": Gertrude Stein and Pablo Picasso' in *Gertrude Stein on Picasso* (New York, 1970), 109. The other epithets that Leo used to describe both Gertrude and Picasso's work included 'haemorrhoids' and 'cubico futuristic tommy-rotting'. See D. Souhami, as in note 6, 109.

14 Stein was later to write of this period:

> One must never forget that the reality of the twentieth century is not the reality of the nineteenth century, not at all and Picasso was the only one in painting who felt it, the only one. More and more the struggle to express it intensified. Matisse and all the others saw the twentieth century with their eyes, but they saw the reality of the nineteenth century, Picasso was the only one in painting who saw the twentieth century with his eyes and saw its reality, and consequently his struggle was terrifying, terrifying for himself and for the others, because he had nothing to help him, the past did not help him, nor the present, he had to do it all alone . . . G. Stein, *Picasso*, reprinted in E. Burns, *Gertrude Stein on Picasso* (1970), 30.

When Stein describes the *Demoiselles* as 'too awful', therefore, she does not condemn it but articulates its awesome power. The use of this phrase to describe her response has often been quoted out of context and used as evidence of her hostility to the painting which she is said to have shared with her brother. Stein's own recollections of this period do not support such an interpretation of her response. For Stein's representation of the divergence of her views from those of Leo's and of her 'enthusiasm' for Picasso's new work including 'a large canvas of nude women with strangely distorted bodies and primitive masklike faces', see B. Pollack, *The Collectors: Dr Claribel and Miss Etta Cone* (New York, 1962), 98–9.

15 See *Picasso*, 35, quoted in Daix, as in note 4, 80.

16 L. Katz, as in note 13, 60.

17 See L. Katz, as in note 13, 60.

18 'I was alone at this time in understanding him', she later said. 'Perhaps because I was expressing the same thing in literature'. See D. Souhami, as in note 6, 145.

19 "'[T]o kill the nineteenth century'", Stein believed, 'the art of this century – paint-ing and writing – must organize compositions that are "de-centralized", object-ori-entated, and expressed in a conceptual iconography which itself becomes the object of the composition'. See L. Katz and E. Burns (1970), 116.

20 Fernande Olivier writes of Matisse's, Derain's, and Braque's horror at encountering the picture, and Yve-Alain Bois connects this suggestively to castration anxiety. See Yve-Alain Bois (1988), as in note 1.

21 On Stein's relationship with her father and her views on fathering, see D. Souhami, as in note 6, 25–49.

22 Stein would have had as little invested in the maintenance of idealised modes of picturing the feminine, whether as beneficent maternal creature or pliant sex god-dess, as she had in this radical recasting of the female form.

23 Gertrude Stein, *The Autobiography of Alice B. Toklas* (London, 1960) (first pub-lished 1933), 26.

24 See J.R. Mellow, *Charmed Circle: Gertrude Stein & Company* (New York, 1974), 113.

25 For accounts of the gendering of genius, see C. Duncan, as in note 7, and Chris-tine Battersby, *Gender and Genius, Towards a Feminist Aesthetics* (London, 1989).

26 'From the Notebooks', reprinted in Edward Burns (ed.), *Gertrude Stein on Picasso*, 97.

27 The question of Stein's Jewishness raises interesting problems. *The Autobiography of Alice B. Toklas* contains a number of anti-Semitic passages indicating Stein's internalization of cultural stereotypes, but at the same time she described Alice B. Toklas as 'her little jew', one of the many terms of affection used for her lover. See D. Souhami, 157. But as Toklas took on the conventional position of 'wife' to Stein's 'husband', it may have suited the power structure of the relationship for Toklas to be defined as such 'as if' from the outside. For a theorization of the inter-nalization of anti-Semitic stereotypes by Jews, see Sander Gilman, *Jewish Self-Hatred: Anti-Semitism and the Hidden Language of the Jews* (Baltimore: Johns Hopkins University Press, 1986).

28 See Carroll Smith-Rosenberg, 'Discourses of Sexuality and Subjectivity: The New Woman, 1870–1931' in M.B. Duberman, M. Vicinus, G. Chauncey, Jr. (eds.), *Hid-den from History: Reclaiming the Lesbian Past* (London: Penguin, 1991), 267. See also G. Chauncey, Jr., 'From Sexual Inversion to Homosexuality: Medicine and the Changing Conceptualization of Female Deviance', *Salmagundi* 58 (1982–83).

29 The 'mannish lesbian' is described as 'a figure who is defined as lesbian because her behaviour or dress (and usually both) manifest elements designated as exclu-sively masculine. From about 1900 on this cross-gender figure became the public symbol of the new social/sexual category "lesbian"'. E. Newton, 'The Mythic Man-nish Lesbian: Radclyffe Hall and the New Woman' (1984), in Duberman et al., as in note 28, 283.

30 As in note 28, 288–9.

31 See G. Stein, *The Autobiography of Alice B. Toklas*, 53.

32 See, for example, Catherine R. Stimpson, 'Gertrude Stein and the Transposition of Gender' in Nancy K. Miller (ed.), *The Poetics of Gender* (New York: Columbia University Press, 1986), 1–18, and Shari Benstock, *Women of the Left Bank* (Lon-don, 1994), 143–93.

33 Stein invented a secret language for describing the range of rich erotic experience that she shared with Toklas. See D. Souhami, *Gertrude and Alice* (London: Pandora Press, 1991), 157–62.

34 For a useful discussion of the Freudian notion of 'sublimation', see J. Laplanche and J.B. Pontalis, *The Language of Psychoanalysis* (London, 1973), 431–3.

35 See L. Katz, 56.

36 See Mellow, 90.

37 See B. Wineapple, *Sister Brother: Gertrude and Leo Stein* (Bloomsbury, 1996), 264.

38 Later on Stein had Toklas say, 'Fernande was the first wife of a genius I was to sit with. The geniuses came and talked to Gertrude Stein and the wives sat with me'. See *The Autobiography of Alice B. Toklas*, 90.

39 On the erotic poetry and its implications for Gertrude and Alice's sexual relationship, see D. Souhami, 157–161.

40 The interpretation of the *Portrait of Gertrude Stein* that follows is indebted to Robert Lubar's argument in 'Unmasking Pablo's Gertrude: Queer Desire and the Origins of Cubism', *The Art Bulletin* 74 (March 1997), 57–84.

41 See Lubar, as in note 40.

42 For my own analysis of this phenomenon, see my 'Visuality and Sexuality in Cézanne's late Bathers', *Oxford Art Journal* 19, no. 2 (1996), 46–60, and 'Cézanne's Late Bathers: Modernism and Sexual Difference' in *Bodies of Modernity; Figure and Flesh in Fin de Siècle France* (London: Thames & Hudson, 1998), 196–220. The 'Bathers' owned by the Steins at this point was a picture of a group of male bathers, c. 1895, now in the Baltimore Museum of Art, The Cone Collection. It is reproduced in a photograph of Stein taken in the rue de Fleurus, c. 1905. See Museum of Modern Art (1970), 53.

43 G. Stein, *The Autobiography of Alice B. Toklas*, 37.

44 Interestingly, Stein recognised herself as portrayed in her portrait. 'I was and still am satisfied with my portrait; for me it is I, and it is the only reproduction of me which is always I, for me' she was to write in 1938. She had her self photographed numerous times in front of the painting and took great pride in it as an image that was 'completely' her. The portrait offered a happy confluence of her empathy with a male artist and her identification with the image of her that he had created.

45 See David Lomas, 'A Canon of Deformity, *Les Demoiselles d'Avignon* and Physical Anthropology', reprinted in this volume in a revised form.

46 For a contemporary discussion of the 'masculinity' of the prostitute, see C. Lombroso, *The Female Offender* (London, 1895), 102–14.

47 This Proudhonian binary was revivified by Otto Weininger in whom Stein showed an enormous interest. For her interest in Weininger, see B. Wineapple (1996), 264–5.

48 The period between the completion of the *Demoiselles* and the execution of the *Homage a Gertrude* (sic) was a period of renewed interest in Cézanne, culminating in the *Three Women*, a composition bought by Stein and probably the most Cézannesque of the figure compositions of the period. See Leo Steinberg, 'Resisting Cézanne: Picasso's Three Women', *Art in America* (November–December 1978), 114–33.

49 For a detailed discussion of *The Eternal Féminin*, see my *Bodies of Modernity*, as in note 42, 178–95.

50 Edouard Manet, *The Bunch of Violets*, 1872. Oil on canvas, 27 × 27 cm. Private Collection.

51 It did indeed remain there for nearly thirty years. After Stein moved from the rue de Fleurus to 5 rue Christine, it rested on the fireplace in her bedroom. See 'Catalogue' in *Gertrude Stein on Picasso*, as in note 6.

52 I am grateful to David Solkin for discussions with him about this aspect of the painting.

53 Gertrude Stein, *Picasso*, 1909, reprinted in *Gertrude Stein on Picasso*, as in note 6, 80.

5

PATRICIA LEIGHTEN

Colonialism, *l'art nègre,* and *Les Demoiselles d'Avignon*

In 1888 the body of a man was stolen from his grave in southern Africa by a Spanish 'scientist', Francesc Darder. He stuffed and mounted the body, with spear and shield (origin unknown), and presented the result to visiting multitudes at the Barcelona World Exposition: 'El Negro', a specimen of 'natural history'.[1] Although no one can be complacent about racism and economic apartheid at the turn of the millennium – from strategies of inner-city crime containment to First World dumping of toxic waste and 'recycled' plastic on the Third World – we can measure some of our cultural difference from the fin de siècle, in conception and in rhetoric, by contemplating this exhibit. Certainly a continuum thrives, such that one finds the figure still in place in 1992 in the tiny Darder Natural History Museum in Banyoles, site of that summer's Olympic rowing competition, where its presence among stuffed monkeys caused unforseen problems for Olympic officials faced with a threatened boycott by the outraged African teams. Nonetheless, the taxiderm's creation and acquiescent reception help chart the distance of the present from the colonial world in which modernism developed, a world whose appetite for the exotic could evidently not be satisfied by the living Africans walking around the streets of Europe's cities.

Turn-of-the-century avant-garde artists and their primitivist aesthetic manoeuvers operated in and against this world; Pablo Picasso and other modernists could simultaneously share in and be sharply critical of such colonial attitudes in an atmosphere we can no longer experience and in a measure we must work to understand. In regard to Africa, for example, far from extending their social criticism to a radical critique of the reductive view of Africans promoted by the French government for colonial justification, the modernists embraced a deeply romanticised view of 'Africa' – conflating many cultures into one – as the embodiment of humankind in a precivilised state, worshipping idols and enacting violent rituals whose presumed meanings they preferred to mystify rather than to examine. The modernists subverted colonial stereotypes, both of the right and the left, but their subversive revisions necessarily remained implicated in the prejudices from which they derived, so that they now appear no less stereotypical and reductive than the racist caricatures they opposed. The modernists' aim was to critique civilisation by embracing an imagined primitiveness whose authenticity they opposed to a 'decadent' West. They wanted to subvert Western artistic traditions – and the social order in which they were implicated – by celebrating a Nietzschean return to those imagined 'primitive' states whose suppression they viewed as having cut off a necessary vitality.[2]

Primitivism focuses colonial issues tellingly, revealing complex and ambivalent relations to issues of race, gender, and power on the part of socially critical modernists grappling with political material. In this light, it is important to recognise how little primitivism, in the hands of all the modernists, speaks of the alien cultures they want to appropriate and how much it speaks of the culture to whom their works were addressed, even if only purposely to scandalise it. By evoking an alien, exotic, or paradisal world, they speak of the inadequacies and oppressions of 'home'.[3] At the deepest level, primitivists sought a contemporary parallel to an edenic moment in the artists' own white European 'race', looking to 'primitive' cultures – visible in Paris via the French colonies – for a naïveté, spontaneity, and directness European culture had putatively lost. Some sought this liberation for more than themselves. Certainty that 'the white race' once enjoyed political and amoral freedom on the model of an imagined and perfect *sauvagerie* in Tahiti, Guinea, and the Congo animated the anarchist critique of France's civilising mission to those lands as tainting the colonies' hitherto uncorrupted primitiveness.

In 1990 I published 'The White Peril and *l'art nègre*: Picasso, Primitivism, and Anticolonialism',[4] in which I considered the Africanism of Picasso and others in Paris as operating both within the French popular image of the 'dark continent' and in an anticolonialist milieu at a charged moment of colonial scandal and political debate around 1905–7. In that essay I expanded an understanding of Picasso's Africanism by considering the relations between, on the one hand, French political and popular culture and, on the other, the French Congo, to which Picasso potently alluded through the masks invoked in his *Demoiselles d'Avignon* of 1907 (Fig. 1). I looked at the history of French popular attitudes towards 'Africa' as a locus of the grotesque and the horrific; at the systematic and casual abuse in the French Congo; at the political scandals in Paris resulting from the revelations of the behaviour of French officials; and at the anticolonialist reaction among the Parisian left wing, including Picasso's own anarchist circle. Here, I summarise the important features of that article, expand on its arguments, and address questions raised by subsequent scholarship and criticism.

That article, in developing a complex and problematic view of Picasso's primitivism, has itself, like the painting, been subjected to reductive readings that would equate its argument with an uncritical celebration of the *Demoiselles d'Avignon* as a simple sign of political protest against French policies in the Congo. Such a critique does not correspond to my multivalent reading of Picasso's primitivism; its proponents have themselves sometimes gone on to posit reductive readings of the work, readings that would identify the *Demoiselles* with a direct manifestation of Picasso's fears of syphilis (William Rubin, 'The Genesis of *Les Demoiselles d'Avignon*') or anthropological notions of degeneracy (David Lomas, in this book).[5] If we accept Bakhtin's concept of heteroglossia, however, the artist's agency in manipulating the cultural languages of form, gender, race, and sexuality remains of real significance.[6]

By 1907 when he painted *Les Demoiselles d'Avignon,* Picasso had long moved his work towards simplification and crudity under the influence of the Barcelona *modernistes,* who already admired Iberian and Catalan Romanesque art in the 1880s and 1890s[7]; he first introduced Iberian forms in his work during 1906. What is new for Picasso in his work of 1907, starting from *Les Demoiselles,* is not only a more brutally primitivising style, but resonances of the popular view of Africa and its unavoidable part in the French Empire.[8] The 'dark continent' captured the imaginations of artists and writers working in an anarchist vein as a result of political scandals and the resulting outcry of the anticolonial opposition of anarchists and socialists to French colonial policy in Africa. These revelations broke upon the world in 1905–6, the same period that Picasso, Maurice Vlaminck, André Derain, and others were inspired to 'discover' an African art that had been visible in Paris since at least the 1890s.[9] Reference to African art not only allowed Picasso to primitivise his figures, it allowed him to introduce Africa into his work as an allusion whose associations for his French viewers were widely known. By conflating his figures with recognisably African forms – such as the Kota sculpture brought from the French Congo to the Musée d'Ethnographie in 1883 (Fig. 17) – he violently subverted the formal treatment of the human figure. Synthesising aspects of a variety of masks and statues, all from various parts of the French Empire,[10] it was the *idea* of Africa that Picasso sought. I argue that *Les Demoiselles* and the primitivising work it generates necessarily constituted both an act of valuing the products of African culture and an allusion to French brutality that contradicted the nation's image of itself as a 'civilising' force, pointing up their 'hypocrisy' and 'bankrupt' cultural traditions at a charged period of political debate.

At the same time, African sculpture evoked the primitivist mythology of a society in that early stage of culture through which Europe supposedly had long ago passed: the stage of the 'childhood' of the European races, a time before 'history'.[11] This experience was suppressed (but not erased) by the rigours and falseness of civilisation, hence the need on the part of European modernists to find what they took to be 'primitive' expressions of thought and feeling that would help them exorcise the interiorised strictures separating them from the authenticity of their own childhoods and of the childhood of their 'race'. Needless to say, the trope of the black as childlike followed all too easily from this, along with an imagined primal savagery that thoroughly merged with images of and references to African sculpture for any artist or audience of prewar France.

Yet the appearance of such forms in Picasso's already 'grotesque' painting also echoed popularised images and associations of superstition, irrationality, and horror, adding to Picasso's considerable arsenal of anticlassical devices with which he assaulted European traditions of representation and taste, including geometrification of form, flattening of space, unnaturalistic color, and crudity of execution. 'Africa', as imported into the work, represented not an idyllic, pre-European society, but the very opposite of 'civilised' Europe and a threat to it. As such Picasso's painting is disturbingly continuous with Darder's gruesome primitivist construction at the Barcelona exposition, even if also operating, I shall argue, as an anticolonialist critique.

With the rest of France, the modernists were influenced by popular sources of information about Africa. Beginning in the late nineteenth century, the Jardin d'Acclimatation and international expositions concocted displays of colonial peoples in live exhibits. Prior to 1906, African peoples, supplied by wild animal importers, were regularly exhibited. For Picasso's generation, the best known such spectacle in Paris was held at the Exposition Universelle of 1900, which mounted enormous ethnographic exhibits including recreations of Dahomean and Congolese villages complete with 'pikes on which were stuck the actual skulls of slaves executed before the eyes of Bahanzin', last king of Dahomey, and performances of 'the rites of

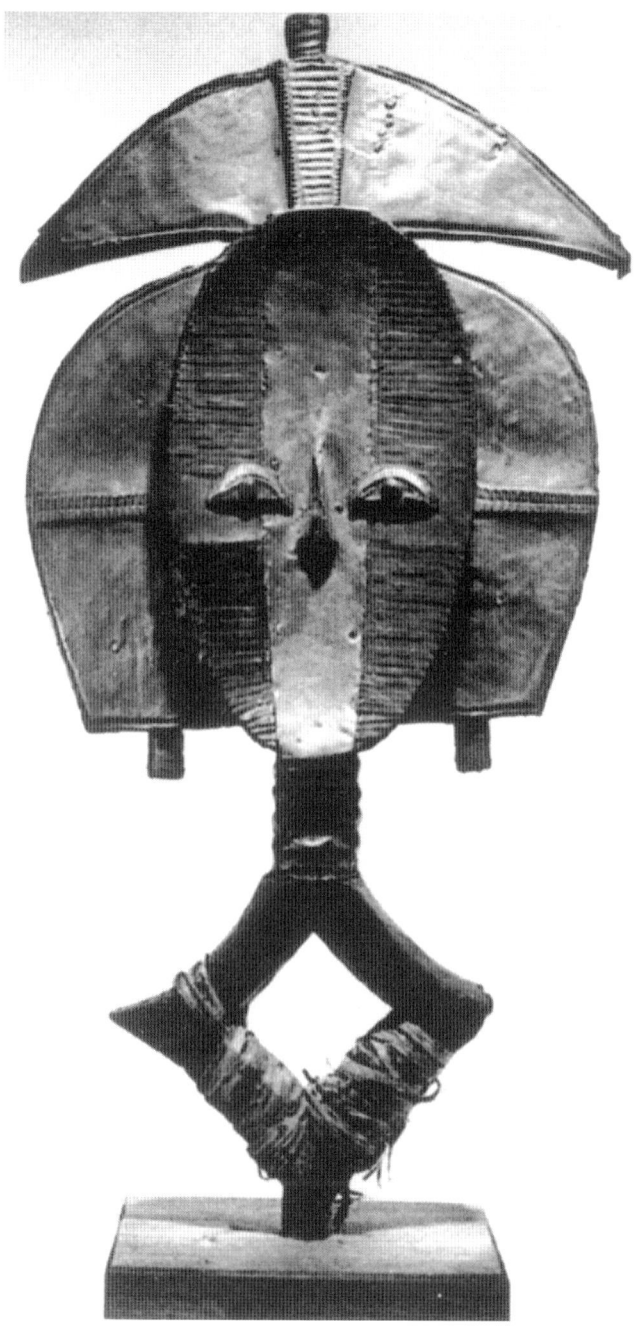

FIGURE 17. Reliquary Figure. Kota. People's Republic of the Congo. Paris, Musée de l'Homme. (© Musée de l'Homme.)

fetichism, performed by haggish witch-doctors and priests in their native costumes', as one guidebook advertised.[12] Part of the aim of these government-sponsored exhibits was to propagandise French colonial possessions around the world and rationalise their cultural transformations, each colony having its own section.[13] Picasso may well have visited this part of the exposition on his first trip to Paris as he was exhibiting a painting with the Spanish section at the Grand Palais.

Another major source of images and information about Africa was the popular press – itself influenced by prejudice, fantasy, and political interests – reinforced by novels and soldiers', missionaries', and explorers' accounts, the latter often accompanied by lurid, exotic, and fantastical illustrations.[14] In the Dahomean Wars of 1890 and 1892, during the 'scramble' for colonies, the French conquered Dahomey.[15] Travellers who ventured into the interior earlier in the century had returned with fantastical tales of animism, human sacrifice, and cannibalism – forming a frightening image of Africans as savage, primeval spirits – that were made much of in the French press. Such mass illustrated magazines as *Le Journal Illustré*, *L'Illustration*, and *Tour du Monde* and the illustrated supplements of the newspapers *Le Petit Journal* and *Le Petit Parisien*, emphasised the purported savagery of customs they misconstrued in accordance with their preconceptions.[16] For example, in a 'Scene of Human Sacrifice' published in *Tour du Monde* in 1863 (Fig. 18),[17] the Dahomeyan king watches from beneath a canopy while the priests sacrifice his chosen victims, holding their heads aloft.

During the Dahomean Wars the French popular press played up such tales in an attempt to justify French conquest. The press followed the wars only superficially, concentrating instead on the legendarily grotesque practices of the natives and illustrating their accounts with uncredited and rather free remakes of earlier engravings.[18] Figure 18, for instance, accompanies a text whose author confesses that he himself had only witnessed the sacrifice of a hyena.[19] The implication of cannibalism in these rites was likewise asserted and popularly believed. Though all tales of cannibalism did not actually come from the Dahomean kingdom, so little distinction was popularly made between various groups and regions of Africa that such images resonated around the word 'Dahomey'. The sensationalism of such accounts was given lurid play in the popular press, and in a remarkably short time Dahomey came to represent in France all that was most thrillingly barbaric, savage, and elemental on the 'dark continent'.

The French and Belgian Congos summon the other side of the image of Africa, which mixed in telling ways with the 'Dahomean'. The scandals following government inquiries into events in both the French and Bel-

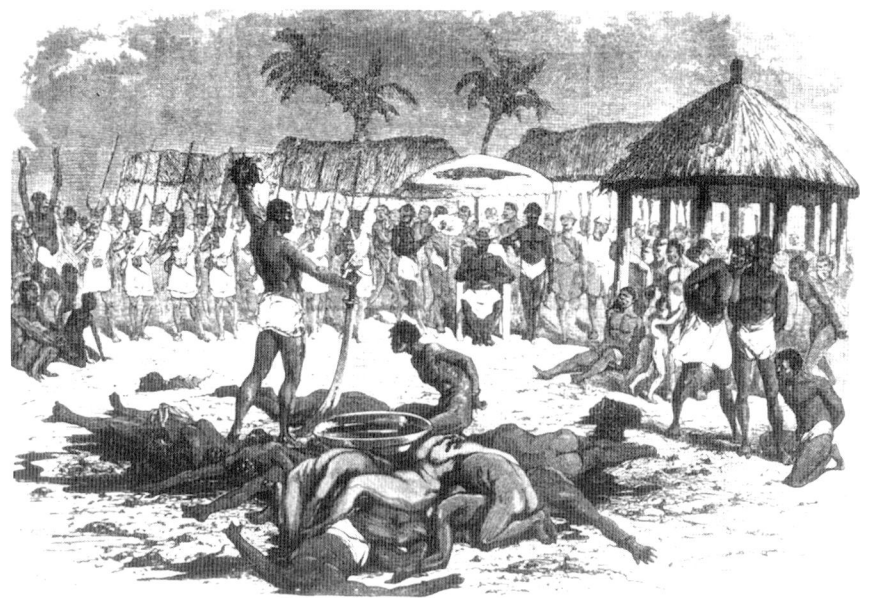

FIGURE 18. 'Sacrifices humaines au Dahomey'. From Dr. Répin, 'Voyage au Dahomey', *Tour du Monde*, VII, 1863.

gian Congos aroused socialist and anarchist opposition, inspiring a heated debate of which modernist writers and artists could not possibly have been unaware, even had they been uninterested.[20] Indeed, members of Picasso's circle articulated forcefully critical attitudes towards events in the Congo in political cartoons, most notably André Salmon, Kees van Dongen, and Juan Gris, as I discussed in the original version of this essay (see note 4). The Belgian Congo represents the most staggering instance of brutality, but the French Congo closely followed the Belgian model and inspired the equal censure of the left wing.

The Congo Free State – all of whose land became the 'personal property' of King Léopold of Belgium – was legitimised by the General Act of the Berlin Conference of 1885, which attempted to direct the European powers (or represent them as directed) towards development, rather than rape, of the colonies.[21] Article VI read,

> All the Powers exercising sovereign rights or influence in these territories pledge themselves to watch over the preservation of the native populations and the improvement of their moral and material conditions of existence, and to work together for the suppression of slavery and of the slave trade.[22]

King Léopold himself freely interpreted the charge enacted here, to which Belgium and France were both signatories, and in 1898 defended a rather ominous view of Belgium's 'civilising mission':

> The mission which the agents of the State have to accomplish on the Congo is a noble one. They have to continue the development of civilisation in the centre of Equatorial Africa, receiving their inspiration directly from Berlin and Brussels. Placed face to face with primitive barbarism, grappling with sanguinary customs that date back thousands of years, they are obliged to reduce these gradually. They must accustom the population to general laws, of which the most needful and the most salutary is assuredly that of work.[23]

The Force Publique, or military arm, of the Congo Free State at first enjoyed popularity in Europe for its destruction of the Muslim slave trade, still flourishing in the early 1890s.[24] But soon there were reports of rapacious exploitation. As King Léopold's agents struggled to establish control of the vast region, Africans were forced into labour for their new rulers and into service in the Force Publique.[25] Between 1892 and 1914, 66,000 Africans passed through the ranks of the Force Publique, which constituted for many Congolese their major contact with the West.[26] In the French Congo, too, colonial laws imposed forced labour so many days a year – legally fluctuating between ten and eighty – on all males between the ages of 18 and 60, a practise not discontinued until 1946.[27]

By far the worst abuses in the Congo involved the collection of rubber from the wild vines that grew in the forests.[28] The delegation of this labour to the Force Publique and its mercenaries invited coercion and violence[29]; profitable procedures included hostage taking, mutilations, and executions, sometimes on a large scale. Nominally most of these methods were illegal, but in practice considerations of profit remained sufficient rationale for what amounted to a system of atrocity. This system was criticised by the Report of the Congo State Commission of Inquiry that Léopold was eventually forced to initiate and was published in 1905.[30]

Rumours of these abuses of the Berlin Act came periodically to Europe, but more (and more appalling) details were published after the turn of the century, growing by 1905 into a scandal that rocked the French and Belgian governments. Parisian artists responded strongly in a series of cartoons in the anarchist journal *L'Assiette au beurre*. For example, Caran d'Ache, in a special issue of 1902 on the distribution of French government medals (Fig. 19), depicts, in front of a huddled mass of underfed Africans, a vicious dog and a brutish overseer reading the following letter from the

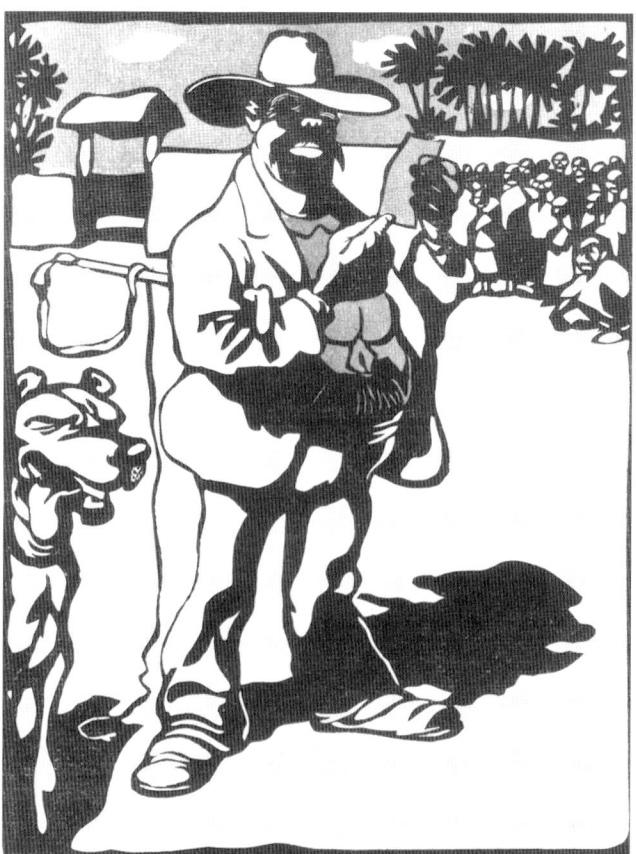

FIGURE 19. Caran d'Ache, 'La Lettre du ministre', *L'Assiette au beurre*, 21 January 1905. (© Photo Morris Library, University of Delaware.)

minister: 'Dear Friend, here people have reported that you have sold blacks, what slander! In any case, between now and July 14th, just barter them and I guarantee you [your decoration]'.[31] A series by Auguste Roubille in 1905 (Fig. 20) illustrates the thought of the bourgeois that 'If the worker is sometimes vile [when he strikes and rebels in France] . . . he is often sublime [when he commits "legal" atrocities in the army]'.[32] Anarchist leader Charles Malato and Juan Gris, a neighbour and close friend of Picasso, suggest that the infamously cruel Turks can *learn* cruelty from the French, whose deeds – as outlined in the inquiries – Gris illustrates (Fig. 21). In words that echo the rationale of the Parti colonial, the caption

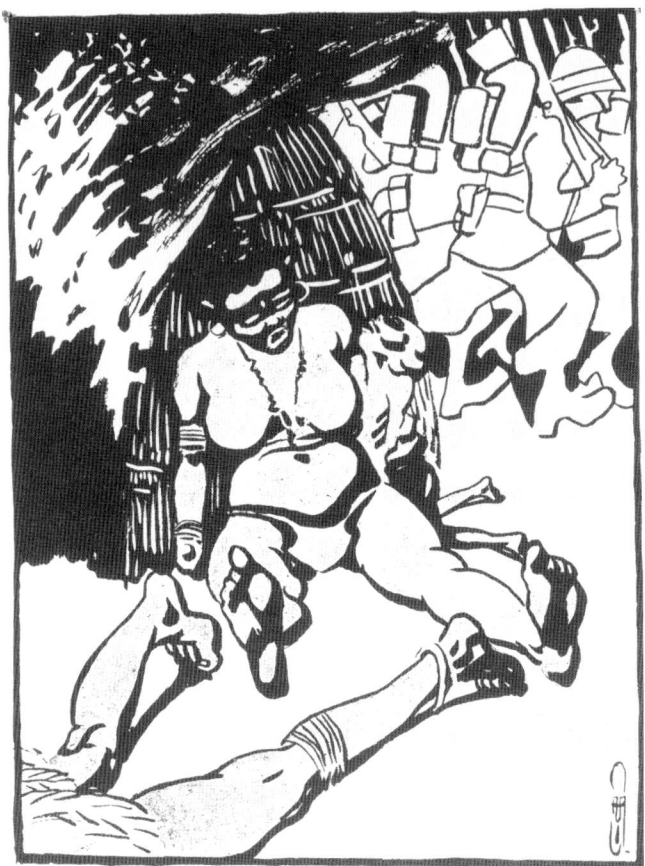

FIGURE 20. Auguste Roubille, '. . . il est souvent sublime', *L'Assiette au beurre*, 21 January 1905. (© Photo Morris Library, University of Delaware.)

reads, 'Guided by a need for expansion proper to every civilised nation, the Turks will go into the savage lands to bring civilised ways'.[33] Another figure close to Picasso, the poet and journalist André Salmon, wrote the captions and the following song parodying the Belgian national anthem for a special issue devoted to Léopold's Congo in 1904:

> Ignoring your happiness, in order that Cabourg and Co. prosper,
> Work with a boot in the rear, Belgians of color!
> Grumble no more, poor devils, the price of rubber will rise again.
> Inscribe on your banners: King, Law and Liberty.[34]

Simultaneous with the revelations of the Belgian inquiry into Léopoldian excesses (and inefficiencies) mentioned here, a scandal broke

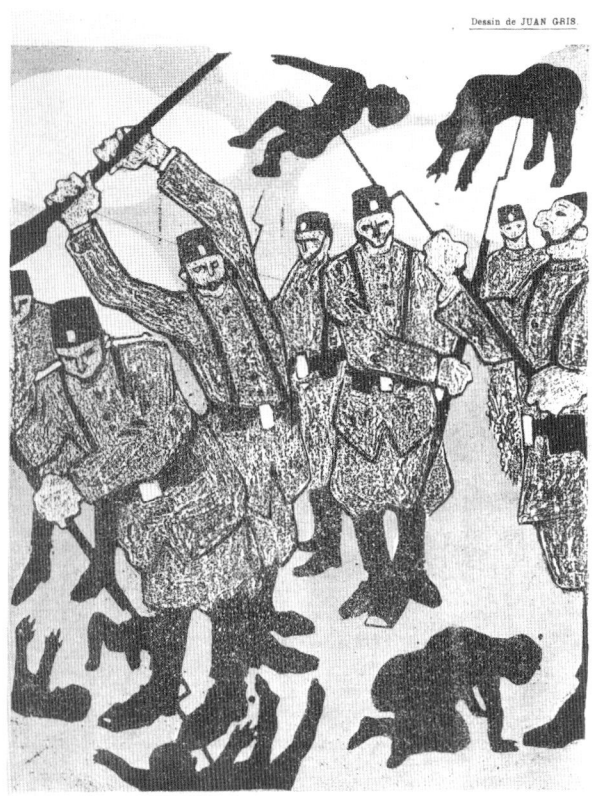

Dessin de JUAN GRIS.

Guidés par un besoin d'expansion propre à toute nation civilisée, les Turcs iront dans les pays sauvages, porter les procédés de civilisation.

FIGURE 21. Juan Gris, 'Guidés par un besoin', *L'Assiette au beurre*, 29 August 1908. (© Photo Bibliothèque Nationale.)

in France that resulted in a government inquiry – the Brazza mission – into conditions in the French Congo. The Gaud-Toqué affair, which involved the exposure of two colonial administrators, revealed numerous arbitrary executions and grotesque murders; these were described in the Parisian press and commented on in the inflammatory *l'Assiette au beurre*'s special issue of 11 March 1905 on 'The Torturers of Blacks'. The most famous case of brutality was the dynamiting of an African guide (as a sort of human firecracker) on Bastille Day, 1903, whose stated, and doubtless successful, purpose was to 'intimidate the local population'.[35] And in images that could have come straight out of *Heart of Darkness* (written following Conrad's trip up the Congo River in 1890),[36] Bernard Naudin and Aristide Delannoy suggest, depicting 'hunts' and enormous piles of bones,

that such methods were rather more systematic than spontaneously patri-
otic.[37] Indeed Toqué's confession, reported in *Le Temps* in 1905, blames
French colonial policy generally.[38]

Though the scandal was eventually hushed up, the report of the Brazza
mission suppressed, and the perpetrators released after a short time in
prison, there was widespread outrage in the newspapers and heated
debates in the Chamber of Deputies. The Socialist leader Jean Jaurès led
a joint attack on the forced labour system, though eventually all that
resulted was minor juridical reform, and essentially the same methods
continued. André Gide saw scenes of coercion identical to those described
here during his trip up the Congo River in 1926.[39]

The arguments of the so-called anticolonialists ranged from critics who
wanted a colonial empire, but one that was both more humanitarian and
more efficient, to those who refused to recognise the right of France to
impose its will, even in the name of civilisation, on other people.[40] Jaurès,
for example, originally accepted the concept of France's 'civilising mission', which he saw as benevolently spreading Enlightenment principles
and, eventually, socialist egalitarianism.[41] By 1905, however, Jaurès had
fundamentally altered his position on colonialism, especially its role in the
French economic system and the threat of pan-European war over competition for new markets and new colonial possessions.[42] His outrage at the
tales emerging from the French Congo was scathing, and his newspaper
l'Humanité – in an unrelenting series of articles by Gustave Rouanet –
played the major role in exposing the scandals in 1905 and 1906.

In a response more explicitly humanitarian, Charles Péguy – beginning
to shift from his early socialism to his later nationalism – published in *Les
Cahiers de la Quinzaine* the exposés of conditions in the two Congos by
Pierre Mille and Félicien Challaye, a member of Brazza's mission whose
reports the leading newspaper *Le Temps* had refused to publish.[43] Though
Péguy declared his devotion to 'the liberty of peoples', like Mille and Challaye, he called for reform rather than withdrawal. When the pacifist Challaye published an expanded form of this pamphlet in 1909, he wrote,
'Colonisation is a necessary social fact. . . . But justice demands that the
domination of the whites should not involve the worst consequences – slavery, robbery, torture, assassination – for the blacks. Justice demands that the
natives should derive some advantages from our presence among them'.[44]

More revolutionary thinkers rejected colonialism and its 'civilising'
premise altogether. Socialist Paul Louis wrote a well-known analysis of the
evils of the colonial enterprise in *Le Colonialisme* of 1905, asserting that,

'there is no peaceful colonisation, . . . all colonisation is based on violence, war, the sacking of towns, sharing out of the loot, and slavery, however well or thinly disguised'.[45] Among the anarchists, the former colonial doctor Paul Vigné d'Octon attacked the colonial system both in the Chambre des Députés and in his book, *Les Crimes coloniaux de la IIIe République*, of 1907, published by the revolutionary socialist Gustave Hervé in whose journal, *La Guerre sociale*, Vigné d'Octon also kept up a stream of articles.[46]

The Comité de Protection et de Défense des Indigènes held protest meetings and published numerous pamphlets from 1905 to at least 1910.[47] At the meeting of 31 October 1905, called jointly by the comité and the influential Ligue des Droits de l'Homme, speakers included the pacifist Frédérick Passy; the socialists Francis de Pressensé and Rouanet; and Pierre Quillard, a well-known anarchist and close friend of Alfred Jarry.

Quillard's speech, like Salmon's illustrated anticolonial diatribe of 1904, is of special interest because he knew members of the Apollinaire-Picasso circle well. He inflamed the crowd with his radicalism: 'Just now we were told that there is in the French press an indifference to colonial issues, an indifference to the crimes that were committed in the Congo and elsewhere. There is no indifference, there is something worse, there is vindication, there is glorification of these crimes'.[48] Whether this speech was heard by Picasso or his friends that night, such rhetoric reappeared in the daily papers and would have been repeated in the highly politicised circles in which they moved in these years. The debates and scandals brought a new and heightened awareness of France's African colonies and, for a politicised avant-garde, concentrated a range of politically charged meanings on everything to do with 'Africa'.

Alfred Jarry was especially important because he almost certainly knew Picasso and indisputably constituted one of his strongest influences.[49] Absurdist playwright, master of black humour, and anarchist artist par excellence, Jarry is of particular interest because, like Quillard, he made colonialism one of his major targets at the same time that he summoned up in his works an irrational world of 'Dahomean' intertribal slavery and cannibalism. In contrast to Jarry and Picasso, the ordinary range of colonial debate stayed within the confines of Enlightenment principles, swinging between an image of the black as noble savage (in a state out of which whites had long ago evolved) and an image of the black as degenerate savage (from which condition the native must be saved). Picasso (in the *Demoiselles*) and Jarry implicitly reject both positions by pointedly revelling in ethnic difference and evoking 'tribal' life and art that they see as irrational, magic, and violent, by embracing precisely the symptoms of its so-called degeneracy. Their works conjure with the idea that it is these very qualities that make Africa *superior* to European culture, especially as it is represented by Jarry.

Jarry was the quintessential anarchist artist, whose political satire would have been shockingly obvious to his contemporaries.[50] In *Ubu colonial* of 1901, Dr. Gasbag meets Père Ubu on his return from a self-described 'disastrous voyage of colonial exploration undertaken by us at the expense of the French government'; like the bloated, self-satisfied bourgeois that Ubu represents, seeking profits for himself at the public's expense, he brags of his adventures in terms that illuminate colonial mentality:

> Our first difficulty in those distant parts consisted in the impossibility of procuring slaves for ourself, slavery having unfortunately been abolished; we were reduced to entering into diplomatic relations with armed Negroes who were on bad terms with other Negroes lacking means of defense; and when the former had captured the latter, we marched the whole lot off as free workers. We did it, of course, out of pure philanthropy, to prevent the victors eating the defeated, and in imitation of the methods practiced in the factories of Paris.[51]

This anticolonial and cannibalistic theme – with its parallel between the exploitation of poor workers at home and the search for even cheaper labour abroad – recurs frequently in Jarry's work. In a piece of vicious 'nonsense' in the conclusion of *Ubu colonial*, Ubu in his disingenuous way attacks Dr. Gasbag for failing to appreciate the black as a completely different animal from the Frenchman:

> PA UBU: I remember a little pickaninny who arrived each day from a distant part of town just to empty a lady's chamber pot under the windows of our dining room, presenting the contents for our inspection with the remark:
> *Hey you folks look heah: me black me make yellow crap, ma mistress she white she make black crap.*

Dr. Gasbag is thunderstruck:

> GASBAG: This would merely prove that the white man is simply a Negro turned inside out like a glove.
> PA UBU: Sir, I am astonished that you should have discovered that all on your own. You have clearly profited from our discourse and deserve advancement. Possibly, when turned inside out in the manner you have described, you may suitably replace the specimen of black slave.[52]

Jarry here confronts and manipulates colonial stereotypes and rhetoric as circulated in the French press, revelling in a deliberate vulgarity satirising the prejudices of French colonials. His stunningly offensive play with the theme of anticolonialism is the other side of his primitivism: the worship of puppets, instinct, violence. By giving a political context to the African figures in such works as these, Jarry refuses to trade in the essentialised, timeless image of the noble savage. Instead he contextualises it, acknowledging the political realities that have brought the African 'fetishes' into the view of the avant-garde. And, like a good modernist subversive, he plays off the political oppressions foisted on natives by men like Ubu against an image of the African as a cannibal rather than a mere innocent, combining the 'Dahomean' with the 'Congolese' image of the black. He likewise satirically celebrates a whole range of other racist and furtively titillating stereotypes that colonial rhetoric traded in: nudity, rampant sexuality, and lack of inhibition of all sorts, as Bonnard confirms in his illustration for this play (Fig. 22).

Picasso's allegiance to concepts of primitivism that date back to his fin de siècle Nietzschean period and his parallel anarchism would have encouraged an interest in the Congo revelations and subsequent debates, and this could very well have led him and others to look freshly at what already surrounded them. Vlaminck, by his own account, had looked at African art with Derain at the Musée d'Ethnographie several times before his 'revelation' – at the time of the scandals – in the bistro in Argenteuil that resulted in his first acquisition of masks.[53] African sculpture offered a model of formal simplification based on folk traditions that were believed to go back into prerecorded history, representing to modernists 'authentic primitive' expressions of thought and feeling. As Frances Connelly has demonstrated, as early as the sixteenth century French aestheticians connected concepts of the 'grotesque' in two dimensions with caricature, ornament, and the fantastical, while the 'grotesque' in three dimensions suggested the monstrous and the horrific and was specifically associated with Africa.[54] African sculptures, as a result, were viewed as 'idols' and 'fetishes' and represented to Europeans manifestations of the 'irrational, mute, and fearful world' in which they imagined the 'primitive' to live. Conversion to Christianity routinely involved destruction (or exportation) of such too powerful three-dimensional art, and the shock felt by eighteenth-century Europeans gradually took on shades of sarcasm and contempt as colonialisation proceeded.[55]

Thus an imagined primal savagery was thoroughly merged with images

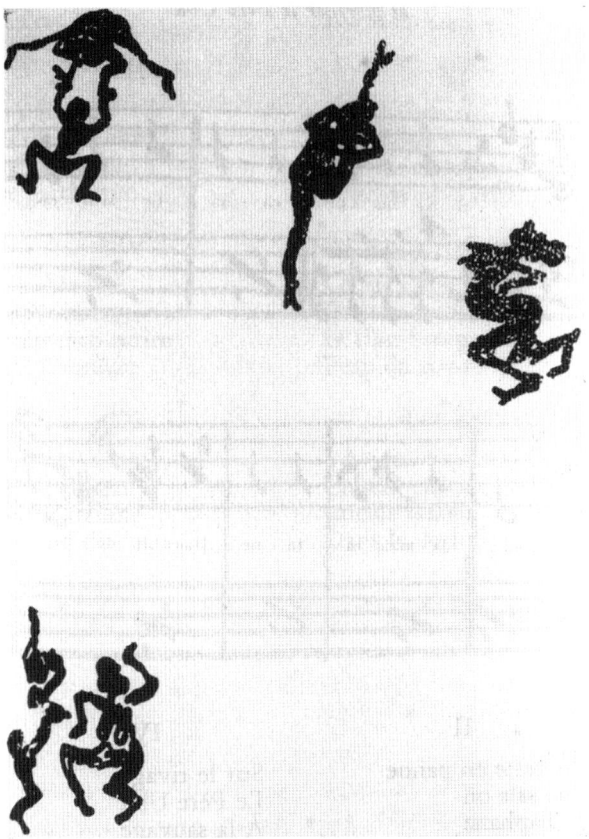

FIGURE 22. Pierre Bonnard, Illustration for Alfred Jarry, 'Ubu coloniale', from *Almanach illustré du Père Ubu* (Paris, 1901).

of and references to African sculpture for any artist or audience of prewar France, and their appearance in Picasso's already 'grotesque' *Demoiselles d'Avignon* (Fig. 1) echoed inherited images and associations of superstition, irrationality, darkness, and horror, adding to his already considerable anti-classical arsenal. Salmon asserted in *La Jeune peinture française* that 'in choosing savage artists as guides', Picasso 'was not unaware of their barbar-ity'. He was 'the apprentice sorcerer always consulting the Oceanic and African enchanters'.[56] Elsewhere, Salmon called Picasso's collection of African and Oceanian sculptures 'grimacing idols' and 'primitive mar-vels'.[57] What Picasso produced in response to this influence were 'forbid-ding nudes, grimacing and perfectly worthy of execration', a human effigy that 'appears to us so inhuman and inspires in us a sort of horror'.[58] Apollinaire used similar language characterising the Congolese objects owned by Vlaminck and Derain, admiringly naming them 'masks and fetishes', 'grotesque and crudely mystical works', and 'barbaric sculptures'.[59]

In *Les Demoiselles d'Avignon* the Iberian faces of the two central figures and their crudely simplified forms ally them with Spain's prehistoric past and announce Picasso's origins and preoccupations as outside (and against) the French classical tradition.[60] The context of the brothel points up the prostitutes' loss of freedom: like slaves they are bought and sold. At the same time, the exaggeration of their sexual display threatens the spectator/customer as they turn their attention from the room to the world beyond the frame. Their 'primitive' power and hypnotic gaze are anything but alluring, yet they pale in comparison with the 'violence' of the two right-hand figures, whose faces are transformed by African rather than Iberian models and whose presences considerably increase the voltage of the work; they mock such sexual display and aggressively challenge the 'bankrupt' Western imagery of the classical 'nude' as Africanised figures.

What Picasso's primitivism does to European art it also does to Europe's idealisations of sexuality. The radical treatment of the traditional nude female announces the end of the old world of art with a new violence. The violence comes not only from the distortion of the faces and forms of the two Africanised figures, and from the transformation of usually passive nudes in tamed attitudes into aggressively challenging mock temptresses, but also from the very allusion to 'Africa' embedded in them. The tremendous powers of 'primitive' spirituality overwhelm the European tradition in a flamboyant act of rebellion. More than this, all those thrillingly nightmarish and well-publicised tales of 'Dahomey' inevitably echo in the African forms imported into this work, summoning up an imagined ruthless barbarity that the male modernist makes it his mission to confront.

As Sander Gilman has shown, racist assumptions about African female sexuality spilled over to the European prostitute, linked by what was seen as a parallel process of physical and social degeneration. The late nineteenth century saw the initiation of sociological and police classification systems for categorising 'biological determinants' of criminal behaviour, the very concept of which denies economic motive.[61] Gilman shows that the physiognomic traits attributed to the prostitute were precisely those associated with the African female, all of which 'point to the "primitive" nature of the prostitute's physiognomy'.[62] The logical conclusion of this chain of signifiers was that the sexual activity and resulting syphilis of the European prostitute became a sign of her physiological regression to the condition of the Hottentot Venus. Picasso's prostitutes – in the early sketches attendant on both customer (the sailor) and 'medical student' (or inspector)[63] – necessarily function within this system, as their overt and aggressive sexuality affirms cultural and racial attitudes shared by the artist and his audience even as their formal treatment underscores their threat to the client/viewer. If the prostitutes represent the savage within Europe's borders, delivering a Dionysian thrill of sexual promiscuity and violence – complete with its promise of escape from both decorum and ordinary consciousness – the Jarry of *Ubu colonial* is a potent precursor.

All this 'horror' can come together – in a way that self-evidently did not seem contradictory – with outrage at the brutality of the white colonialists. Jarry, as we have seen, exhibits a fascination with both sides of this strange African coin. So does Conrad; in the beginning of *Heart of Darkness*, Marlow is appalled to see Europeans using chain gangs of blacks, overworked and dying; but, finally, for Conrad it is the indigenous evil of human sacrifice, to which Mr. Kurtz succumbs through his participation and which the primeval forest somehow compels, that is the worst. The attraction to the grotesque, the artist's obligation to acknowledge, even to experience on some level, the most horrific human truths, was already thoroughly established in the Symbolist period by the Decadents, with precedents going back to the Romantics of the early nineteenth century. Mario Praz's classic study of this subject details a whole literature's fascination with a catalogue of horrors that includes incest, murder, vampirism, Satan worship, and necrophilia.[64] That this embracing of 'horror' could be conflated with a larger agenda of social criticism and 'liberation' was likewise explored by the previous generation. The new venue was Africa itself.

Thus both stylistically and thematically these 'African' figures in *Les Demoiselles* are not only unsympathetic to the art and life of established European culture, they are its enemy. This painting's 'rhetoric' owes much to those anticolonial satires on black Africa that are central to Jarry's oeuvre. The raw sexuality of his black characters, their perverseness, like that of Picasso's 'African' demoiselles, stands against the rational, orderly, decorous world of colonialist Europe; and behind it all lies the exploitation, and the brittle and vainglorious cultural superiority that Jarry ridiculed.

Ultimately, Picasso's primitivism, like all primitivism, subverts aesthetic canons of beauty and order in the name of 'authenticity'.[65] For Picasso and other anarchists, this is a way of contravening the rational, liberal, 'enlightened' political order in which they are implicated. The deliberate ugliness of the *Demoiselles* asserts the persistence, within a self-congratulatory 'modern' culture, of ugly realities that a complacent modernity would prefer to elide. The artist conjures with the anxiety that civilisation has done its work too well, made Europeans too tame, and thus cut them off from sources of magic, fear, and dread, sources on which a more 'primitive' art might still draw and to which it might still be able to return them.[66] His imagery asserts that the culture of such 'savages' has a power and a beauty all its own. Picasso's primitivising proposes a more subversive alternative ruled out of the accepted terms of debate, namely that the African is neither an inferior brute nor a misunderstood equal, but something more like an absolute other who remains possessed of primordial powers with which 'modern' culture has lost touch – much to its disadvantage.

Picasso's primitivising style thus aspires, like the African sculptures he so admired, to an act not of mere decoration, but of *power*, a bid to recapture kinds of representational 'power' that the arts of civilised, enlightened Europe had lost. The multivalent strategies of his work speak to many levels of public and private experience as well as to conventions of inherited tradition, which this public would have recognised and which Picasso would have expected it to recognise. And part of this recognition, by virtue of 'masking' his figures, would have inescapably involved the complicated mixture of ideas, fantasies, political postures, and racial and sexual attitudes relating to Africa as the French public 'knew' it in 1907, a public recently agitated by reports of nearly unbelievable yet documented cruelty and illegal exploitation in a colony viewed by so many as undergoing a process of 'civilisation' at the hands of their own 'superior' culture.

Avant-garde painters for a century and more – David, Géricault, Delacroix, Courbet, and others – had offered finely calculated provocations of subject and theme at moments of political anxiety, crisis, and scandal. Picasso's provocation is similarly motivated, but additionally grapples with a central problem of modernism in general: how to radicalise structure and form, and abandon realism and narrative, without also abandoning centrally important real-life concerns. Picasso by 'masking' his figures conflates an exotic and exploited group external to Western society with an equally exploited group within Western society, analogising the ironically more visible periphery with the corrupt center of French culture. In their power both to attract and repel the male beholder, the Africanised prostitutes capture the ambivalent character of Picasso's primitivism. By conflating African masks with an image of European 'idols', Picasso identifies the prostitute as a 'grotesque other', yet at the same time he identifies his own avant-garde status as a self-styled 'primitive' with this same 'other', thus overturning European cultural values that would identify the 'primitive' with the degenerate. For colonialists France had a civilising mission in Africa; for anarchist avant-gardists, African art and culture had a primitivising mission for Europe. Like Jarry and Conrad before him, Picasso simultaneously condemns the colonial policies that brought such masks to Europe, yet embraces the very stereotypes that would see African culture as a recuperative cure to degeneration 'at home' rather than abroad.[67] Thus Picasso's ambivalence is the ambivalence of modernism: a customer of prostitutes and an appreciative exploiter of 'Africa', he operated in and against a colonialist world, addressing himself to audiences equally immersed in the assumptions and animating questions of the day. That his contemporaries and supporters were 'horrified' by his ambitious painting tells us he went too far[68]; but that, in our own time, we have forgotten that 'Africa' carried these meanings for modern culture, only tells us something about ourselves.

NOTES

1 D. Cress, 'Racial Discord Flares over Museum Mummy in Small Spanish Town', *New York Times* (5 February 1992). My thanks to Tracy Meyers for bringing this article to my attention.

This chapter is part of a larger study, *The Politics of Form: Art, Anarchism and Audience in Avant-Guerre Paris*. I would like to express my gratitude to the J. Paul Getty Foundation, the American Philosophical Society, the University of Delaware, and the National Endowment for the Humanities for support in the early stages of this project, and the Center for Advanced Study in the Visual Arts for a Samuel H. Kress Senior Fellowship in 1989–90. My thanks also go to Steven Helmling, Jody Blake, and Suzanne Preston Blier for discussions on various aspects of this subject and, especially, to Mark Antliff for a close reading of the manuscript.

2 See M. Antliff and P. Leighten, 'Primitive', in R. Nelson and R. Shiff (eds.), *Critical Terms for Art History* (Chicago: Chicago University Press, 1996), 170–84, for a fuller discussion of this concept in colonial and modernist discourse and Antliff and Leighten, *Cubism and Culture* (London and New York: Thames and Hudson, 2001), for its context in the larger Cubist movement.

3 C. Miller, *Blank Darkness: Africanist Discourse in France* (Chicago and London, 1986), 5, has analyzed this paradigm in more general terms: 'Africa has been made to bear a double burden, of monstrousness *and* nobility. . . . The gesture of reaching out to the most unknown part of the world and bringing it back as language . . . ultimately brings Europe face to face with nothing but itself, with the problems its own discourse imposes'. For extended discussions of primitivism, see J. Clifford, *The Predicament of Culture* (Cambridge, Mass., 1988); G. Perry, 'Primitivism and the "Modern"', in C. Harrison, F. Frascina, and G. Perry (eds.), *Primitivism, Cubism, Abstraction: The Early Twentieth Century* (New Haven and London, 1993); S. Price, *Primitive Art in Civilized Places* (Chicago and London, 1989); G. Stocking, *Race, Culture, and Evolution: Essays in the History of Anthropology* (Chicago and London, 1968, 1982); M. Torgovnick, *Gone Primitive: Savage Intellects, Modern Lives* (Chicago and London, 1990).

4 *The Art Bulletin* 72 (December 1990), 609–30; reprint in *Race-ing Art History*, K. Pinder (ed.) (London: Routledge, forthcoming, 2002).

5 W. Rubin, 'The Genesis of *Les Demoiselles d'Avignon*', in *Les Demoiselles d'Avignon* (New York, 1994), 13–144, updated version of 'La Genèse des *Demoiselles d'Avignon*', in *Les Demoiselles d'Avignon*, vol. 2 (Paris: Musée Picasso, 1988), 367–487. Rubin's frequent dismissals of my work on the political milieu of the prewar period are methodologically based on a strictly biographical approach to Picasso's art. Thus he not only condemns my work but that of scholars as diverse as Carol Duncan, Michael Leja, and Hal Foster, all on the same basis; see C. Duncan, 'The MOMA's Hot Mamas', *Art Journal* 48 (Summer 1989), 171–8; M. Leja, '"Le Vieux Marcheur" and "Les Deux Risques": Picasso, Prostitution, Venereal Disease, and Maternity, 1899–1907', *Art History* 8 (March 1985), 66–81; and H. Foster, 'The "Primitive" Unconscious of Modern Art or White Skin Black Masks', *October* 34 (Autumn 1985, 45–70), reprinted in *Recodings: Art, Spectacle, Cultural Politics* (Seattle, 1985). For Rubin the only approach free of the taint of a political point of view is his own supposedly value-neutral grounding in the 'private', usually unconscious, motivations of Picasso, propped up by a unique and miraculous access to Picasso's psyche. In Rubin's hands, Picasso's work emerges not in relation to history, society, or contested issues within his aesthetic milieu, but as a compulsive, solipsistic exercise. Premised on the conviction that all meaning in a work of art is generated by the maker, with no awareness of the hermeutic governing the relation of present to past in historical scholarship (see Catherine Belsey, *Critical Practice* [London, 1980], 37–47), this notion accounts for Rubin's false distinction between private motivations and the broader historical matrix in which such motivations are inevitably inscribed.

   Lomas, 'A Canon of Deformity: *Les Demoiselles d'Avignon* and Physical Anthropology', *Art History* 16 (September 1993), 424–6, and here, pp. 104–127 (in revised form) alternatively claims that the *Demoiselles* has become 'detached from the social and cultural context of its production', but 'that the audacious departure from a classical canon of the body in *Les Demoiselles d'Avignon* relies on and brings into play what were, in effect, highly denigratory stereotypes of cultural otherness' (425, 427). Here he notes my essay and dismisses it as offering a 'contrasting, rosier picture of Picasso's primitivism', ignoring its arguments concerning the political context of colonialism, the problematic negative aspects of modernist primitivism, and Picasso's 'anticlassicism' (442). Whereas I view Picasso's anticlassicism as an assault on established cultural 'norms' of classical beauty, Lomas drains this act of its avant-gardism and makes a direct correlation between Picasso's primitivism and contemporaneous anthropological and criminological representations of degeneracy, without the mediating element of avant-garde politics or purpose. Lomas's 'anthropological' reading of anticlassicism thus fails to account for the stylistic dimension of Picasso's departure from academic norms and could not be distinguished from pre-modernist representations of degenerate Africans, from Herbert Ward to Gérôme. Lomas nonetheless makes an important contribution in focusing on the association of prostitution, criminality, and degeneration in relation to this painting.

6 Mikhail Bakhtin, in such works as 'Discourse in the Novel' (originally published Moscow, 1975), translated in *The Dialogic Imagination: Four Essays* (Austin, 1981), saw all languages as 'heteroglot', representing 'the co-existence of socio-ideological contradictions between the present and the past, between differing epochs of

the past, between different socio-groups in the present, between tendencies, schools, circles and so forth' (291). For Bakhtin 'discourse' is individual language in active dialogue with other kinds of language – many kinds of language – including 'official' ones: 'language not as a system of abstract grammatical categories, but rather language conceived as ideologically saturated' (271). Thus 'the social life of discourse outside the artist's study, discourse in the open spaces of public squares, streets, cities and villages, of social groups, generations and epochs' (259) not only necessarily echoes throughout any work of art but also constitutes the myriad of languages with which the artist necessarily conjures, whether within the dominant discourse or as 'counter-discourse'. My forthcoming study, *The Politics of Form: Art, Anarchism, and Audience in Avant-Guerre Paris*, deals with the variety of languages left-wing artists negotiated in this period in terms of subject, medium, venue, and stylistic form.

7 See P. Leighten, *Re-Ordering the Universe: Picasso and Anarchism, 1897–1914* (Princeton, 1989), 78–84.

8 For considerations of Picasso and Africanism, see R. Goldwater, *Primitivism in Modern Painting* (New York, 1938; rev. ed., 1967); J. Laude, *La Peinture française (1905–1914) et 'l'art nègre'* (Paris, 1968); W. Rubin, 'From Narrative to "Iconic" in Picasso: The Buried Allegory in *Bread and Fruitdish on a Table* and the Role of *Les Demoiselles d'Avignon*', *The Art Bulletin* 65 (December 1983), 615–49, and 'Picasso', in W. Rubin (ed.), *'Primitivism' in 20th Century Art* (New York, 1984), 241–343; Foster, 'The "Primitive" Unconscious of Modern Art, or White Skin Black Masks'; Y.-A. Bois, 'Kahnweiler's Lesson,' *Representations* 18 (Spring 1987), 33–68; S. Gilman, 'Black Bodies, White Bodies: Toward an Iconography of Female Sexuality in Late Nineteenth-Century Art, Medicine, and Literature', in H.L. Gates, Jr. (ed.), *'Race', Writing, and Difference* (Chicago, 1986), 223–61; K. Herding, *Pablo Picasso, 'Les Demoiselles d'Avignon': Die Herausforderung der Avantgarde* (Frankfurt am Main, 1992); and Lomas, 'A Canon of Deformity', as in note 5.

9 See J. Paudrat, 'From Africa', in *'Primitivism' in 20th Century Art*, as in note 8, 125–75, for a discussion of what was available in Paris at this time. The 'discovery' of African sculpture by the Fauves and the date of Picasso's first encounter has been much debated by scholars; Paudrat, 137–41, proposed autumn 1906 as the date of the first real impact of African art on Vlaminck, Derain, and Henri Matisse; Rubin (1984), 248, and J. Flam, 'Matisse and the Fauves', in *'Primitivism' in 20th Century Art*, 216–17, concur in this date, though Flam later suggested, if I read him correctly in *Matisse: The Man and His Art, 1869–1918* (Ithaca and London, 1986), 173–4, that Matisse's first purchase was in the spring of that year.

10 See J. Donne, 'African Art and Paris Studios, 1905–20', in M. Greenhalgh and V. Megaw (eds.), *Art in Society: Studies in Style, Culture, and Aesthetics* (London, 1978), 105–20, for a discussion of the exclusively colonial origins of the African art Picasso was able to see. For a brilliant study of the denial of history and 'coevalness' to the 'primitive', see J. Fabian, *Time and the Other: How Anthropology Makes Its Object* (New York, 1983).

11 For the French views of 'Africa' and traditions of primitivism, see Miller and F. Connelly, 'The Origins and Development of Primitivism in Eighteenth- and Nineteenth-Century European Art and Aesthetics', Ph.D. Diss., University of Pittsburgh, 1987, and *The Sleep of Reason: Primitivism in Modern European Art and*

Aesthetics, 1725–1907 (University Park, Penn., 1995). For Gauguin and primitivism, see K. Varnedoe, 'Gauguin', in *'Primitivism' in 20th Century Art,* 179–209.

12 J. Boyd, *The Paris Exposition of 1900* (Chicago, 1900), 449–50; my thanks to Jody Blake, who kindly brought this reference to my attention.

13 For example, an enormous book, L. Brunet and L. Giethlen, *Dahomey et Dépendances: Exposition Universelle de 1900 – Les Colonies françaises* (Paris, 1900), accompanied the Dahomean exhibition, detailing Dahomey's history and its current – that is, French – organisation, administration, ethnography, production, agriculture, and commerce, all in the most glowingly propagandistic terms.

14 For example, N. Baudin, *Fetichism and Fetich Worshippers* (New York, Cincinnati, and St. Louis, 1885) (translation of French original). See W. Cohen, *The French Encounter with Africans: White Response to Blacks, 1530–1880* (Bloomington and London, 1980), 258 ff.; Miller; Connelly (1987); and W. Schneider, *An Empire for the Masses: The French Popular Image of Africa, 1870–1900* (Westport, Conn., and London, 1982). For a highly readable history of the imperial procedures of this period, see E. Hobsbawm, *The Age of Empire, 1875–1914* (New York, 1987).

15 See Général Duboc, *L'Epopée coloniale en Afrique Occidentale Française* (Paris, 1938), 395; and J. Fage, *A History of West Africa* (Cambridge, 1969), 175. For Dahomey and French West Africa, see J. Webster and A. Boahen, *History of West Africa: The Revolutionary Years – 1815 to Independence* (New York and Washington, 1970); and R. Cornevin, *Histoire du Dahomey* (Paris, 1962). Dahomey, ruled from the central city of Abomey, had a truly urban social structure by the eighteenth century, another misunderstood aspect of the African culture modernists distorted in their admiration; see R. Thompson, *Flash of the Spirit: African and Afro-American Art and Philosophy* (New York, 1983), and M. Fried, *The Notion of the Tribe* (Menlo Park, 1975). C. Diop, *Precolonial Black Africa, a Comparative Study of the Political and Social Systems of Europe and Black Africa, from Antiquity to the Formation of Modern States,* trans. H. Salemson (Westport, Conn., 1987), 72–5, discusses the extent to which this was true for all of Africa.

16 See V. Champion-Vincent, 'L'image du Dahomey dans la presse française (1890–1895): Les sacrifices humains', *Cahiers d'études Africaines* 7 (1967), 27–58; Fage, 199–200; Cohen, 257–60; and Schneider, 97–109.

17 Dr. Répin, 'Voyage du Dahomey', *Tour du Monde* 7 (1863), 65–110.

18 Figure 18 was reproduced, at the beginning of the French conquest, in *Le Journal Illustré* on 9 March 1890 and in *Le Petit Parisien* a week later, neither with any indication that the engraving was nearly thirty years old; see Schneider, 97–109.

19 Cohen, 258.

20 See J. Suret-Canale, *Afrique noire* (Paris, 1964), vol. 2: *L'Ere coloniale 1900–1945,* trans. T. Gottheiner (New York, 1971), 34–6; and M. Loutfi, *Littérature et colonialisme: l'expansion coloniale vue dans la littérature romanesque française, 1871–1914* (Paris, 1971), 119.

21 On the Belgian Congo, see L. Gann and P. Duignan, *The Rulers of Belgian Africa, 1884–1914* (Princeton, 1979); and R. Anstey, *King Leopold's Legacy: The Congo under Belgian Rule, 1908–1960* (London, New York, and Ibadan, 1966).

22 A. Doyle, *The Crime of the Congo* (New York, 1909), 8.

23 Translated in J. Conrad, *Heart of Darkness* (Norton Critical Edition, R. Kimbrough, ed.) (New York, 1971), 86.

24 Gann and Duignan, 55–8.

25 As one witness, G. Burrows, *The Curse of Central Africa* (London, 1903), 22 and 174–5, wrote,

> As the State established its authority . . . a regular system of recruiting was instituted, each district being called upon to furnish a certain number of conscripts. . . . The *commissaires de district* have orders to see that their quotas are promptly forthcoming, and each naturally enough delegates the duty of recruiting to his *chefs de zone* who, in their turn, call upon the more subordinate *chefs de poste* to levy upon the local chiefs for the men required. The native chieftain usually makes his selection from the worthless and recalcitrant slaves of the village, who, when they reach the station, are promptly placed in the chain, or "collier national" as the Belgians call it, so that they cannot escape.

Guy Burrows, a former district commissioner of the Congo Free State, exposed many abuses of Léopold's rule; though he presents such evils in a heated and occasionally exaggerated form, his book is considered reliable; see Gann and Duignan, 77.

26 Gann and Duignan, 79; Burrows, 92–3.

27 Webster and Boahen, 271.

28 Gann and Duignan, 104.

29 Anstey, 4–5; Gann and Duignan, 136.

30 Congo Independent State, 'Report of the Commission of Inquiry', *Bulletin officiel* (Brussels, September–October 1905), 135–285.

31 *L'Assiette au beurre* no. 40 (4 January 1902): 'Cher ami, ici l'on a raconté que vous vendiez des nègres, quelle infamie! Dans tous les cas, d'ici au 14 juillet, ne faites que de simple échanges et je vous garantis que vous le serez. Agréez, etc.', translated in S. Appelbaum, *French Satirical Drawings from "L'Assiette au Beurre"* (New York, 1978), 10. This cartoon is the more interesting because Caran d'Ache was generally conservative, but was here moved to attack the government.

32 *L'Assiette au beurre* no. 199 (21 January 1905): 'Quant à l'ouvrier, s'il est quelquefois ignoble . . . il est souvent sublime' (author's translation).

33 *L'Assiette au beurre*, special issue on 'La Turquie regénérée', no. 386 (29 August 1908): 'Guidés par un besoin d'expansion propre à toute nation civilisée, les Turcs iront dans les pays sauvages, porter les precédés de civilisation' (author's translation).

34 *L'Assiette au beurre* no. 181 (17 September 1904) (text by André Salmon): 'Ignorants de votre bonheur,/Pour que Cabourg et Cie prospèrent,/A coups de pied dans le derrière/Travaillez, Belges de couleur!/Ne vous plaignez plus, pauvres hères,/Le caoutchouc va remonter./Inscrivez donc sur vos bannières:/Le Roi, la Loi, la Liberté' (author's translation).

35 *L'Assiette au beurre* no. 206 (11 March 1905) (special issue on 'Les Bourreaux des Noirs'), accompanied by an excerpt from the press.

36 Joseph Conrad wrote *Heart of Darkness* in 1898–9, and first published it serially in *Blackwood's Magazine* in 1899; it first appeared in a separate volume in 1902.

37 Both are from *L'Assiette au beurre* no. 206 (11 March 1905) (special issue on 'Les Bourreaux des Noirs').

38 *Le Temps* (23 September 1905), translated in Suret-Canale, 35.

39 A. Gide, *Voyage au Congo* (Paris, 1927). Gide dedicated his book 'To the Memory of Joseph Conrad'.

40 See R. Betts, *Assimilation and Association in French Colonial Theory, 1890–1914*

(New York and London, 1961); see also C. Andrew and A. Kanya-Forstner, 'The French Colonial Party: Its Composition, Aims and Influence, 1885–1914', *Historical Journal* 14 (1971), 99–128; and R. Girardet, *L'Idée coloniale en France de 1871 à 1962* (Paris, 1972). On anticolonialism, see H. Brunschwig, *Mythes et réalités de l'impérialisme colonial français, 1871–1914* (Paris, 1960), 173–84; C. Ageron, *L'Anticolonialisme en France de 1871 à 1914* (Paris, 1973); and R. Jeaugeon, 'Les sociétés d'exploitation au Congo et l'opinion française de 1890 à 1906', *Revue française d'histoire d'outre-mer* 48 (1961), 353–437.

41   In 1903 Jaurès said to the Chamber of Deputies: 'If we have always combatted the politics of colonial expansion by war, the politics of armed expeditions and of violent protectorates, we have always seconded and we are always ready to second the peaceful expansion of French interests and of French civilisation'; see Jaurès's speeches in the Chambre des Députés, *Journal officiel*, March and 24 December 1895; and H. Goldberg, *The Life of Jean Jaurès* (Madison, Wisc., and London, 1968), 202–3.

42   See Goldberg, 348.

43   See F. Challaye and P. Mille, *Les Deux Congos: Devant la Belgique et devant la France* (Paris, 1906); and Challaye, *Le Congo français* (Paris, 1906).

44   F. Challaye, *Le Congo français* (Paris, 1909), 313, translated in Suret-Canale, 127.

45   P. Louis, *Le Colonialisme* (Paris, 1905), 109, translated in Suret-Canale, 125.

46   P. Vigné d'Octon, *Les Crimes coloniaux de la IIIe République* (Paris, 1907), 8, translated in Suret-Canale, 139.

47   Published by the Comité de Protection et de Défense des Indigènes in Paris; see also 'Abus financiers dans les colonies', 'Au Congo; les considerations d'un arrêt du Conseil d'état', and 'Projet de statuts d'une union internationale pour la protection et la défense des indigènes (adoptés par le comité dans sa séance du 4 février 1908)'.

48   'Discourse de Pierre Quillard', *Les Illégalités et les crimes du Congo*, Comité de Protection et de défense des Indigènes – Meeting de protestation 31 octobre 1905, Paris, 54–7: 'Tout à l'heure on nous disait qu'il y a dans la presse française une indifférence pour les choses coloniales, une indifférence pour les crimes qui se commettent au Congo ou ailleurs. Il n'y a pas d'indifférence, il y a quelque chose de pire, il y a l'apologie, il y a la glorification de ces crimes (author's translation).

49   John Richardson, following Hélène Parmelin, asserts in *A Life of Picasso, Volume I: 1881–1906* (New York: Random House, 1991), 362, that Picasso never met Jarry. Max Jacob, *Chronique des temps héroïques* (Paris, 1956), 48–9, describes a banquet with both Jarry and Picasso present, though Richardson doubts its reliability. Given the number of witnesses to their mutual gathering places and acquaintances, especially Apollinaire from 1904 on, I think it virtually impossible that the two never met. In either case the poet was enormously influential on the artist, as Richardson agrees.

50   See Leighten (1989), 63–9 and 135–9.

51   A. Jarry, 'Ubu Colonial', *Almanach illustré du Père Ubu* (Paris, 1901); translated in R. Shattuck and S. Taylor (eds.), *Selected Works of Alfred Jarry* (New York, 1965), 53–4.

52   Translated in Shattuck and Taylor (1965), 59.

53   M. Vlaminck, *Portraits avant décès* (Paris, 1943), 106.

54 See Connelly (1987), 164 and 237.

55 Connelly (1987), 260–1 and 266–9.

56 Salmon, *La Jeune peinture française* (Paris, 1912), 44–51 (author's translation).

57 Ibid., translated in E. Fry, *Cubism* (London, 1966), 89; and Salmon, 'Pablo Picasso', *Paris-Journal* (21 September 1911), translated in Fry, 68.

58 Salmon (1912), 48 and 51 (author's translation).

59 G. Apollinaire, 'The Beginnings of Cubism', *Le Temps* (14 October 1912), translated in L. Breunig, *Apollinaire on Art: Essays and Reviews, 1902–1918* (New York, 1972), 259–61.

60 For a lengthy consideration of Picasso's relation to the 'classical tradition', see E. Fry, 'Picasso, Cubism, and Reflexivity', *Art Journal* 47 (Winter 1988), 296–310.

61 See Gilman; R. Nye, *Crime, Madness, & Politics in Modern France: The Medical Concept of National Decline* (Princeton, 1984); D. Pick, *Faces of Degeneration: A European Disorder, c. 1848–c.1918* (Cambridge, 1989); and A. Sekula, 'The Body and the Archive', in R. Bolton (ed.), *The Contest of Meaning: Critical Histories of Photography* (Cambridge, Mass., 1989), 343–89.

62 Gilman, 243.

63 See Leja's convincing discussion of the 'medical inspector', 75–6; see also Rubin (1994), 42 ff., for a lengthy discussion of this figure.

64 M. Praz, *The Romantic Agony* (Oxford, 1933 and 1970).

65 L. Trilling argued in *Sincerity and Authenticity* (Cambridge, Mass., 1971) that the idea of 'authenticity' has governed much of modernist art, which rejects received canons of beauty and order because these are implicated in other received structures of social order and dominance that the adversarial artist aspires to subvert, and points out that 'authenticity is implicitly a polemical concept, fulfilling its nature by dealing aggressively with received and habitual opinion, aesthetic opinions in the first instance, social and political opinion in the next. One topic of its polemic, which has reference to both aesthetic and social opinion, is the error of the view that beauty is the highest quality to which art may aspire' (94).

66 Beginning with 'Picasso' in his *"Primitivism" in 20th-Century Art* of 1984, William Rubin has recognised the artist's shamanistic motives; for instance, in 'The Genesis of *Les Demoiselles d'Avignon*' (1994), 13, he has written,

> Picasso's ambition became nothing less than the recovery of the magical function that first led humankind to make images: the power to change life. Picasso understood instinctively that the Western tradition had been losing contact with that primordial, talismanic aim of image-making – indeed, had lost it altogether in the nineteenth-century definitions of art shared by his painter-father, the schools he attended, and the Salons that insured prevailing values. But for Picasso, it was less the nature and conventions of art than those of life – and most important, of his own life – that were at stake.

Though I agree that Picasso viewed himself in this manner, an attitude I have worked to contextualise within Nietzschean modernism, I find Rubin's assertion problematic, making assumptions, on the one hand, about 'primordial' humankind and, on the other, about nineteenth-century art as divorced from 'the talismanic aim of image-making'. I cannot share such faith with Picasso or Rubin in the transformative value of modernist art.

67 For a compelling discussion of Conrad's relation to this process, see C. McNelly

[Kearns], 'Nature, Women, and Claude Lévi-Strauss', *Massachusetts Review* 16 (1975), 7–29.

68 Salmon (1912), translated in Fry, 84, wrote, 'nudes came into being, whose deformation caused little surprise – we had been prepared for it by Picasso himself, by Matisse, Derain, Braque, Van Dongen, and even earlier by Cézanne and Gauguin. It was the ugliness of the faces that froze with horror the half-converted'. According to Roland Penrose, *Picasso: His Life and Work,* rev. ed. (New York, 1973), 133–4, Gertrude Stein was silent and Leo Stein laughed. Even Apollinaire was taken aback and worried that Picasso might destroy the reputations they had both worked hard to establish; according to Pierre Cabanne, *Pablo Picasso: His Life and Times* (New York, 1977), 119, he said only one word: 'révolution'. Picasso leaned his huge painting against a wall of his studio and did not exhibit it until 1916; see J. Cousins and H. Seckel's superb 'Chronology of *Les Demoiselles d'Avignon,* 1907–1939', in *Les Demoiselles d'Avignon* (1994), 145–205.

6 DAVID LOMAS

In Another Frame

LES DEMOISELLES D'AVIGNON AND PHYSICAL ANTHROPOLOGY

Studies of human morphology which each day assume greater importance bring art and science together on a terrain rich in lessons. Anthropologists, doctors, artists, archaeologists, etc. can only benefit from it.[1]

*L*es Demoiselles d'Avignon has an almost mythic stature as the source from which cubism was engendered along with the rest of modern art. The poet André Salmon, whose role as myth maker was far from negligible, in 1921 proclaimed the *Demoiselles* 'the ever-glowing crater from which the fire of contemporary art erupted', adding that 'Picasso has invented it all'.[2] At that moment, the tide of opinion in France had turned against what was portrayed as the convulsive disorder of prewar culture in favour of a more ordered classicism. Salmon was a staunch defender of modern art against this hostile reaction, and his exaggerated claim that the vital strands of modern art all originate from Picasso must be understood in this light. Yet the potent appeal of this mythic account of the *Demoiselles* – inseparable from its status as the foremost icon of artistic modernism – is such that it has proven remarkably tenacious, even in art history where it is often maintained that the picture marks an absolute breach with the artistic and cultural past.

It needs to be borne in mind that the reputation of the *Demoiselles* began to accrue even before it had ventured from the artist's studio. Eyewitnesses relayed to the wider world their shock at its willful travesty of accepted canons of female beauty: a company of five brazen whores defiantly confront a once venerated classical past (which their poses and drap-

104

ery mockingly recall). This, above all, must have struck Salmon as totally new and unheralded, a volcanic eruption in the cultural landscape of his time. Unprecedented in art it might have been, however this chapter seeks to demonstrate that Picasso's transgressive schema for depicting the body recapitulates features of an established visual iconography of the female prostitute already formulated by physical anthropologists in the latter part of the nineteenth century. Contrary to Salmon, I argue that the *Demoiselles* was thus firmly embedded in a cultural terrain that provided the visual terms with which it could be read.

The discursive context of physical anthropology and the specific meanings it imputed to the prostitutional body have been largely neglected in the existing art historical literature. Leo Steinberg, the first writer seriously to address the issue of sexuality in relation to the picture, asserts that it was in order to embody a Dionysiac eroticism unconstrained by civilised mores that Picasso conflated the prostitute with the primitive. These libidinous women, 'nature beings who dwell behind all civilisation', are said by Steinberg to 'personify sheer sexual energy as the image of a life force'.[3] Now, although prostitution was much discussed during the period, it was never evoked in such glowing terms, but rather in association with the syphilis scourge was considered an alarming symptom of the malaise of modern urban society. Michael Leja has convincingly shown that Picasso was aware of the prevailing views about prostitution and they inform numerous images dealing with the theme painted after his arrival in Paris in 1901.[4] For such reasons, it is unlikely he would have chosen the prostitute to symbolise either a Nietzschean vital life force (syphilis was on the contrary life threatening), or a human nature unspoilt by civilisation (the very fact of bringing Cézanne's bathers indoors, which Steinberg remarks on, seems to foreclose this reading). It will be seen that a more cogent explanation for these fearsome hybrids lies in widespread fears about degeneracy at the turn of the century which led anthropologists on a quest to define a recognisable prostitutional physiognomy and body type. At the outset, it needs to be said that my intention in situating *Les Demoiselles d'Avignon* within this nonartistic framework is not to add just another item to an already burgeoning list of sources; instead, I hope it will permit us to elicit the interconnected beliefs, attitudes, and fears that underlay its breach of classical proportion.

Classicism and a range of perceived deviations from it constitute a fundamental set of binary terms in the discourse and representational practices of physical anthropology as they do in Picasso's art, a fact that affords a convenient link between these two seemingly unrelated spheres of activity. Encapsulated in a famous statement in 1935, Picasso's artistic stance was one predicated on transgression of an implied classical ideal – a practice that is inaugurated by *Les Demoiselles d'Avignon*. 'Academic training in beauty', he maintained, 'is a sham. The beauties of the Parthenon, Venuses, Nymphs, Narcissuses, are so many lies. Art is not the application of a canon of beauty but what the instinct and the brain can conceive beyond any canon. When we love a woman we don't start measuring her limbs'.[5] The conceptual space of physical anthropology was similarly organised around a canon of ideality (or normality) defined by the classical body. In the colonial encounter with other races, the classically conformed body functioned as a potent signifier for the Western subject whose superiority it affirmed. Moreover, as France came to regard itself as the sole legitimate heir to Latin culture in the lead-up to the First World War, the classical body was able to mediate a sense of French national identity, as well as being a focus for its anxieties and discontents.[6] Quantifiable deviations from this norm were taken to denote inferiority – whether racial, moral, or intellectual – and when applied to a reviled subgroup worked as a virulent mode of exclusion from the social body. Consequently the classical ideal had a normative, prescriptive power, serving to organise and secure a group identity in the face of a multitude of threatening others, outside France and within, whose contours it delineated and over whom it facilitated a regime of surveillance and control. Bound up with this overarching binary opposition of a normative classicism and an aberrant or pathological other were a number of key terms operative in anthropological discourse. Most significant from the viewpoint of my essay are the twinned concepts of degeneration *(dégénérescence)* and regeneration *(regénérescence)*, which not only permeated fin de siècle medical and anthropological discourse, but also left their stamp on the literary and artistic culture of the period.[7]

Physical anthropology emerged as a separate discipline in France with the founding of the Société d'Anthropologie in 1859, headed by the eminent neurologist Paul Broca.[8] Its membership was largely drawn from medically trained professionals who tended to share a positivist scientific outlook and avowedly Republican politics – Broca himself became a senator under Leon Gambetta. From these few facts much of the programme of the Société follows. Pioneers of the new discipline favoured an anatomical, strictly empirical approach. Craniology, the measuring and comparative study of skulls, a passion for which originated early in the century with the phrenology of Gall, came to epitomise the new science. Joy Harvey, in her doctoral thesis on the Société d'Anthropologie, remarks that, aided by new forms of instrumentation, craniology became 'a world-wide enterprise, with the collection of skulls carried on with the enthusiasm of shell collection, being shipped from all areas of the world to the Société d'Anthropologie, until it could boast many thousands of specimens'.[9] Correlations were said to exist between skull and brain size, and thus with intellectual and cultural development. Proponents of craniometry were of the opinion that raging controversies of the day surrounding the role and status of women or the potential for development of colonised peoples might be settled by this ostensibly neutral, because empirical and scientific, technique.

Anthropometry, as the new science was called, recorded data in the form of ratios derived ultimately from artistic canons of proportion, as a leading exponent of the method concedes: 'the first attempt at anthropometry for the purpose of determining the proportions of the human body, and craniometry, for analysing the physiognomy, are due to artists', wrote Dr. Paul Topinard.[10] The truth of this admission is confirmed by glancing at the earliest book on anthropometry by the Belgian social statistician Adolphe Quetelet where a diagram of the *homme moyen*, or average man, unashamedly copies Leonardo's famous drawing of a male body based on Vitruvius's system of proportion.[11] Where Academic treatises on ideal beauty once advised painters to generalise from the model in nature, eliminating accidental deformities to extract 'an abstract idea of their forms more perfect than any one original', anthropologists calculated statistical averages from their precise measurements in order to put this procedure on a surer, more scientific footing.[12] Topinard predicted that art would, in its turn, prosper by obeying the limits anthropology set: 'Art, then, ought to rest upon anthropology, in that its whims are tolerated, though under the express condition that they do not go beyond the individual variations which anthropology reveals to it'.[13]

Quetelet and Topinard encapsulate two antithetical viewpoints regarding the use of proportional systems. Guided by religious faith in the unity of the species, Quetelet affirms one type of beauty in both men and women. His main priority is to define this general human type *(type général)* and only then to differentiate groups on the basis of secondary features. 'Our species admits one type or module of which one can easily determine the different proportions', Quetelet insisted.[14] From statistical analysis of his Belgian subjects, he concluded that this general type conforms almost miraculously to the old *beau idéal* of classical antiquity: 'everything tends to establish that the human type, in our climate, is identical with that which is deduced from observation of the most regular ancient statues'.[15] The universal truth of the Greek ideal was thenceforth verified by science! Topinard, on the other hand, hotly disputed this stance, arguing that 'It had not occurred to the ancients that there are differences in the proportions of the various races of mankind. . . . It is now generally admitted, and we look for the negro ideal, or the Mongol ideal, as well as for the white ideal'.[16] Physicians at the Société like Topinard were by and large secular materialists whose polygenic theory of the separate origin and parallel development of human races was a challenge to the biblical doctrine of the common origin of mankind. Hostility to religion lay behind Topinard's efforts to rid anthropology of any residual metaphysical taint: 'Art by its nature is idealist, unitary', he wrote, 'it admits but one canon and one human type and around it simple variations, whereas anthropology, necessarily realist, accepts multiple types and canons'.[17]

Although my primary objective is to identify a shared mentality rather than specify causal connections, it might reasonably be asked whether channels existed whereby an artist could have gained information about a specialised discourse conducted within the institutional bounds of anthropology. From at least the middle of the nineteenth century, the potential benefits to artists from having a knowledge of anthropometry had been extolled.[18] In 1878 Topinard wrote,

> We are not now living in the time of Albert Dürer and of Rubens when artists were satisfied with delineating the forms and features of those around them to represent those of foreign nations. Our annual exhibitions testify the progress which has been made in this direction . . . and at the Ecole des Beaux-Arts, the professor of anatomy knows that he must teach the different forms of the beautiful, as seen in every country and under every climate, and, therefore, must be an anthropologist.[19]

As a site where the interests of medical men and artists overlap and reciprocally inflect one another, the Ecole des Beaux-Arts was central to the dissemination of medical knowledge about the body of particular interest to visual artists. Dr. Paul Richer, who as assistant to Jean-Marie Charcot, had contributed to the *Iconographie de la Salpêtrière*, was from 1903 professor of anatomy at the Ecole des Beaux-Arts and was the author of several books promoting and diffusing physical anthropology for the guidance of artists.[20] Texts by Richer incorporated advice on proportion and translated the raw data of anthropology into a more palatable form by constructing

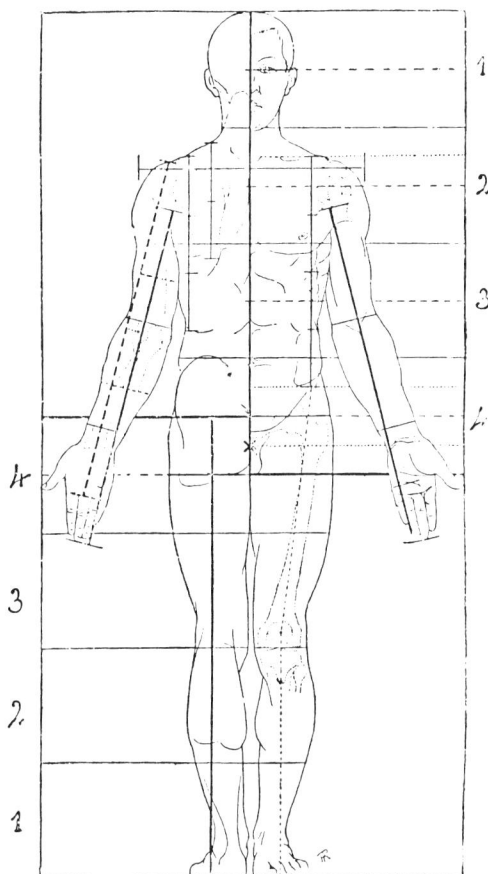

FIGURE 23. Canon of an average male. From Paul Richer, *Anatomie artistique* (Paris, 1890), 173.

diagrams artists could follow (Fig. 23). Although it cannot be established with any certainty that Picasso's training in academic procedures would have acquainted him with texts of this sort, nevertheless a cluster of proportional studies in which he endeavours to formulate a distinct canon of the primitive body must count as the first, belated response by an artist of his stature to the proselytising efforts of physical anthropologists since the middle of the previous century.

These sketches of a figure standing erect with hands clasped (Fig. 24), some drawn onto blank pages of a Daumier catalogue, were a startling revelation of the exhibition held at the Musée Picasso in Paris in 1988.[21] As a group, they can be assigned with reasonable certainty to April-May 1907, thus coinciding with preparatory studies for the final phase of work on the *Demoiselles*. The exercise was quite informal, but a system of numbering allows one to surmise that some calculation, now indecipherable, must have taken place. They have been seen as a nostalgic backward glance to an academic mode of figuration Picasso was about to jettison, but a meticulous study by Pierre Daix shows beyond doubt that the studies are of a piece with the primitivising trend that predominated in his art at this moment.[22] They afford vital evidence that Picasso was looking to the African body and its conformation as a counterweight to the classical canon that up until that point had reigned supreme in Western art.[23] In broad terms, he traces a similar path to physical anthropologists whose study of non-Western races had led them to reject the notion of a universal canon *(type général)* in favour of a multiplicity of distinct bodily types.

Though purporting to dispense with the sovereignty of the old *beau idéal*, Harvey notes that in reality doctors at the Société clung onto pejorative beliefs 'about other human societies as well as the innate superiority of civilised European man'.[24] Polygenism, with its emphasis on human diversity, dovetailed with a ranking of race and culture in which the classical ideal, now identified with the white race and placed at the summit of human development, provided a measure against which other groups subjected to anthropological scrutiny were invariably found wanting.[25] A typical example of this sleight of hand is Dr. René Verneau's *Physical Characteristics of Women in Different Races*, published in 1908 as the first installment of a four-volume compendium on the subject of *Woman*.[26] Verneau ranks different races according to their greater or lesser degree of physical charm, venturing the opinion that 'each of the types encountered in ethnic groups corresponds to a stage of human evolution'.[27] The book is copiously illustrated with unflattering mug shots of female natives, photographic evidence that is backed up by verbal testimony from missionaries and explorers. But this humiliating scrutiny was thought unbecoming for the European woman in whose place the *Medici Venus* is discreetly substituted. It is noteworthy that Polynesian races whose bodily proportions were said to rival even those of classical antiquity fared better than so-called *peuples barbares* under the spurious hierarchies fabricated by these authors. A similar perception might have governed Picasso's turning away from Gauguinesque imagery, Polynesian in inspiration, to 'barbaric' African and Oceanic sources as he seeks to convey a more extreme departure from the classical canon.

Anthropometric techniques were applied with equal relish to marginal

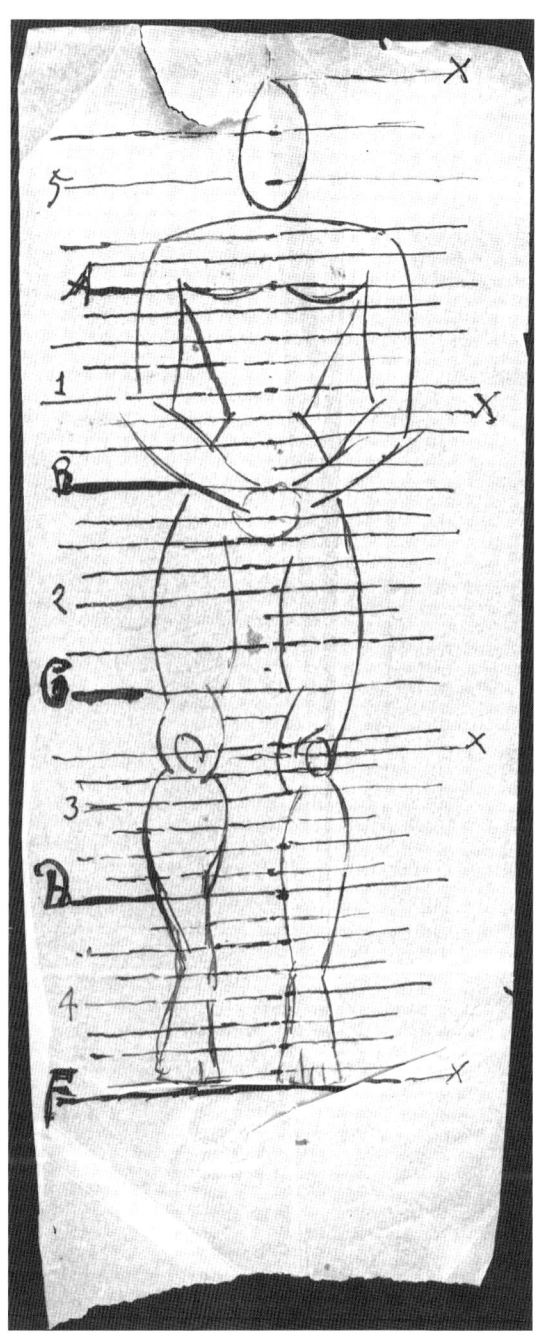

FIGURE 24. Pablo Picasso, *Proportion Study*, April–May 1907. Ink on tracing paper, 31 × 12.6 cm. Musée Picasso (MP 535). (© Photo Réunion des musées nationaux – Picasso.)

subgroups in the metropolitan French population. Robert Nye has argued that, in the aftermath of its ignominious defeat in the Franco-Prussian War, there emerged in France 'a medical model of cultural crisis'.[28] Signs of pathology were discerned everywhere in the social body. The notion of *dégénérescence*, understood as evolution in reverse, came to encapsulate the pessimistic belief that society was in a state of decadence and decline. The term first gained currency in psychiatry, being often invoked as an etiological factor in mental disorders following the publication in 1856 of Auguste Morel's *Traité des dégénérescences*. It has been plausibly suggested that psychiatrists were faced in the mid-century with statistical evidence of an increase in rates of mental illness and, lacking any effective response to this situation, proved receptive to the idea of an irremediable, inherited disposition to madness.[29] Sheer vagueness of definition paradoxically enhanced its utility until, by the end of the century, it seemed that any and every ill besetting the French populace could be gathered under the rubric of degeneration.[30]

Physical anthropologists avidly joined in the search for stigmata of degeneration. Male criminals and their female counterparts, prostitutes, were targeted by researchers who zealously looked for physical clues denoting atavistic regression. The fallen woman had, so to speak, toppled down the evolutionary ladder, and the stigmata of degeneration were read from her face, which took on the contours of a grotesquely deformed mask. No qualms were felt about applying highly subjective aesthetic criteria of beauty and proportion in the evaluation of these subjects. An authoritative and much cited study of female prostitutes published in Paris in 1889 by Dr. Pauline Tarnowsky concluded that 'anomalies of the face present frequently as asymmetry, prognathism, or a perceptible disproportion of the diverse parts of the face'.[31] At the same time, doctors associated with the Société were pioneering methods for identifying criminals on the basis of physical characteristics that were, Nye remarks, essentially a revamping of older phrenological systems.[32] A notable example was the criminologist Alphonse Bertillon's compilation of tables in which he exhaustively catalogued the protean variations of the human ear (Fig. 25).[33]

Physical deformities were the index of an underlying moral monstrosity, also innate and held to explain the prostitute's attraction to vice. Tarnowsky reported in her sample of Russian prostitutes 'a diminution of the principal diameters of the cranium by several millimetres', this being 'entirely to the detriment of the intellectual and moral development of prostitutes'.[34] In his withering critique of physical anthropology, Stephen Jay Gould has demonstrated that faulty inferences were made from minuscule differences

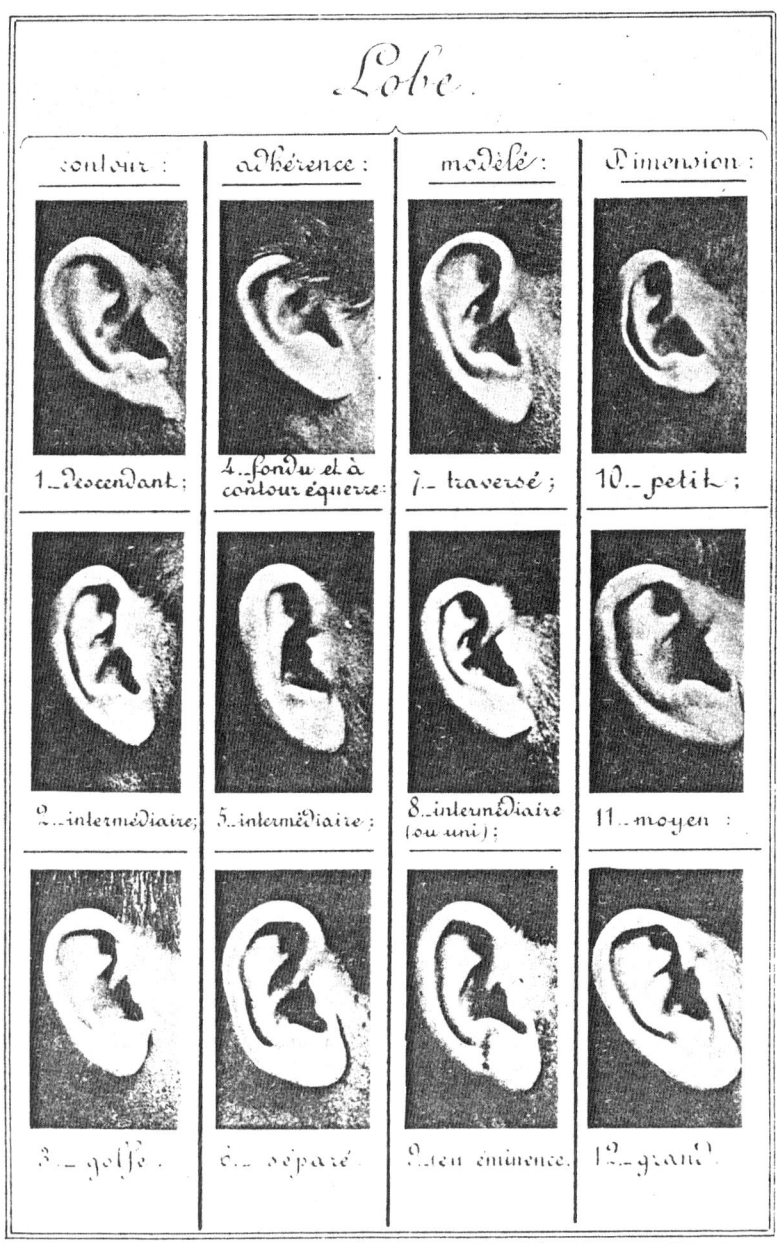

FIGURE 25. Classification of ear lobes. From Alphonse Bertillon, *Identification anthropomorphique. Instructions signalétiques* (Paris, 1893), Plate 53.

between populations that, in many cases, were smaller than the margin of error of the instruments used to calibrate them.[35] In reality, the evidence adduced by Tarnowsky and others merely served to confer a scientific aura on banal stereotypes through which Belle Epoque society channelled its fears and anxieties, principally about syphilis, into a scapegoating of the presumed source.[36] If the gruesome picture these authors painted of the prostitute had been in any way an accurate reflection, rather than a projection of their own phantasms, one could be excused for wondering how the unfortunate wretches managed to attract any customers at all.

The epiphany that occurred at the Musée de l'Homme when Picasso reports he was suddenly overwhelmed by the incantatory power of African masks is held to account for the fearsome, masklike faces of the *Demoiselles*. Punctuating the two phases of work on the picture, it was allegedly this event that caused him to overpaint the demoiselle on the left as well as the two right-hand figures. However, attempts to relate particular masks to the *Demoiselles* are fraught, an exhaustive study of this matter by William Rubin concluding that Picasso could not have seen most of the masks traditionally compared with the picture, nor did he slavishly follow those he did see. Moreover, the asymmetry of Picasso's solution to the problem of representing the primitive is at odds with the almost exclusive bilateral symmetry of archaic art (Rubin concedes it is highly improbable that Picasso could have known a rare type of asymmetrical *masque de maladie* which he compares to the *Demoiselles*).[37] On the other hand, there are striking parallels between the way Picasso registers a deviation from classical ideals in the primitivised masks of the *Demoiselles* and the degenerate physiognomy as recorded by anthropologists. The former is characterised by Pierre Daix in terms of a 'disequilibrated deformity of the face', 'uneven levels of the eyes', and 'a jutting jaw'.[38] Tarnowsky, meanwhile, includes a selection of photographs to illustrate the salient features of *dégénérescence* (Fig. 26), captions beneath drawing attention to the presence of asymmetry, prognathism, or disproportion of the lower third of the face, misshapen ears, and curiously 'deviation of the nose, [or] a deep depression of the root of the nose' (a perception that may have arisen from analogy with the typical saddle-nose deformity of congenital syphilis).[39] One irresistibly recalls the bizarre scroll-like ear in studies for the *Demoiselles* (Fig. 27), for which the specific artistic source was an Iberian head, and the renowned nose *en quart de Brie*. For both artist and anthropologist the telltale sign of atavism is, above all, physiognomic asymmetry. The degree of overlap is so striking one is inclined to speculate that Picasso,

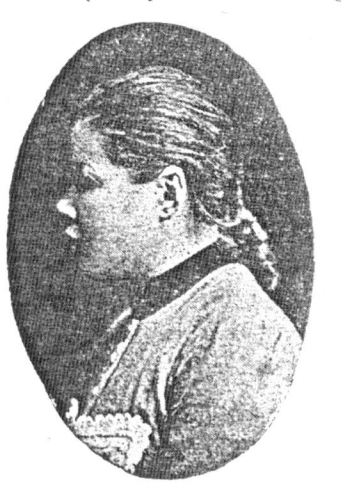 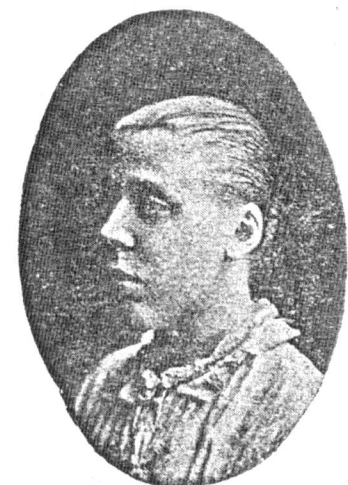

Fig. 4.   Fig. 5.

Fig. 4. Prognatisme de la partie inférieure du visage. Nez camus. Développement de la région temporale.

Fig. 5. Disproportions de la partie inférieure du visage. Tête plate. Oreille difforme.

FIGURE 26. Photographs of facial anomalies in prostitutes. From Dr. Pauline Tarnowsky, *Etude anthropométrique sur les prostituées et les voleuses* (Paris, 1889), 37, figs. 4 and 5.

who went to the lengths of actually visiting the Hôpital St-Lazare to study at firsthand the prostitutes incarcerated there, might have consulted Tarnowsky's book in the course of these researches or at least garnered some knowledge of it from the medical doctors he encountered.

If medical and anthropological studies were able to confer a legible stamp on the face of the prostitute, troubling uncertainties of identification in the urban crowd would be resolved. It is also significant that at this moment regulationists were pressing for more policing and harsher controls of clandestine prostitutes operating outside the *maisons de tolérance*.[40] Accordingly, the issue of visibility is a central concern of Cesare Lombroso's treatise on *La Femme criminelle et prostituée*.[41] Lombroso alleges that female prostitutes, because of a perverse natural selection imposed by their vocation, 'disclose fewer of the anomalies which produce ugliness, but are marked by more of the signs of degeneration'. They manage to conceal these blemishes by dint of a certain facility in the art of applying makeup, but he warns sternly, 'when youth vanishes, the jaws, the cheekbones, hidden by adipose tissue, emerge, salient angles stand out, and the face grows virile, uglier than a man's; wrinkles deepen into the likeness of scars, and the countenance, once attractive, exhibits the full degenerate type which early grace had concealed'.[42]

In the moralising contrast sketched in by the sanctimonious Lombroso, it is perhaps not too farfetched to see an analogy with the polarity some commentators have discerned in *Les Demoiselles d'Avignon* between the relatively gracious Iberian courtesans at the centre of the composition and the scarified masks of the whores on the right, though by a Picassean twist of an otherwise hackneyed plot it is the masks that render visible the truth which earlier grace (and art) had concealed.

As for the prostitute's body, it too was pronounced devoid of usual female charm, coarsened by a *métier infâme* coupled with the ugly taint of degeneration. Lombroso recorded a virile appearance in prostitutes due to excessive body hair and a high incidence of masculine voices owing to hypertrophy of the larynx and vocal cords. This he cites as evidence of a 'tendency to atavistic return to the period of hermaphrodism'.[43] Lumping the prostitute together with the primitive on grounds of a manly body habitus could be justified by recourse to a theory that viewed sexual differentiation as linked with the progress of civilisation. In the *Bulletins de la Société d'Anthropologie*, for example, it was asserted that

> there exists among different races a sort of seriation which corresponds roughly to how ancient their civilisation is. The race which presents the greatest difference between men and women is the yellow race, the first to be civilised; then comes the European race, then the Americans. The negroes and arabs, who present the least advanced degree of civilisation, where women work with men at the same hard labour, present the smallest sexual difference.[44]

According to this theory, femininity could be fully expressed in modern civilised societies like France only where women were spared the same labour as men. Lombroso found in the prostitute, a working woman par excellence, supposedly incontrovertible proof of this view. One suspects that this scientific argument was fuelled by the same sentiment as a popular stereotype that portrayed the modern, emancipated woman as a mannish virago, a kind of *hommesse*, in the words of one commentator.[45] Physical anthropologists supplied a welter of vital statistics ranging from their smaller brain size to a larger child-bearing pelvis to persuade a broader public of the unsuitability of women for any kind of work that might lead them to stray from the hearth and home.[46]

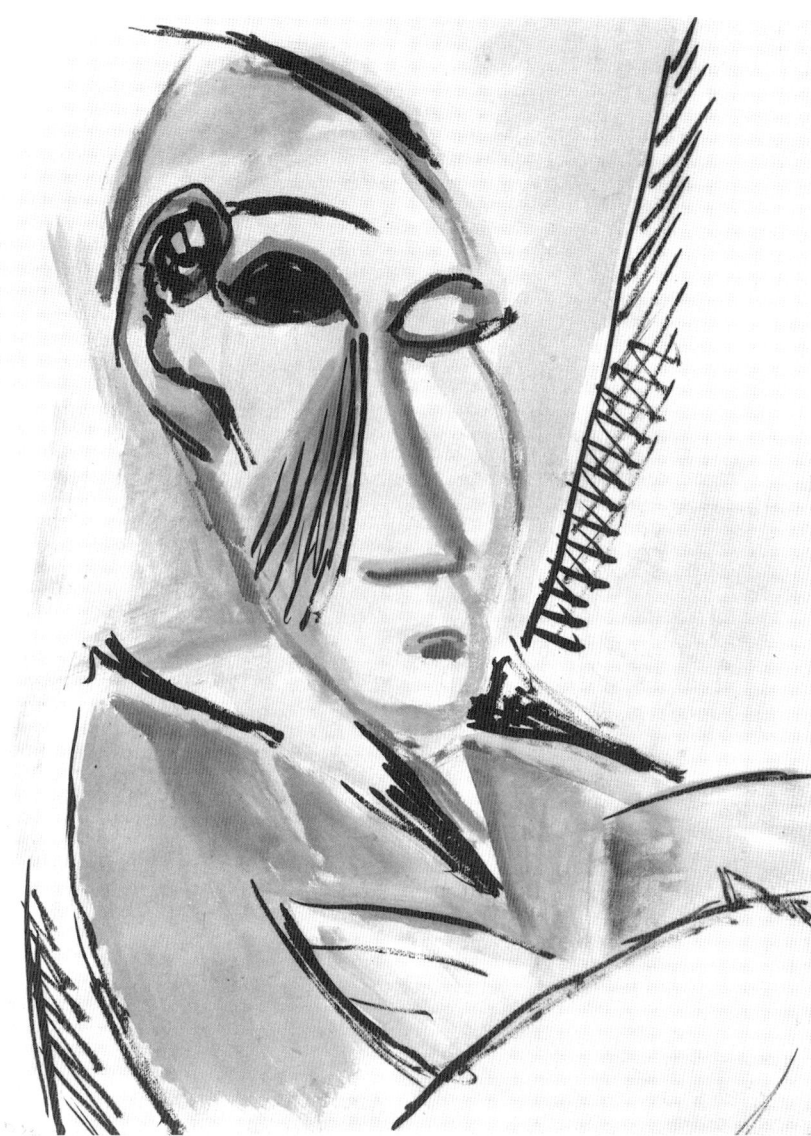

FIGURE 27. Pablo Picasso, *Head of a Sailor, Study for 'Les Demoiselles d'Avignon'*, June 1907. Gouache and watercolour on paper, 60.3 × 47 cm. Museum of Modern Art, New York. A. Conger Goodyear Fund. (Photo © 1998 The Museum of Modern Art, New York.)

Ambiguous gendering of body types from the period of Picasso's work coinciding with the *Demoiselles* is often noted, but its significance rarely explained. Though masculine traits are muted in the final picture by comparison with individual studies, the mannish character of its women is not infrequently remarked on. The marked ambiguity of a number of sketch-book drawings led Zervos to identify mistakenly as male a study of the seated demoiselle found in earlier states of the composition. Additionally, it was noted that the proportion sketches which punctuated work on the *Demoi-selles* are of a single androgynous prototype that spawns both male and female progeny. It seems unlikely that Picasso is reverting here to the unisex *type général* advocated by Quetelet among others. The more probable explanation is that he is registering the view popularised by Lombroso that female prostitutes display features of atavistic return to a more masculine type. Why Picasso should look to the androgynous dying slaves of Michelangelo as a source for one of the demoiselles, initially baffling given his rebellion against Renaissance conventions of figuration, can be understood in the light of this anthropometric discourse on the prostitute: Michelangelo was, after all, renowned for the masculine body cast of his women.

Studies for individual figures in the *Demoiselles* portray the body as an amalgam of distinct male and female parts, in the same way that medical authorities were busy espousing a detailed morphology of gender. Alexandra Parigoris has demonstrated that the *Seated Demoiselle* (Fig. 28), for example, is derived from male antique statuary, adopting the pose of the Roman *Spinario*, or thornpicker, and pastiching the *Belevedere Torso* which has been adorned with female breasts.[47] In another sketch the arm, and the powerful deltoid and pectoral muscles are those of a male, whereas the pelvis belongs to a female body. At this very moment, anthropometry was similarly engaged in producing an exact typology of gender applicable to every part of the body and every organ. These attempts to ground gender difference in anatomy tended to naturalise the unequal social opportunities of men and women and, as suggested above, may have been in part a conservative backlash to growing demands by women for emancipation. A wry comment by Thomas Laqueur on a parallel situation in eighteenth-century France that 'wherever boundaries were threatened arguments for fundamental sexual differences were shoved into the breach' was no less applicable to the urgent task of anthropologists a century later.[48] The desire to demarcate the sexes on the basis of anatomy was accompanied by inordinate anxiety about borderline cases such as effeminate males, bearded women, and hermaphrodites – numerous attempts

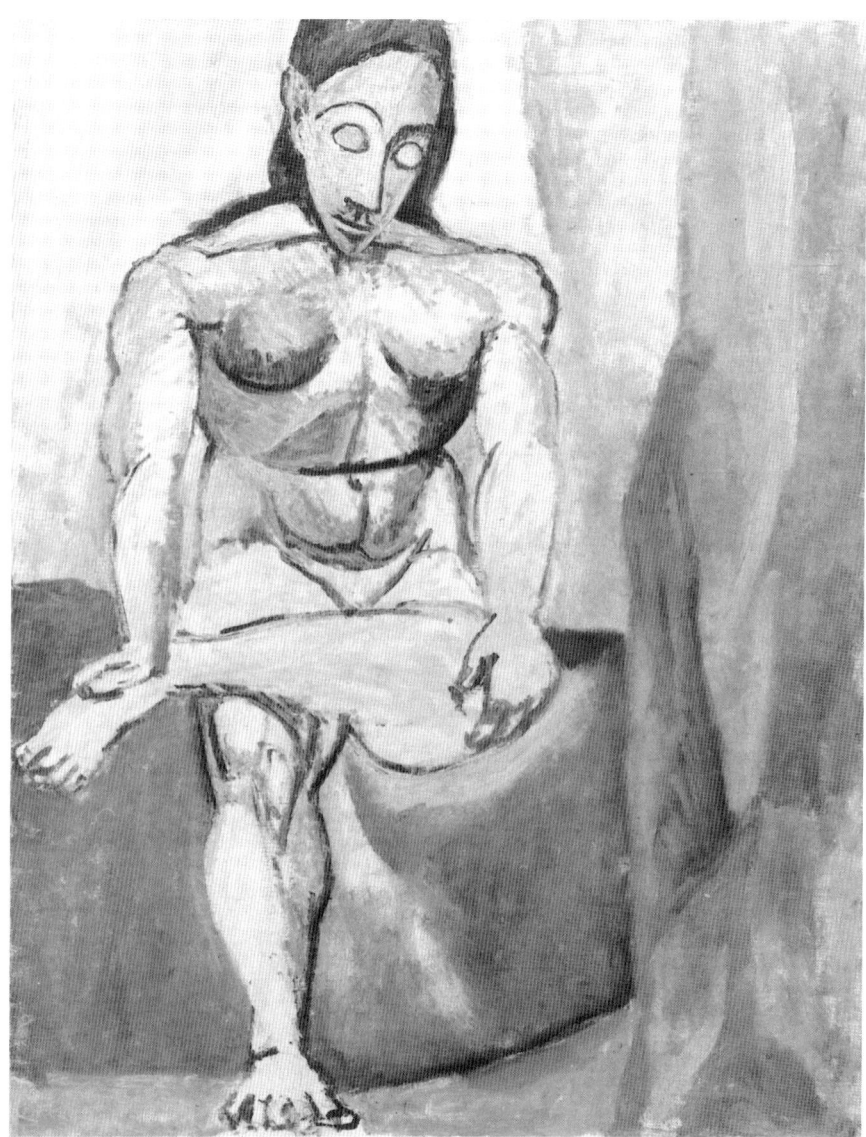

FIGURE 28. Pablo Picasso, *Seated "Demoiselle"*, *Study for 'Les Demoiselles d'Avignon'*, winter 1906–7. Oil on canvas, 121 × 93.5 cm. Musée Picasso, Paris. (Photo © Réunion des musées nationaux – Picasso.)

being made to classify the assorted types of this latter anomaly. In an article published in *L'Anthropologie* in 1895, Dr. Henry Meige undertook a close examination of antique sculptures of hermaphrodites, as Picasso may have done, claiming that their composite nature should not be dismissed as mere artistic licence, because 'there exist in nature corporeal anomalies of which they are the exact reproduction'.[49]

Alongside the deeply pessimistic doctrine of *dégénérescence*, remedies for the ailing body were also forthcoming from the medical profession. Dr. Francis Heckel, writing in 1908, reproaches those experts too preoccupied with ideas of 'hereditary and ineluctable physical degeneration' for overlooking 'the degree to which the *matière* is malleable and keen to regenerate'.[50] Like many others in the period, this author was convinced that vast individual and social benefits would accrue from properly conducted exercise: 'If the State promotes equally physical and intellectual education, it increases individual gain and economic gain; it augments the national wealth; . . . it also increases the possibility of expansion beyond the metropole, and it remedies depopulation in giving to each man confidence in himself and in his descendence'.[51]

Repudiating 'the man hypertrophied in his muscular apparatus', Heckel appealed to antiquity for a model of physical health based on balance and equilibrium. In a paraphrase of classical beauty, he describes as the desirable outcome of his *méthode myothérapique* a 'harmoniously balanced appearance of all the segments of the body', a point comically underscored by a plate that depicts the unlikely transformation of a flabby present-day Frenchman into a live simulacrum of the *Apollo Belvedere*. Nye remarks that amidst 'the extraordinary explosion of sport and physical culture in the *fin de siècle* . . . the body became an ideological variable in the first burst of modern sportive nationalism'.[52] And, as the case of Dr. Heckel proves, 'medical terminology was deeply embedded both in the discourse of sport and fitness and in the pronouncements of the purity crusaders who wholeheartedly believed in the healing properties of exercise'.[53]

The fad for physical culture may be implicated in the resurgence of classicism in the work of Picasso around 1905 and 1906, accompanied as it was by a spate of images of gymnasts, an archetypal embodiment of balance, and circus strongmen. Coinciding with the appearance of these subjects in his painting, from 1905 the fitness magazine *La Culture physique* ran a series of articles on circus acrobats with the aim of documenting this colourful, but fast disappearing, part of French life. Two extremely curious articles by Apollinaire that appeared in subsequent issues of *La Culture physique* in February and March 1907 closely echo the pronouncements of medical men by advocating sport as a panacea for the twin risks of depopulation and degeneration.[54] The first of the articles, on dance as a sport, insists without evident irony that 'Alcoholism and depopulation, these scourges of France, would find a sure remedy in the proliferation of balls and dances'. The second on 'Guy de Maupassant athlète' is less adamant in tone. The subject of the study who, 'by certain sides of his talent is attached to the most French if not the most classical' tradition, in spite of devoting 'an important part of his existence to physical development', had the misfortune to end his days in madness; *une saine vie* plainly did nothing to preserve de Maupassant's sanity.

In a preface to the farcical drama *Les Mamelles de Tirésias*, outwardly concerned with the issue of repopulation, Apollinaire confesses to being unable to decide whether he ought to be taken seriously or not. Ironic equivocation also informs the attitude of Picasso to physical culture, as a caricatural drawing of Apollinaire from 1905 portraying the poet as a strongman, clutching a copy of *La Culture physique* in reference to his current enthusiasm, reveals.[55] Proponents of physical culture strenuously objected to excessive and unbalanced development of muscles, yet this is precisely what Picasso depicts. Though irony serves to distance him from the jingoistic rhetoric that surrounded physical culture, Picasso's drawing and the related articles by Apollinaire on the regenerative value of sport indicate they were both acutely aware of what was merely the obverse side of a discourse on degeneracy.

Returning to *Les Demoiselles d'Avignon*, I briefly wish to consider a case of contested identity that copious expert testimony has so far failed to resolve. Earlier studies for the picture (Figs. 8, 9, and 11) include a male figure on the left who clutches, rather enigmatically, a human skull or a book. As the composition develops, this character undergoes a sudden transformation into a partially clad female, whereupon the puzzling attributes disappear. Lingering on the threshold of a brothel scene, he is lacking a wholly convincing alibi. Picasso testified at many years remove that he was a medical student, but this leaves the reason for his presence unexplained. A consensus view held that he was a memento mori symbolising the wages of sin, but this does not tally with Picasso's presumed bohemian disregard for conventional morality. Various alternative readings have been proposed: Leo Steinberg contends he stands for distanced knowledge as opposed to action in the realm occupied by his counterpart, the sailor. That the medical student is also a partial self-portrait is strongly implied by the presence of a profile drawing on one of the sheets (Fig. 8).

The meaning of this protagonist continues to perplex; indeed, it is likely that a penchant for symbolist ambiguity guided Picasso's choice of this highly resonant motif. However, one further association of a medical man clutching a skull may now be added: physical anthropology, closely allied with medicine and for the layperson synonymous with measuring skulls. Drawing aside a curtain to render its company of prostitutes visible, he – the artist as anthropologist – enacts a cardinal function of anthropometry in its relentless dedication to calibrating limbs. Though this figure drops out of the picture as we know it, its ultimate form owes much to the fin de siècle science he may well represent.

POSTFACE

An implication to be drawn from this study, as I stated in the originally published article, is that Picasso (albeit inadvertently) relies on and brings into play what were, in effect, highly denigratory stereotypes of cultural otherness. Physical anthropology, by ascribing to the prostitute a catalogue of physical 'stigmata' of degeneracy, forced her to bear the sins of a society that created the very conditions of inequality and exploitation in which prostitution flourished. Once marked out and ostracised, having been declared physically and morally monstrous, all sorts of indignities and violations of their basic rights were then inflicted on these women. At the level of visual representation, Picasso is as guilty of complicity in this process of scapegoating as physical anthropology was.[56]

We naturally resist such an assertion because it contradicts a widely held belief that formal experiment in modernist art is the correlate of a certain idea of freedom. It may be nothing more than a residual prejudice of this sort that causes me to raise a number of factors in mitigation of my own earlier conclusions. Nonetheless, I think it is true to say that art historians have tended to overlook the degree of ambiguity in the *Demoiselles* as concerns its location and its theme. As we saw, the composition evolved consistently in the direction of open-endedness. On the visual evidence alone, one would be hard-pressed to say that this is unequivocally a picture of five prostitutes in a brothel; it was probably deliberately intended by Picasso that the *Demoiselles* should retain a strong reminiscence of the Cézanne bather topos from which it was derived. One might say that this generalising impulse shows an interpretation like mine to be too literal; however, the less charitable view of the matter would be that the prostitute as threat becomes universalised as every woman.

In response to the argument of my article, it has been said that Picasso manipulates diverse visual codes for representing the body, playing one off against the other, but without falling prey to the ideologies subtending them. The stylistic heterogeneity that is such a salient feature of the *Demoiselles* can be understood in this manner. In addition, we have seen how a set of physical traits that anthropologists used to define otherness and aberrancy are applied indiscriminately by Picasso even to figures that it has been argued are surrogate self-portraits. But it must be admitted that these 'studies for' are finally incidental to an analysis of the work itself and the meanings we can ascribe to it. The portrayal of Picasso as a deconstructor of ideologies looks suspiciously like a form of special pleading and is potentially anachronistic. Though it offends against entrenched assumptions about the transcendant nature of genius, it perhaps says nothing more than that Picasso was a creature of his own times to conclude that, even within the revolutionary format of *Les Demoiselles d'Avignon*, he was in fact playing by dominant cultural rules.

NOTES

1   Henri Meige, 'L'Infantilisme, le féminisme et les hermaphrodites antiques', *L'Anthropologie* 6 (1895). Meige was a physician who published widely on art and medicine during this period. He was later appointed professor of anatomy at the Ecole des Beaux-Arts in Paris.
2   André Salmon, 'Picasso', *L'Esprit Nouveau* no. 1 (May 1920), 61–80. Quoted from Marilyn McCully (ed.), *A Picasso Anthology* (London, 1981), 138–44.
3   Leo Steinberg, 'The Philosophical Brothel', *October* 44 (spring 1988), 53–4.
4   Michael Leja, '"Le Vieux Marcheur" and "Les Deux Risques": Picasso, Prostitution, Venereal Disease, and Maternity, 1899–1907', *Art History* 8, no. 1 (March 1985), 66–81.
5   'Statement by Picasso: 1935', Alfred H. Barr, *Picasso. Fifty Years of His Art* (New York, 1966), 273.
6   Charles Maurras, leader of the Royalist *Action française*, promulgated a return to classicism as the cultural counterpart to his organic ideal of nationhood rooted in a sense of racial and geographic belonging – an ideology of *le sang et la terre*. Though it pertains to a slightly later period than that being considered here, for a detailed study of the link between classicism and nationalism in French cultural ideology, see Kenneth Silver, *Esprit de Corps. The Art of the Parisian Avant-Garde and the First World War, 1914–1925* (London, 1989). See also Athena Leoussi, 'Nationalism and Racial Hellenism in Nineteenth-Century England and France', *Ethnic and Racial Studies* 20, no. 1 (January 1997), 41–68.
7   There is a growing body of literature in this area. See, inter alia, Sander Gilman, *Difference and Pathology: Stereotypes of Sexuality, Race and Madness* (Ithaca and London, 1985); Mary Cowling, *The Artist as Anthropologist* (Cambridge, 1989); Anthea Callen, *The Spectacular Body. Science, Method and Meaning in the Work of Degas* (New Haven and London, 1995).
8   Joy Harvey, 'Races Specified, Evolution Transformed: The Social Context of Sci-

entific Debates Originating in the Société d'Anthropologie de Paris 1859–1902',
Ph.D. Diss., Harvard University, 1983.

9 Harvey, as in note 8, 127.

10 Paul Topinard, *Anthropology* (London, 1878). Introduction.

11 Adolphe Quetelet, *Anthropométrie, ou Mesure des différentes facultés de l'homme*
(Brussels, 1870), 243.

12 The growth of physical anthropology was one manifestation of what has come to
be known as the probabilistic revolution, a nineteenth-century revolution not so
much in mathematical statistics per se as in its wide applications. On this question,
see Lorenz Krüger et al. (eds), *The Probabilistic Revolution* (Cambridge, Mass.,
and London, 1987), 2 vols.

13 Topinard, *Anthropology*, 316. See also articles by Patin, 'Projet de canon scien-
tifique à l'usage des artistes', *L'Anthropologie* 9 (1898) and 'Application des données
anthropologiques au contrôle des canons de proportions artistiques', *L'Anthropologie* 10 (1899). Numerous articles in *L'Anthropologie* reiterate the optimistic predic-
tions of these authors about the benefits accruing to both sides from the
rapprochement of art and anthropology (see note 1).

14 Quetelet, *Anthropométrie*, 13.

15 Quetelet, as in note 14, 83. The authority Quetelet cites is Gérard Audran, *Les Proportions du corps humain mesurées sur les plus belles figures de l'antiquité* (Paris,
1683).

16 Topinard, *Anthropology*, 316.

17 Paul Topinard, *L'Homme dans la nature* (Paris, 1891), 125.

18 Charles Rochet, erstwhile professor at the Ecole des Beaux-Arts, was one of the earliest proponents of anthropometry as an aid for artists. See his *Cours d'anthropologie appliqués à l'enseignement des beaux-arts* (Paris, 1869) and *Traité d'anatomie
d'anthropologie et ethnographie appliquées aux Beaux-Arts* (Paris, 1886).

19 Topinard, *Anthropology*, 12.

20 The intersections of art and medicine in the work of Paul Richer (1849–1933) are
deserving of a separate study in their own right. Included among his writings on
anthropology and artistic proportion are *L'Anatomie dans l'art. Proportions du corps
humain. Canons artistiques et canons scientifiques* (Paris, 1893) and *Anatomie artistique. Descriptions des formes extérieures du corps humain au repos et dans les prin-
cipaux mouvements* (Paris, 1890).

21 *Les Demoiselles d'Avignon*, 2 vols., exh. cat. (Paris: Musée Picasso, 1988).

22 Pierre Daix, 'L'Historique des *Demoiselles d'Avignon* révisé à l'aide des carnets de
Picasso', in *Les Demoiselles d'Avignon*, vol. 2, 505–6.

23 That Picasso was interested in actual bodies and not just artistic representations of
them (i.e., masks and statues), is confirmed by the collection of ethnographic photographs in his possession, revealed in a recent exhibition at the Musée Picasso.
See *Le Miroir noir. Picasso, sources photographiques 1900–1928* (Paris: Musée
Picasso, March–June 1997).

24 Harvey, as in note 8. Neo-Lamarkian precepts lay behind the belief 'that physical
and cultural evolution were intimately tied, and that any cultural hierarchy was
paralleled by an organic hierarchy'.

25 Physical anthropology helped legitimise the position of the colonising west by the

proofs of moral and physical superiority it purported to uncover. See Harvey, as in note 8, 115–16 and 128 ff. on the Société d'Anthropologie and colonialism.

26 René Verneau, 'Les Caractères physiques de la femme dans les races', in *La Femme. Dans la nature, dans les moeurs, dans la légende, dans la société*, vol. 1 (Paris, 1908). There were equivalent German and English texts: H. H. Ploss, *Das Weib in der natur und Volkerkunde. Anthropologische Studien* (Leipzig, 1884), which was reprinted in numerous editions and translated into English in 1935, and T.A. Joyce and N.W. Thomas (eds.), *Women of all Nations. A Record of Their Characteristics, Habits, Manners, Customs and Influence* (London, 1908).

27 Ibid., 511. Stephen Jay Gould, *The Mismeasure of Man* (New York, 1981), 32 remarks on the blithe intrusion of highly subjective judgements into the descriptions of physical anthropologists.

28 Robert Nye, *Crime, Madness and Politics in Modern France. The Medical Concept of National Decline* (Princeton, N.J., 1984), Chapter 5. Nye states succinctly that by the turn of the century 'the German menace was regarded as the sign of French decadence'. Daniel Pick has shown that anxieties about the nation-state were associated with the popularity of the concept of degeneration Europe-wide. See Daniel Pick, *Faces of Degeneration. A European Disorder, c.1848–c.1918* (Cambridge, 1989).

29 See Ruth Harris, *Murders and Madness. Medicine, Law, and Society in the Fin de Siècle* (Oxford, 1989).

30 The most notorious instance of this extension of the notion of degeneracy to the area of cultural analysis is Max Nordau's highly influential book *Degeneration*, first published in 1892. It is worth recalling that the era under discussion was characterised by medical expansionism as doctors rushed to fill a moral vacuum left by the decline of religious authority.

31 Dr. Pauline Tarnowsky, *Étude anthropométrique sur les prostituées et les voleuses* (Paris, 1889), 36. See, in addition, Dr. Emile Laurent, 'Prostitution et dégénérescence', *Annales médico-psychologiques* t.X (November 1899), 353–81. The main authority cited in this article is Tarnowsky; Lombroso (note 42) also based the claims in his book on her findings.

32 Nye, as in note 28, 65.

33 Alphonse Bertillon, *Identification anthropométrique. Instructions signalétiques* (Paris, 1893). On Bertillon, see Alan Sekula, 'The Body and the Archive', *October* (Winter 1986).

34 Tarnowsky, *Étude anthropométrique*, 25.

35 Gould, *Mismeasure of Man*. Tarnowsky employed methods for measuring the head and face that had been pioneered by Broca and Topinard. She used Broca's goniometer to measure the facial angle which, since the time of Lavater had been regarded as a reliable index of the level of evolutionary development.

36 The issue of syphilis in its relation to the *Demoiselles* has been comprehensively treated by William Rubin, most recently in *Les Demoiselles d'Avignon. Studies in Modern Art* 3 (New York: Museum of Modern Art, 1994). There are aspects of his study with which I disagree, but there can be no doubt that worries about syphilitic contamination did contribute to the creation of the monstrously deformed creature described by anthropology – underlying it is a sort of phantasmatic of horror that Picasso was also prey to.

37 Rubin implies that these very distinctive masks portray the ravages of syphilis. To my mind it seems more likely that they depict the effects of facial nerve paralysis which skews the lower part of the face in just this manner. Leprosy, not syphilis, would be a possible cause.

38 Daix, as in note 22, 530.

39 Tarnowsky discounts *acquired* syphilis as a cause of facial deformities in any of her subjects, but allows that *congenital* syphilis might well be implicated in some cases. 'From this point of view', she writes, 'parental syphilis joins those other pernicious influences transmitted by parents to their descendants, such as alcohol abuse, consumption, nervous and mental illness etc.'. Tarnowsky, *Étude anthropométrique*, 35.

40 See Alain Corbin, *Women for Hire: Prostitution and Sexuality in France after 1850* (Cambridge, Mass., and London, 1990). For a valuable discussion of the deeper motivations underlying studies of physiognomics in the nineteenth century, see Ludmilla Jordanova, 'Reading Faces in the Nineteenth Century', *Art History* 13 no. 4 (December 1990), 570–5.

41 Quotations are from C. Lombroso and G. Ferrero, *The Female Offender* (London, 1895), 85. A French translation from the original Italian was made in 1896. It is worth stressing that, unlike Tarnowsky and Lombroso, earlier authors such as Parent-Duchatelet had tended to conclude that the female prostitute could *not* be readily distinguished by her physical traits from other women (Corbin, as in note 40, 8).

42 Lombroso and Ferrero, as in note 41, 102.

43 Cited by Corbin, who notes that the views of Tarnowsky and Lombroso, although a subject of controversy, were nonetheless rapidly diffused and very influential in the discourse on prostitution in France during the period of concern. As in note 40, 441.

44 G. M. Soularue, 'Recherches sur les dimensions des os et les proportions squelettiques de l'homme dans les différentes races', *Bulletins de la société d'anthropologie de Paris* (18 May 1899), 346.

45 Quoted in Debora Silverman, *Nature, Nobility, and Neurology: The Ideological Origins of 'Art Nouveau' in France, 1889–1900*, Ph.D. Diss., Princeton University, 1983, Chapter 3.

46 See, for example, Dr. René Verneau, *Le Bassin dans les sexes et dans les races* (Paris, 1895).

47 Lecture at the Royal Academy of Arts (London, November 1988).

48 Thomas Laqueur, 'Orgasm, Generation, and the Politics of Reproductive Biology', *Representations* 14 (Spring 1986), 1–41. Laqueur comments that in eighteenth-century France feminist and antifeminist writers alike increasingly endeavoured to find 'in the facts of biology a justification for cultural and political differences between the sexes' (18).

49 Meige, as in note 1. The distortion of the word *feminism* by these authors evidently packed a reactionary political punch.

50 Dr. Francis Heckel, *Culture physique et cures d'exercise (myothérapie)* (Paris, 1913). The preface to this book avers that 'physical degeneration is like the defect of civilised peoples who neglect the culture of the body'.

51 As in note 50, 494.

52 Nye, as in note 28, 319.

53 As in note 52, 327.
54 Guillaume Apollinaire, 'La Danse est un sport', *La Culture physique* (February 1907) and 'Guy de Maupassant athlète', *La Culture physique* (March 1907). On the depopulation issue, driven by fears of the greater strength of neighbouring Germany, see Dr. Jacques Bertillon, *La Dépopulation de la France* (Paris, 1911).
55 Zervos XXII, 286. 'Portrait-charge de Guillaume Apollinaire'.
56 There are grounds for viewing degeneracy theory as a 'persecution text' in the sense defined by René Girard in his book *The Scapegoat* (Baltimore, 1986).

7 CHRISTOPHER GREEN

'Naked Problems'? 'Sub-African Caricatures'?

LES DEMOISELLES D'AVIGNON, AFRICA, AND CUBISM

In the summer of 1905, Henri Matisse engaged in a curious cultural ritual: he dressed his wife as a Japanese, posed her on rocks beside the sea at Collioure in the South of France, and painted her. In the small quickly worked canvas that resulted, Matisse pulled off the orientalising trick by making the arabesques of her Japanese robe the heart of his mark-making, colour-placing exercise.[1]

If there was much that was new in Matisse's handling of colour here, there was little beyond banality in his decision to orientalise a Western woman (there were many precedents); but it is a decision that underlines the fact that Matisse's sole exhibit at the Salon des Indépendants of 1906, his *Bonheur de vivre* (Fig. 29), possessed an orientalising aspect. This orientalising aspect did not lie in the subject matter, or the figure drawing, it lay in the decorative mark making and the weightlessness of the colour; and, even though the picture was shown the month before his first visit to North Africa, it is orientalising with reference, not to Japan, but to the Middle East and North Africa; above all, to Islamic carpets, ceramics, and textiles, objects in which Matisse had shown an interest at least since the Universal Exhibition of 1900. Pierre Schneider has argued that such an internalisation of learned decorative principles amounts to something more than orientalism, something he calls 'orientality'.[2] According to such a view, the Matisse of *Bonheur de vivre* took an explicitly European subject, the golden age, and an explicitly Ingresque approach to figure drawing, and literally fused them with an internalised understanding of certain things 'Oriental'.

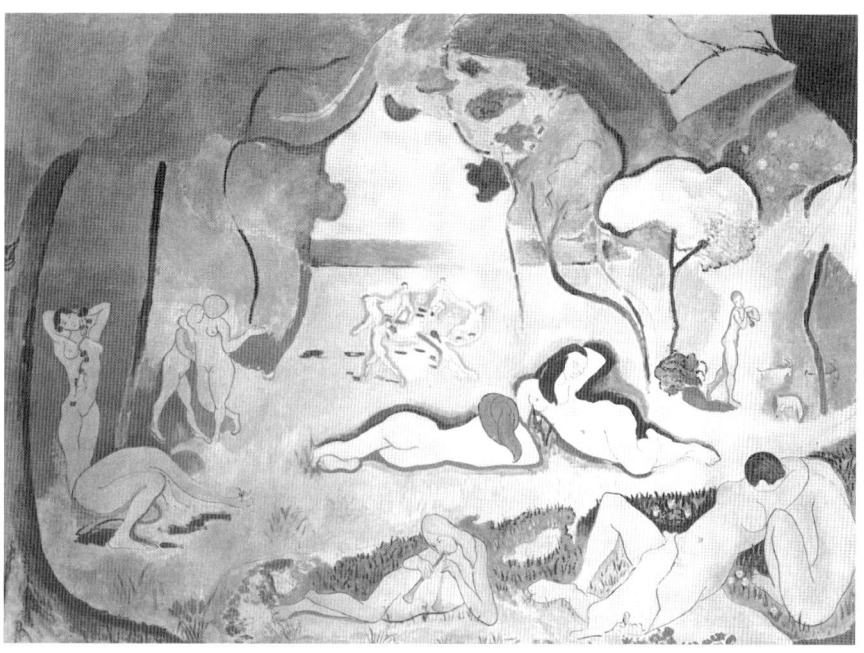

FIGURE 29. Henri Matisse, *Le Bonheur de vivre*, autumn–winter 1905–6. Oil on canvas, 174 × 238.1 cm. The Barnes Foundation, Philadelphia. (BF 719)

It has often been asserted that Picasso dedicated himself to the production of his Salon-scale canvas, *Les Demoiselles d'Avignon*, in the first six or seven months of 1907 at least partly in a spirit of rivalry with Matisse's *Bonheur de vivre*. It takes a subject – naked women on display – that has as obvious European precedents as Matisse's, reaching back via Cézanne's *Bathers* at least as far as the Rubens and Titian he knew from the Prado.[3] Indeed, it has precedents both in Ingres and in orientalism, most obviously in Ingres's own orientalist *The Turkish Bath* of 1862 (Fig. 3); but it totally reformulates that subject in terms of a harshly antidecorative approach, and in terms of a figuration that is explicitly primitivising, combining echoes of European archaism with the strongest possible invocations of African tribal sculpture. Where in Matisse's picture, whatever could be called oriental is so totally fused with the European that there is no sense of cultural confrontation, of difference, in Picasso's picture, pink (that is, white) bodies are Africanized by what is instantly seen in the two 'demoiselles' on the right as the donning of masks. The effect of cultural confrontation is accentuated by the dislocations of masking; difference is brutally present. Hence the startled immediacy of such early responses as that of the American journalist Gelett Burgess in 1910, who probably referred to the *Demoiselles* when he described seeing 'sub-African caricatures' in Picasso's studio,[4] and of Picasso's friend André Salmon in 1912, who placed the picture in the context of 'images from . . . Dahomey', writing of 'masks almost entirely freed from humanity'.[5]

By juxtaposing Matisse's *Bonheur de vivre* and Picasso's *Demoiselles*, my intention has been not to revive the well-worn scenario of rivalry between emerging vanguard heroes, but to bring out strongly contrasting stances in relation to non-European cultures: on the one hand, an 'orientality' that conflates the European and the non-European, on the other, a 'primitiveness' that dramatises difference through confrontation. Discussion of the two pictures has so far ignored the fact that they reiterate a fundamental distinction between French attitudes to the 'Orient' and to 'l'Afrique noire' in the early twentieth century.

When Salmon mentioned 'images of . . . Dahomey', he also mentioned those of Polynesia; when Burgess mentioned 'African caricatures', he also mentioned 'Alaskan totem poles'. William Rubin, the scholar to have studied the *Demoiselles* most exhaustively in terms of its non-European sources, has found in it nothing Alaskan, but he has made a strong case for the presence of colour contrasts and stylisations in the heads on the right related to masks from Vanuatu (formerly known as the New Hebrides) (Fig. 5), as well as accepting the case first made by John Golding for links with the striation patterns of West African Kota reliquary figures (Fig. 17).[6] At the same time, Rubin has noted a tendency in early twentieth century France to lump together under the single simplistic concept of the 'primitive', the African, the Oceanic, and indeed anything that could be considered especially remote in cultural terms.[7] The idea of Africa could be highly reductive and generalised, so generalised as to include anything at all disturbingly 'Other' in relation to Europe; such an idea of Africa, at its most reductive, was inevitably fearful. Patricia Leighten, the scholar to have most deeply explored the early twentieth century French idea of Africa as it connects with the *Demoiselles*, points out in Chapter 5 that in the decade before 1907, Dahomey (the French colony mentioned by Salmon) became almost synonymous as a name with an especially terrifying notion of the 'primitive Other', one built around travellers' tales that had produced an entire mythology of human sacrifice and cannibalism.[8]

Such attitudes, however crude, are revealing of the assumptions that sustained both French colonial rhetoric and policy in the Third Republic, from the administration of Jules Ferry in the 1880s through to the peace negotiations that followed the 1914–18 war.[9] Ferry's colonialism was driven both by grandiose nationalist ambition and by the post-Enlightenment ideal of the 'civilising mission', with its underlying ethos of European racial and moral superiority. In January 1892 Ferry wrote,

> One must believe that if Providence has deigned to confer on us a mission by making us masters of all the earth, this mission consists not in realising an impossible merger of the races but simply in spreading or in awakening in the breasts of the other races, the superior notions of which we are the guardians. To proclaim everywhere the law of work, to teach a purer morality, to spread and transmit our civilization, that task is beautiful enough to honour the great colonial enterprise.[10]

Throughout the period from the 1880s to the early 1920s, this ideal of the civilising mission (racist, as Leighten insists, yet more associated then with the liberal left than with the conservative right) went with an aspiration that the historians Betts and Charles Ageron have called 'assimilationist'.[11] This was the aspiration to the assimilation of the colonies by France, that is, to the acceptance of the colonised (whatever their race) *as French*: the gradual effacing, in other words, of cultural difference, so that other colonised cultures could be finally absorbed into, become part of French society and culture. This aspiration went with the phrases '*la plus grande France*' (greater France), and '*la France d'outre-mer*' (overseas France), and centred most concretely on the possibility of a French-dominated political and cultural order, cemented by the French language, centred on the shores of the Mediterranean, where Algeria and Morocco would in some ideal future become extensions of the French nation: new 'départements'.[12] But what was known as 'l'Afrique noire' was, ultimately, set apart from the assimilationist vision, something perhaps most effectively brought home in the context of European colonialism as a whole by Africa's treatment after the First World War. In 1922 the League of Nations conferred on France the once German-controlled West African colonies of Togo and Cameroon as what were termed 'B' mandates. Their populations were classified incapable of self-government 'under the strenuous conditions of the modern world'.[13] France's Middle Eastern mandates, Syria and then Lebanon, were given, by contrast, 'A' mandate status: that is, France was committed to 'facilitate their progressive development as independent states'.[14] Though not mandates, France's Far Eastern colonies were certainly thought of in the same way.[15]

It is obviously a grotesque oversimplification to think of Matisse's *Bonheur de vivre* as merely a reflection of French assimilationist attitudes to the Orient, but there is, nonetheless, a comfortable consonance between the orientality of Matisse's absorption of Middle Eastern and North African decorative principles into a European figurative aesthetic and the aspiration to a 'plus grande France' on the shores of the Mediterranean, a France in which the Islamic cultures of North Africa would be assimiliated into French culture. At the same time, it is obviously a grotesque oversimplification, indeed a grotesque distortion, to think of Picasso's *Demoiselles d'Avignon* as merely a reflection of those fundamentally racist attitudes that consigned the Cameroons and Togo to 'B' mandate status. Yet, nonetheless, the *Demoiselles* is a work that brings out more powerfully than any other of the early twentieth century the sense of distance and difference between Europe and Africa that directed even the idealist colonialism of the civilizing mission. I start with these two works placed in the context of colonialist attitudes and policy not simply to underline Leighten's point that the *Demoiselles d'Avignon* cannot be discussed in terms of 'primitivism' without coming up against issues of power and of race, but also to bring out the importance to such a discussion of stylistic and cultural fusion on the one hand, as we find it in Matisse's *Bonheur de vivre*, and of stylistic and cultural confrontation on the other, as we find it in Picasso's *Demoiselles*. The distinction between fusion and confrontation is central to my treatment of the *Demoiselles d'Avignon* and its immediate so-called African sequel. Picasso recorded his own taste for confrontational juxtaposition in his immediate surroundings when he photographed his Catalan friend Ramon Pichot in his studio on the boulevard de Clichy in the winter of 1910–11 (Fig. 30). He has hung a Puni mask from West Africa as one of an evidently ad hoc, fluctuating assortment of items, including a fragment of European textile, his own drawings, a cubist variant on Ingres's *Grand Odalisque*, and the little Matisse he owned, which is balanced precariously on the dado. No attempt is made at compositional resolution, at muting difference.

When the Musée Picasso in Paris put on its celebrated exhibition of 1988 centred on the *Demoiselles*, it brought together in a kind of ante-room to the painting itself what were dubbed '*choses vues*': things agreed by scholarly consensus to have been seen by Picasso before or during the months he dedicated to the painting in 1907. Here, gathered together in one small space, was a highly selected group of images that may or may not have acted as stimuli for Picasso (Fig. 31): a Kota reliquary figure and an Oceanic mask shown in the Musée d'Ethnographie du Trocadéro early in the century (Figs. 5 and 17), a Fang mask once in the collection of André Derain, one of two ruggedly 'primitive' stone heads from Cerro de los Santos, briefly and illicitly in Picasso's own possession, whose elongated ears are strikingly echoed by those of the two central 'demoiselles' (Fig. 6), a

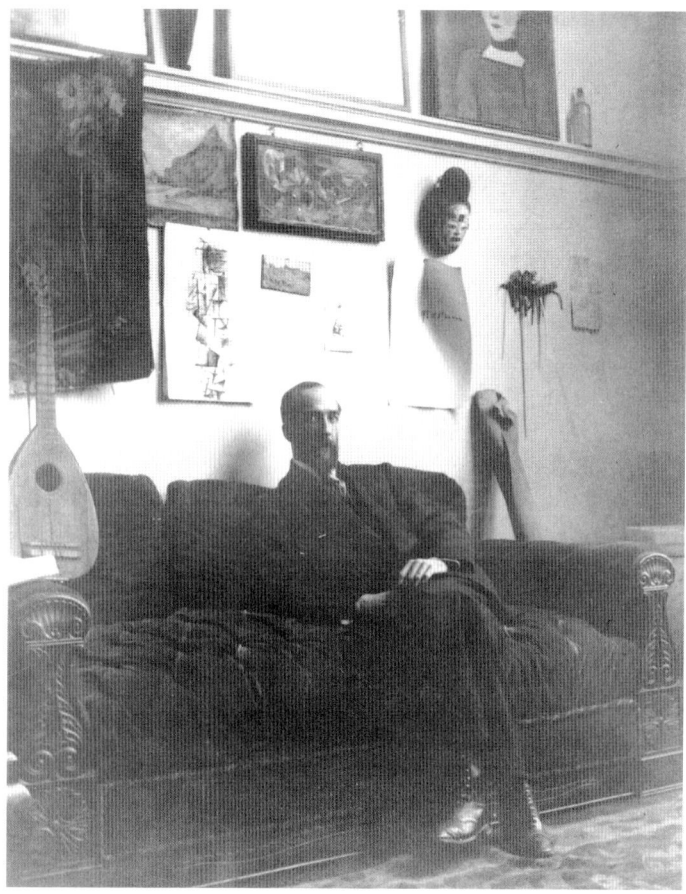

FIGURE 30. Pablo Picasso, *Portrait of Ramon Pichot in Picasso's Studio,* autumn–winter 1910. Photograph, Musée Picasso, Paris, 1988 (Archives). (Photo © Réunion des musées nationaux – Picasso.)

couple of *Bather* compositions by Cézanne (Fig. 4), Derain's primitivising *Bathers* of 1907, whose faces vaguely evoke the Fang mask he owned, and, of course, Ingres's *Bain turque* (Fig. 3). No attempt at museological composition could have made a synthetic unity of such a dissonant group of European and non-European images (Fig. 31). The late 1980s spectator encountered a cacophony of stimuli in juxtaposed confrontation before encountering the cacophonic cultural collisions of the *Demoiselles* itself.[16]

Les Demoiselles d'Avignon may not have been publicly exhibited until 1916, but various reminiscences, first systematically tabulated by Hélène Seckel and Judith Cousins in the catalogue of the 1988 *Demoiselles* exhibition, make it clear that Picasso kept the picture on show in his studio for at

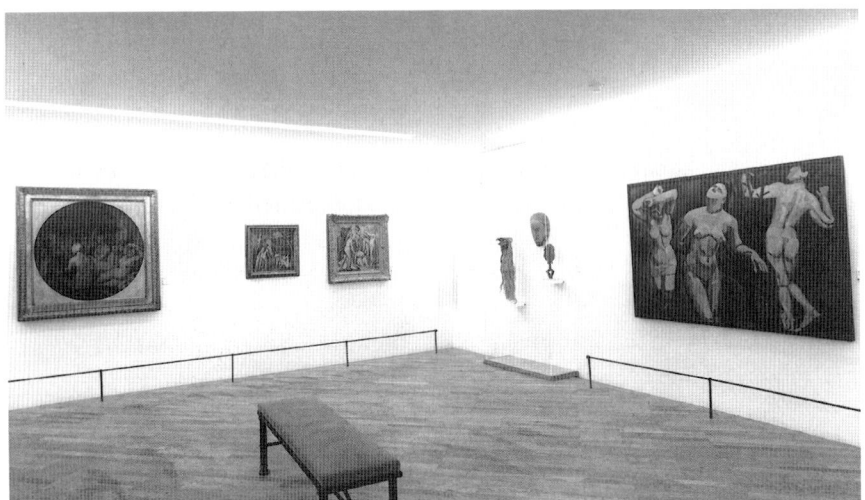

FIGURE 31. 'Choses vues'. Installation photograph of a room in the exhibition *Les Demoiselles d'Avignon*, Musée Picasso, Paris, 1988. (Photo © Réunion des musées nationaux – Picasso.)

least a year after he stopped working on it (probably in July 1907). Apart from his circle of friends, including the poets Guillaume Apollinaire and Max Jacob as well as André Salmon, and the painters Braque, Derain, Vlaminck, and van Dongen, collectors like Gertrude and Leo Stein and the Russian Shchukin saw it, as did Kahnweiler and visitors like Augustus John.[17] The very earliest recorded responses are of two contradictory kinds: horror, on the one side, and calm, level-headed historical assessment, on the other. *The* representative of level-headed historical assessment is Kahnweiler. It is with his little book *Der Weg zum Kubismus (The Rise of Cubism)*, published in Munich in 1920, but conceived in 1915–16, that the two Africanized figures on the right of the canvas (especially the croucher) are first plainly called the 'beginning of cubism'. Kahnweiler manages to write about the painting as if its major concern was the solution of the most basic of pictorial problems: the problem of representing three dimensions on a two-dimensional surface.[18] The accounts of horror as an early response are anecdotal and remembered. They come from contemporary witnesses like Gertrude Stein (who herself was not horrified, as Tamar Garb argues in this book), and include the famous story of Braque declaring that Picasso would ask them to eat tow and drink kerosene next.[19] It is worth mentioning too that Gelett Burgess's article, based on a visit to Picasso's studio in 1908, deploys a journalist's vocabulary of horror to fascinate through shock.[20] The most interesting early response, however, combines both the calm *and* the horrified: it is the response already cited of Picasso's friend André Salmon as published in 1912. For Salmon, famously, the 'demoiselles' are 'naked problems, white numbers on a blackboard', and yet they 'inspire in us a sort of terror'.[21]

The contradictions found in the textual space of Salmon's *La Jeune peinture française* have been echoed in the temporal space of the *Demoiselles*'s historiography. The historical analyses the picture has generated, especially since Alfred H. Barr's treatment of 1939, have been contradictory to an astonishing degree.[22] Between 1939 and 1972, the work was approached predominantly in terms of Kahnweiler's problem-solving metaphor, as proto-cubist, most brilliantly, if circumspectly, by John Golding in the late 1950s.[23] Then, as my Introduction to this book outlines, with Leo Steinberg's two-part article 'The Philosophical Brothel', published in 1972, the *Demoiselles* abruptly became a picture so centrally engaged in the force of sexual encounter, so focused on the relationship between the nudes-as-prostitutes and the spectator-as-male-client, that all its formal characteristics have been sexualised, and the problem solving associated with cubism has been set aside as a formalist irrelevance.[24] Steinberg's rediscovery of the sex in the *Demoiselles* stressed Nietzschian energy above horror; for him, the nudes were primal nature beings. But since 1972 it has been the horror in the picture that has come to the fore, as writing on the *Demoiselles* has followed either the psychobiographical path of William Rubin or the historically contextualising path of Michael Leja, Patricia Leighten, or David Lomas.[25]

In both these types of analysis the themes of sexuality and 'primitivism', of sexual and cultural difference, have become conflated. Rubin reads the confrontation between the two central nudes (those related to archaic Iberian [European] models) and the two nudes on the right (those related to African and Oceanic models) as a confrontation between Eros and Thanatos, between objects of desire and the terrifying aspect of death; he situates this confrontation in relation to the possible effect on Picasso of frightening public awareness campaigns concerning venereal disease, and the breakdown of his relationship with Fernande Olivier in the summer of 1907.[26] For Rubin, the Oceanic and African sculpture in the Musée d'Ethnographie du Trocadéro made such an impact because, caught up in a personal crisis, Picasso understood their magical function as protectors against the mortal danger above all of venereal disease. Rubin gives special prominence to a statement of 1937 recorded by André Malraux where Picasso spoke of the work as 'my first exorcism picture'.[27] For the contextualisers (Leighten and Lomas in this book) the association between the horrifying and the picture's primitivising aspect remains central, but they move beyond Steinberg's imagined male spectator and Rubin's traumatized Picasso into the historical setting. For them, Picasso's decision to bring together the theme of prostitution with the idea of the 'primitive' opened the picture to particular kinds of response in the period which were determined by widespread attitudes to prostitution as well as to 'l'Afrique noire'.

My own approach here, like that of the contextualisers, places the emphasis on how the work, and indeed the whole phenomenon of 'primitivisation', could be responded to in the period, but with one qualification. Where these contextualised rereadings of the work have tended to take its primitivised, horrifying aspects as their primary focus, I want to concentrate, as I have suggested already, on the confrontations in the work: the archaic European in confrontation with the primitivised non-European. Further, unlike both Rubin and the contextualisers, I want to look again at the picture as not just horrifying but also as proto-cubist. What Kahnweiler, Barr, and Golding found in the *Demoiselles* was and is in the painting to be seen, despite its transfixing sexual charge, and it is in its proto-cubist aspect that its *European* control of the conflicts within it is clearest. Late twentieth century spectators of the *Demoiselles d'Avignon* have become so attuned to its horror that perhaps the most astonishing thing about the history of the picture is that there could have been a time after Salmon and before Steinberg when it was understood most essentially to be a problem-solving experiment, a manifestation of European intelligence at its most visually developed.

André Salmon's text of 1912 provides a key means to grasping how this picture, now habitually detached from the very idea of cubism, could have been considered both 'primitive' *and* proto-cubist: the contradictions in his response have never been carefully enough considered. Strikingly, the problem-solving metaphor and the vocabulary of horror coexist in juxtaposed confrontation in Salmon's text. He attempts to accommodate one to the other under the signs of science and the 'primitive', geometry and Dahomey, but geometry emerges dominant. His mention of images from Dahomey, with all their terrifying connotations, is immediately followed by his much quoted report that, for Picasso, such images are *'raisonnable'* (rational and correct). When he mentions the 'barbarity' of what he calls the 'savage artists' Picasso took as his 'mentors', it is only to highlight Picasso's rational view of tribal sculpture. 'Those who see in Picasso's work', he writes, 'the masks of the occult, of symbolism or mysticism, are in great danger of never understanding it'. Bringing to bear the conceptual view of cubist art as the representation of our all-round knowledge of things in simple emblematic terms, he goes on to conclude: 'He [Picasso] is trying . . . to give us a total representation of man and things'. When he describes the final re-painting of the two right-hand 'demoiselles', he brings into close proximity quasi-scientific and exotico-mystical vocabulary thus: 'Soon Picasso attacked the faces, whose noses were for the most part placed full-face, in the form of isosceles triangles. The apprentice sorcerer was still seeking answers to his questions among the enchantments of Oceania and Africa'. Clearly geometry (despite the inconvenient fact that there are no isosceles triangles among the noses of the 'demoiselles') and the solving of problems are to be extracted from these 'enchantments', and clearly Picasso is given the status of 'sorcerer', but what is to be produced is an art which is not magical, an art *without*, Salmon insists, 'the marks of the occult . . . or mysticism'. And when Salmon tackles the strangeness of the figures thus produced, he might call them terrifying, but this is presented merely as a result of their distance from accepted convention, in particular the post-Renaissance conventions of European art. The smile of the Mona Lisa is used as the symbol of all that is denied. Salmon makes of Picasso's primitivised nudes a revaluation of African and Oceanic tribal sculpture, but one that is founded not on the horrifying or on an attempt to appropriate any magical functions they might have, but rather on a new and profoundly European notion of art. That notion is, of course, cubist as he understood the term: it is geometric and highly conceptualised.[28]

William Rubin argues that the precedence given by Salmon to reason and geometry over horror and the magical force of tribal images merely reflects discussions among the cubists and their supporters in 1912 about the conceptual in art.[29] For Rubin, as we have seen, magic as a mode of personal exorcism is the key to the *Demoiselles*, and far more significant than Salmon's text is the much later statement Picasso is reported to have made to André Malraux, where he supposedly talks about the picture as 'my first exorcism picture'. This is a much-quoted passage, where, according to Malraux, Picasso recalled for him his first encounter at the time of the *Demoiselles* with African and Oceanic tribal sculpture, speaking of his realisation that they were 'magic things', produced as 'weapons' against 'unknown, threatening spirits', and remarking, 'If you give spirits a shape you break free of them. Spirits, the unconscious, (. . .) emotion, they're all the same thing'.[30]

In fact, the first to focus attention on this passage in post-Steinberg writing on the *Demoiselles* was Lydia Gasman in a highly influential doctoral dissertation of 1981, whose central thesis was the exorcistic function of magic in Picasso's art after 1925.[31] Gasman suggested that Picasso's openness to the magical in 1907 might have been based, directly or indirectly, on the major social anthropological study of magic published in 1902–3 by

Marcel Mauss and Henri Hubert, their *Esquisse d'une théorie générale de la magie*.[32] There is good reason for both doubting the relevance of Mauss and Hubert's study and questioning the credibility of Picasso's reported statement to Malraux as convincing evidence of his state of mind in 1907. To take the latter first, the equivalence Picasso assumes between 'the unconscious' and 'spirits' along with his talk of breaking free from 'spirits' (the unconscious) by giving them form could only have been possible with at least a rudimentary knowledge of psychoanalysis, something Picasso had in 1937, but could not have had by 1907.[33] As to the question of Mauss and Hubert's theory of magic, Gasman stresses the relevance to Picasso of their observation that magic is based on a belief in a mystical force found in everything, a force known in some languages as *Mana*;[34] but she does not mention the crucial point that Mauss and Hubert viewed magic above all as a collective, social phenomenon. For them, in the sociological tradition of Durkheim, magic could only have a function where it was collectively supported by belief.[35] From such a viewpoint, the highly subjective psychic role imagined for magic by Rubin in Picasso's painting of the *Demoiselles* was of little importance; it was uncommunicable and inaccessible, and could have no major role in a society where the belief in magic was so enfeebled.

Picasso (who took his superstitions very seriously) might indeed have found what he thought of as magic in tribal sculpture, but so sophisticated a postpsychoanalytical reading of its magical function as the exorcism of unconscious fears would not have been available to him. Certainly, as Rubin has shown, the labelling of tribal exhibits in the Musée d'Ethnographie du Trocadéro did on occasion record their reported protective functions against illness and so on, but this merely drew attention to the way fear induced by images could be used against *external* threats; it did not suggest a power that could be turned *inward* to protect the psyche.[36] It is, of course, possible that at an unconscious level Picasso was drawn to an exorcistic power he *felt* in African and Oceanic magic images, but I would turn back to Mauss and Hubert to stress, as they do, the importance of the distinction that must be made between the subjective/private and the social, between – in the case of the *Demoiselles* – any internal psychobiographical meanings to be dredged from the picture, and the possible meanings it could have had for anyone else in Paris before 1914. It is difficult to imagine any spectator reading the work at that time in terms of Picasso's psychic state: the complexity of his desires and fears.

How then are we to take André Salmon's determination to give precedence to the geometric and the rational in so disruptive a picture? To begin with, I accept Rubin's point that Salmon's text is infused with a conceptualist notion of cubism that belongs to 1912, not 1907, but I believe that a further answer is suggested by looking at the most important sequel to the *Demoiselles*, the large canvas, which, despite its inclusion of at least one male figure, is known as *Three Women* (Fig. 32).[37]

In one respect Salmon's text is puzzling.[38] It seems to refer not to two stages in the painting of the *Demoiselles*, but to several, two of which were

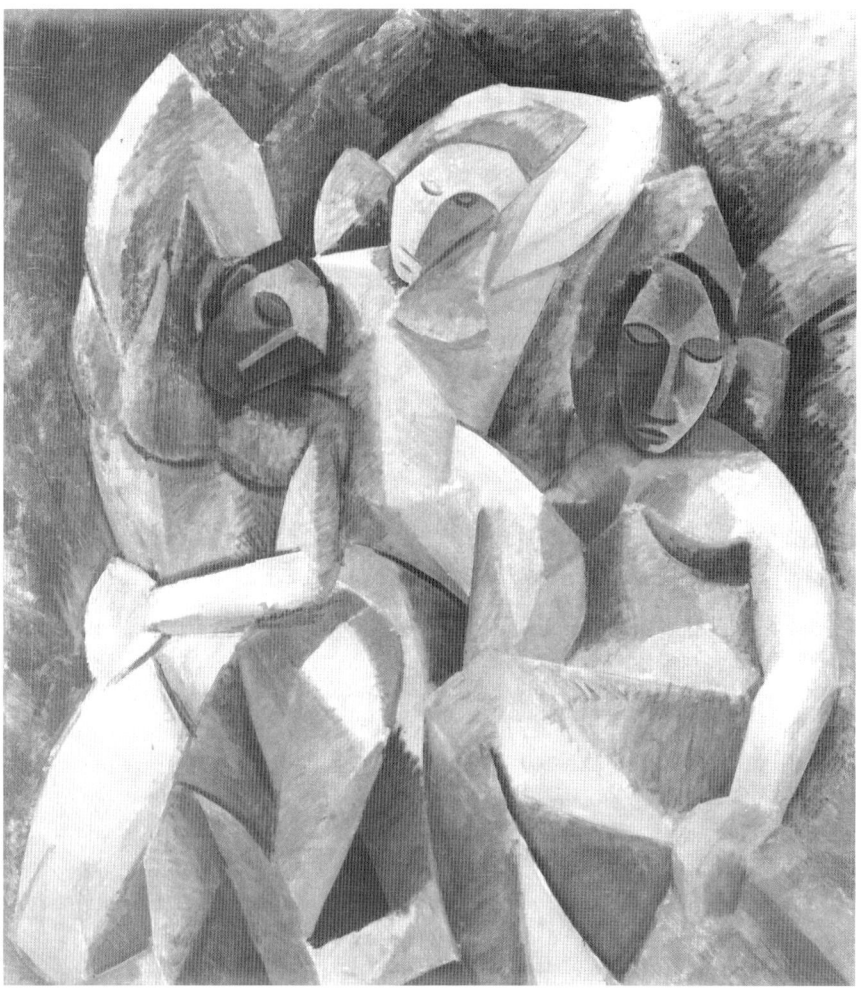

FIGURE 32. Pablo Picasso, *Three Women*, summer 1908 and autumn–winter 1908. Oil on canvas, 200 × 178 cm. The Hermitage Museum, St. Petersburg.

separated by a 'holiday' and led to the introduction of a 'dynamic decomposition of light values' and the making of 'geometrical signs'. Pierre Daix has convincingly suggested that this discussion of later stages applies not to the *Demoiselles* at all, but to *Three Women:* that Salmon brings the two pictures together in the one account.[39] Daix further suggests that *Three Women* went through three stages, moving from a stage late in 1907 when the figures were brutally primitivised and strongly modelled,[40] through a second early in 1908 when Picasso oscillated between a rhythmically linear three-figure idea and a four- or mostly five-figure idea with an outdoor bather setting (strongly reminiscent of Cézanne's late *Bathers*) (Fig. 33), and culminating probably in July 1908 with the thoroughgoing flattening of the initial three-figure composition by the superimposition of geometric faceting, and the introduction of a new close-valued range of greens, reds, and browns (Fig. 32). This late development has rightly been associated by Rubin with a brand of Cézannism that places the emphasis on the picture surface, whose faceting and whose facture is visibly proto-cubist.[41] If Salmon does refer in his 1912 text to both the *Demoiselles* and *Three Women*, he therefore refers to a process of development that did indeed end with the declaration of a distinctly geometric and conceptual agenda (something closer to isosceles triangles is incidentally to be found in the noses of *Three Women*).

And yet, *Three Women* retains clear elements of primitivisation (the central head in particular relates to certain Fang masks); it is not a work open solely to conceptual readings because of its geometric faceting and its close-valued tones. Leo Steinberg has argued with great eloquence, in fact, that it represents at least partly a reprise in new terms of the major themes of the *Demoiselles*. He has read the picture as a representation of origins in the most elemental sense: the origins no less of gender differentiation and of *libido* – sexual identity and sexual energy.[42] Broadly I agree with this argument, but my stress here is on the distinctions to be made between the treatment of sexuality and nature in the two pictures. Three key developments distance *Three Women* from the *Demoiselles* in these terms. First, any stylistic heterogeneity there may be in *Three Women* does not accentuate racial or cultural difference by the confrontational juxtaposition of European and non-European features; second, the nudes are no longer prostitutes in a brothel, they have been taken out into a rocky landscape; and third, the faceting of the surface and its unification by a close-valued colour range encourages the image of a fusion of figures and setting, and thus the idea of the unity of nature (landscape) and the human (the nudes).[43] Such a unity is plainly the theme of the four- and five-figure drawings made during what Daix calls the second phase in the

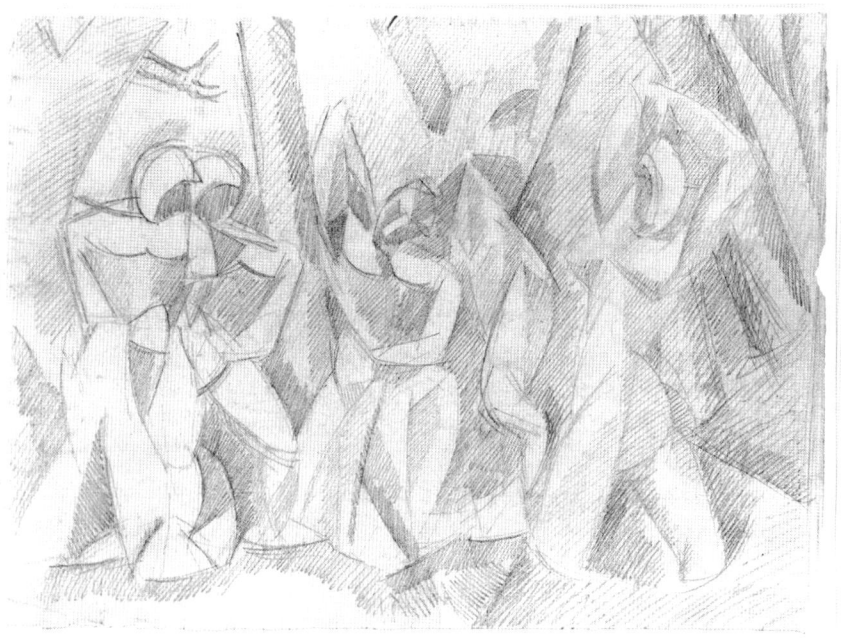

FIGURE 33. Pablo Picasso, *Study for 'Bathers'*, spring 1908. Pencil on paper, 32 × 43.5 cm. Musée Picasso, Paris (MP 603). (Photo © Réunion des musées nationaux – Paris.)

development of *Three Women*, where the figures take on the sexually less active roles of bathers. Indeed, I have argued elsewhere that the raised elbow of the central bather plays the compositional role of the rocky peak found in a couple of landscapes of 1908 (based on memories of the mountain Pedra Forca at Gósol), so that it fuses at one remove figure and rock.[44] As Steinberg maintains, Picasso's *Three Figures* are built as if from the red rocks of Cézanne's Bibémus quarry paintings.[45] Where juxtaposition and confrontation, in stylistic and cultural terms, are basic to the *Demoiselles*, fusion is basic to *Three Women*; and in the latter cultural and racial difference is no longer manifestly at issue. Where the *Demoiselles* stands in all its conflictual complexity against that simple idea of Nietzschian sexual energy – of sex as nature – so easily read in André Derain's *Bathers* of 1907, *Three Women* stands alongside a later large *Bathers* of 1908 by Derain: both fuse sexuality and the natural by painting primitivised nudes as rock.[46] There is still the effect of masking in *Three Women*, especially in the two flanking figures, but these 'women' cannot be read as urban European nudes that have been primitivised: they are in a much more elementary and reductive sense, 'natural' in their primitiveness.

To consider further the readings opened up by the image of fusion found in *Three Women*, it is necessary to return to the contextualised readings of the prostitutes in the *Demoiselles* in terms of the idea of Africa and the 'primitive' offered by Leighten and Lomas. Leighten's reading is not simple. She accepts the negative implications of the racial assumptions that go with the stereotyping of African savagery, but at the same time she allows the strong possibility that the picture presents a powerful anticolonialist critique, fueled by the 1905–6 exposure of the brutal exploitation of the indigenous populations of the Congo.[47] Lomas's reading is far less open to a positive interpretation. It places the *Demoiselles* in a tightly bound network of prejudice, whose strands include white suprematism, late nineteenth-century degeneracy theory, and the tie-up between fears of European degeneration and fears of prostitution. The 'canon of deformity' he reveals in Picasso's Iberian and African prostitutes and the force with which those deformations released a sense of the monstrous are aligned with deeply negative ideas of the primitive and specifically of the black. Certainly the horror the painting provoked in so many of its first spectators was experienced overwhelmingly in negative terms, and it seems indeed likely that such responses were connected with the fears generated not only by the Dahomeyan idea of Africa and of savage fetishes, but by that devastating conjunction of negative associations exposed by Lomas, culminating in the fear of bodily degradation and degeneration, a fear concentrated on the perceived threat mounted by Picasso's prostitutes to the European ideal of beauty.[48]

And yet, as Salmon's text of 1912 makes clear, positive readings *were* possible, readings that gave a positive role to the African and the Oceanic as well as to the Iberian. For Salmon's reading of the work in terms of so conceptual and formalist an idea of African and Oceanic tribal sculpture went, of course, with a belief that Picasso's picture had fundamentally challenged the high status of European art in the cultural hierarchy, had not offered a 'canon of deformity' at all, but a new countercanon of aesthetic value, symbolized by the wiping of the Mona Lisa's smile off the face of European painting.

Even as early as the first decade of the twentieth century, it was possible in France to approach the extreme cultural differences summed up by the confrontation of the European and the non-European in the *Demoiselles* with a positive agenda; and it was possible not only for anticolonialists or those in the circle of Picasso and André Salmon, but even for those working in a scientific discipline dedicated to the study of 'Other' societies and cultures. If physical anthropologists were responsible in the later nineteenth century for constructing an emphatically negative 'scientific' image of the black, sociological ethnographers and ethnologists trained in the methodology then being developed by Emile Durkheim were capable of looking at tribal societies without such a transparently negative bias. In this respect, Marcel Mauss, coauthor with Henri Hubert in 1902–3 of the *Esquisse d'une théorie générale de la magie*, is after all relevant to this discussion.[49] For Mauss was one of the first to react against the racism inherent in an evolutionist approach to the study of non-European peoples (that approach which placed especially the African in some remote, childlike region of origins) and to argue for a different kind of approach. Mauss did not assume a progression from the simple and the false to the complex and the true, but instead approached his topic, magical thinking, as complex but *different* applications of *similar* mental processes to those of European logical thinking structured in *similar* ways.[50] I repeat the point that it is very unlikely that Picasso was aware of Mauss; he certainly did not have adequate French for even a fanciful reading of the *Esquisse*, and there is no evidence that his friends, including Salmon, knew of it. Picasso was to become aware of new sociological approaches to ethnography based on Mauss's teaching at the turn of the 1920s and 1930s, but that awareness touches his primitivising work of the post-1925 period, not the *Demoiselles*.[51] Yet, it is possible to read Picasso's 1907–8 engagement with the idea of the 'primitive' in cross-cultural, humanist terms: that is, not only in terms of the inversion of values, of the African and the Oceanic offered as a countercanon to the European, but in terms of the theme of sameness in difference, the essentialist theme of the unity of humankind. At least, it is possible to do so if one looks not just at the *Demoiselles*, but at the development that links it to *Three Women*, because of course what that development ends in is the *fusion* of the European and the non-European, and the fusion of the human and the natural. The theme of the primal still carries with it strong evolutionist connotations, but in this representation of origins, there are no differences.

From such a point, divergent possibilities were opened up. Derain's frozen image of fusion in petrification, his 1908 *Bathers*, was the first step in a strongly evolutionist evolution that took his work back (after 1910) to what was understood as the origins of the European pictorial tradition, Italy before 1500, and then on (after 1918) towards the seventeenth century and a modern self-consciously European 'classicism': a restoration of the humanist ideal of beauty. Picasso's dionysian image of primal fusion in his 1908 *Three Women* brought him up short before the basics of a new kind of painting that held in tension control (geometry) and an ad hoc responsiveness to things seen (including nudes). It was the starting point of a ruthless investigation of painting as representation (language), which eventually, in 1912, took him back again to African sculpture, this time as an object lesson in how finally to separate the activity of visual sign making from the capture of appearances. To use African (Grebo) masks in the way he would in 1912 was so thoroughly to conceptualize them that any recognisable reference to African imagery with all its connotations disappeared from the constructed metal *Guitar* and its 'synthetic cubist' progeny that resulted.[52] Such a step amounts, of course, to a final European appropriation of the African. More than assimilation, we have the making of sculptural objects that totally obliterate their African 'sources', that mask those sources from view, but it is an appropriation of the African founded on the most positive of revaluations, one compelled by the search for similarity in difference at the deepest level.

I give here, perhaps, the false impression of a single direction in Picasso's work out of the *Demoiselles* and its sequel *Three Women* and into the conceptualised formalism of so-called synthetic cubism as André Salmon knew it in 1912. What happened, in fact, was complex and contradictory, and in the end it is the complexity and the contradictions of the *Demoiselles*, whatever its relationship to *Three Women*, that should be stressed: the fact that it could terrorize *and* induce the idea of an artistic practice so conceptualised that its semiotic liberties would be made manifest. When André Breton, who was to give the *Demoiselles* a new surrealist identity for the mid and later 1920s, wrote to the collector Jacques Doucet to persuade him to buy the picture in 1923, he summed up thus: 'Through it one penetrates right into the core of Picasso's laboratory . . . , it is the crux of the drama, the centre of all the conflicts that Picasso has given rise to and that will last for ever in my opinion'.[53] The conflicts to which Breton responded went with a confrontation between the European and the non-European, the proto-cubist and the noncubist that is dramatically clear, but what that confrontation could signify is still unclear. The meanings of the picture remain ambivalent.

I end by turning to the psychoanalytic implications of the *Demoiselles* as invoked by the work of William Rubin above all. In 1913 Freud published his study of neurosis in relation to totemic belief systems, *Totem and Taboo*. It is not in any way historically connected to Picasso and the *Demoiselles*, and moreover it presents an approach to cultural difference deeply negative in its implications.[54] On the other hand, Freud's account of the mechanisms of displacement and the fundamental importance of emotional ambivalence in neurosis is uncannily consistent with accounts of the Picasso of the *Demoiselles*, a Picasso caught up in a moment, it has been demonstrated, of singular psychic instability.[55]

Ambivalence was central to Freud's understanding of neurosis: the dual existence of, say, love and hatred towards the father, or desire and fear in the male relationship with the mother (relevant, of course, to the 'Medusa effect' explored by Yve-Alain Bois in this book). On this basis, he draws a parallel between the practice of taboos in primitive societies, and the displacement of the loved and hated, the desired and feared object on to other objects (people, creatures, or things) in the obsessional behaviour of neurotics, which usually also involves prohibitions and taboos. The *Demoiselles* is easily, of course, seen in terms of all that is inferred by masking with reference to displacement within the Freudian psychoanalytic tradition, especially with regard to protection against the desired and the feared. I believe that such displacement, however, cannot be said to have occurred in the *Demoiselles*. If it had, we would have had the final and complete substitution perhaps of the bathers for the prostitutes (which is what occurs in *Three Women*) and so we would have had the protective containment of all that is fearful and terrible; in a sense, the themes and subject matter of the picture would have been 'civilized'. *Les Demoiselles d'Avignon* might then have been unequivocally finished, and, had it been, it would have ended closer to Salmon's 'geometry', to what we think of as cubism. In the *Demoiselles*, we have instead something which, in these terms, is profoundly, discomfitingly *un*civilized. One could say we have the conditions of neurosis themselves as Freud understood them. Blatantly displayed, we have the unresolved conflict of ambivalent feelings (desire and dread) that go with the unresolved conflict of sex and death. It is not a representation in which either the objects of desire or of fear are substituted: the ambivalence of Picasso's and of other male responses to female sexuality are exposed, most disturbingly by the primitivisation of the nudes. They are not repressed.

Whether we consider *Les Demoiselles d'Avignon* thus, within a Freudian framework, or within the framework of the comparative analysis of cultures and its early twentieth-century history, we are left with unresolved ambiguity: stylistic, cultural, emotional ambivalence. Hence, perhaps, the need to go on talking about it.

NOTES

1 *La Japonaise: Woman Beside the Water*, summer 1905 (oil & pencil on canvas, 35.2 × 28.2 cm, Museum of Modern Art, New York).
2 Pierre Schneider, *Matisse* (Great Britain, 1984), chapter 7, 155–85.
3 Best known of the *Bathers* Picasso certainly knew at the time of painting the *Demoiselles* is *Trois Baigneuses*, 1879–82 (oil on canvas, 53 × 55 cm, Musée du Petit

Palais, Paris), then owned by Matisse. He could not have seen any of the late *Bathers* until they were shown in the Cézanne retrospective at the Salon d'Automne of 1907, that is, after he had ceased working on the *Demoiselles*. Of the Rubens he knew in the Prado, most relevant is *Diana and Calisto*, where the inward-looking figure on the left and the seated woman, foreground right, are clearly comparable with the curtain-raiser and croucher of the *Demoiselles*. The most relevant Titian precedent is the *Diana and Actaen* from the Duke of Sutherland collection, which he could have known only from reproduction.

4   Gelett Burgess, 'The Wild Men of Paris', *The Architectural Record* no. 5 (New York, May 1910), 408.

5   André Salmon, *La Jeune Peinture française* (Paris, 1912), 'Histoire anecdotique du cubisme', 43. Translated in Edward F. Fry (ed.), *Cubism* (London, 1966), 82.

6   John Golding, 'The *Demoiselles d'Avignon*', *The Burlington Magazine* 100, no. 662 (London, May 1958), 155–63.

7   William Rubin, 'Modernist Primitivism: An Introduction', in Rubin (ed.), *"Primitivism" in Twentieth-Century Art: Affinity of the Tribal and the Modern*, vol. 1 (New York: Museum of Modern Art, 1984), 3.

8   See Leighten, chapter 5.

9   For Ferry's colonial policies in context, see Jean-Marie Mayeur and Madeleine Rebérioux (trans. J.R. Foster), *The Third Republic from Its Origins to the Great War, 1871–1914* (Cambridge, 1973), chapter 3, 72–100.

10   Cited in Charles-Robert Ageron, *France Coloniale ou Parti Colonial?* (Paris, 1978), 66. Author's translation.

11   See R. Betts, *Assimilation and Association in French Colonial Theory, 1890–1914* (New York and London, 1961), and Ageron, as in note 10, especially chapter 6, 'Doctrines et politiques de la France coloniale', 189 ff. The liberal left credentials of assimilationism in particular are conclusively demonstrated in 1936 by Léon Blum and Maurice Viollette's Front Populaire project to give 20,000 Muslim Algerians French citizenship. See Serge Berstein, *La France des années 30* (Paris, 1988), 127.

12   The idea of 'la France d'outre-mer' is discussed by both Betts and Ageron, as in notes 10 and 11.

13   See Christopher M. Andrew and A.S. Kanya-Forstner, *France Overseas: The Great War and the Climax of French Imperial Expansion* (London, 1981), 226, and Robert Aldrich, *Greater France. A History of French Overseas Expansion* (London, 1996).

14   As in note 13.

15   A clear index of this is Albert Sarraut's educational and administrative policies as governor-general of French Indo-China in the period immediately after the 1914–18 war. See Ageron, as in note 10, 227 ff.

16   See Hélène Seckel (ed.), *Les Demoiselles d'Avignon*, 2 vols. Exhibition catalogue (Paris, Musée Picasso, 1988).

17   See Judith Cousins and Hélène Seckel, 'Eléments pour une chronologie de l'histoire des *Demoiselles d'Avignon*', as in note 16. Translated into English as 'Chronology of *Les Demoiselles d'Avignon*, 1907 to 1939', in Judith Cousins, William Rubin, and Hélène Seckel, *Les Demoiselles d'Avignon, Studies in Modern Art* 3 (New York, Museum of Modern Art, 1994).

18   Daniel-Henry Kahnweiler, *Der Weg zum Kubismus* (Munich, 1920).

19   The evidence for specific visits and reactions (1907–10) is summed up with exem-

plary clarity in Cousins and Seckel, as in note 17, 148–59. For Garb on Gertrude Stein's response, see Garb, 55–76.

20 Burgess, as in note 4. Burgess's visit to Picasso's studio is discussed by Cousins and Seckel, as in note 17, 155–6 and 230.

21 Salmon, as in note 5, 43 and 47; in Fry, as in note 5, 82 and 84.

22 Despite Kahnweiler's earlier analysis of the work, I would contend that the historiography proper of the *Demoiselles* begins with Barr's study of the picture on the occasion of the retrospective exhibition at the Museum of Modern Art, New York, in 1939–40. See Alfred H. Barr, Jr., *Picasso: Forty Years of His Art* (New York, Museum of Modern Art, 1939).

23 Golding, as in note 6, and John Golding, *Cubism: A History and an Analysis, 1907–1914* (London, 1959). Golding insists that the picture is not at all cubist, but nonetheless brings out how it opened the way to cubist practices.

24 Leo Steinberg, 'The Philosophical Brothel', *Art News* 71, nos. 5 and 6 (New York, September and October 1972), 22–9 and 38–47. Published in a revised version in *October*, no. 44 (New York and Cambridge, Mass., Spring 1988), 7–74. See Introduction, 9–10.

25 Michael Leja, '"Le Vieux Marcheur" and "Les Deux Risques": Picasso, Prostitution, Venereal Disease and Maternity, 1899–1907', *Art History* 8, no. 1 (Oxford, March 1985), 66–81; Patricia Leighten, 'The White Peril and L'*Art Nègre*: Picasso, Primitivism and Anticolonialism', *The Art Bulletin* 72, no. 4 (New York, December 1990), 609–30 (revised in this book as chapter 5); David Lomas, 'A Canon of Deformity: *Les Demoiselles d'Avignon* and Physical Anthropology', *Art History* 16, no. 3 (Oxford, U.K., and Cambridge, Mass., September 1993), 424–46 (revised in this book as chapter 6).

26 Rubin's analysis has been developed in a series of articles since 1977, but most importantly since 1983. His views are most comprehensively put together in the fundamental study 'La Genèse des *Demoiselles d'Avignon*', published in Seckel, as in note 16, a revised version of which appears in Cousins et al., as in note 17.

27 André Malraux, *La Tête d'obsidienne* (Paris, 1974), 18. Rubin cites this passage in Cousins et al., as in note 17, 16, and discusses the exorcistic character of tribal sculpture as he believes Picasso experienced it, 103–6.

28 Salmon, as in note 5, 43–7 as translated into English in, as in note 5, 81–5.

29 Rubin, as in note 17, 20–1.

30 Malraux, as in note 27, 18.

31 Lydia Gasman, *Mystery, Magic and Love in Picasso, 1925–1938, Picasso and the Surrealist Poets*. Thesis submitted for the degree of Ph.D., Columbia University, 1981. Gasman cites the passage from Malraux, 460.

32 Marcel Mauss and Henri Hubert, *Esquisse d'une théorie générale de la magie* (L'Année Sociologique, Paris, 1902–3); republished in Marcel Mauss, *Sociologie et anthropologie* (Paris, 1966). For Gasman's analysis, as in note 31, 476–82.

33 My doubts are anticipated by Leighten. See Leighten, chapter 5.

34 Gasman, as in note 31, 479.

35 'C'est donc l'opinion qui crée le magicien et les influences qu'il dégage. C'est grâce à l'opinion qu'il sait tout, qu'il peut tout'. Mauss, as in note 32, 32. For Mauss's development and sociological methodologies, see Claude Lévi-Strauss's introduction to Mauss (1966), and Jean Cazenove, *Sociologie de Marcel Mauss* (Paris, 1968).

36 Rubin in Cousins et al., as in note 17, 104 and 141, note 264.

37 In particular, Maurice Raynal's ideas on the conceptual nature of cubist painting find echoes in Salmon's text. See especially his article 'Conception et vision', *Gil Blas* (Paris, 29 August 1912).

38 Another puzzling feature is Salmon's statement that the picture contains 'six large female nudes'. Rubin argues plausibly that this indicates that Salmon had not seen the picture for some time and was depending on far from precise memories. See Rubin, as in note 17, 20.

39 Pierre Daix, 'Les Trois périodes de travail de Picasso sur *Les trois femmes* (automne 1907–automne 1908), les rapports avec Braque et les débuts du cubisme', *Gazette des beaux-arts*, series 6, vol. III, nos. 1428–29 (Paris, January–February 1988), 141–54. The fact that Salmon's memories of the picture as such were inaccurate might well go with confusions concerning the making of the *Demoiselles* and *Three Women*.

40 Visual evidence of this stage survives in the form of a photograph of André Salmon posed in front of the picture, which Rubin has shown is in an earlier state. See William Rubin, 'Cézannisme and the Beginnings of Cubism', in Rubin (ed.), *Cézanne: The Late Work* (New York, Museum of Modern Art, 1977).

41 As in note 40.

42 Leo Steinberg, 'Resisting Cézanne: Picasso's *Three Women*', *Art in America* 66, no. 6 (New York, November-December 1978), 114–33.

43 Picasso was drawn to the idea of the human figure placed outdoors in the landscape during the final phase of work on the *Demoiselles*, producing probably in July the much smaller, quickly worked oil in the Thyssen-Bornemisza Collection *The Harvesters*. I have analysed this picture as a foil to the *Demoiselles* in my entry on it in Christopher Green, *The Thyssen-Bornemisza Collection. The European Avant-gardes: Art in France and Western Europe 1904–c.1945* (London, 1995), 378–83.

44 The landscapes I refer to are nos. 182 and 183 in Pierre Daix and Joan Rosselet, *Picasso. The Cubist Years, 1907–1916. A Catalogue Raisonné of the Paintings and Related Works* (London, 1979). See Christopher Green, 'De la figura al paisatge al *tableau objet*, el lloc que correspon als paisatges cubistes de Picasso' (published in English as 'Landscape into Figure into *Tableau-objet*: Placing Picasso's Cubist Landscapes'), in *Picasso: Paisatges 1890–1912*, exhibition catalogue (Barcelona, Museu Picasso, 1994), 21–36.

45 Steinberg, as in note 42.

46 *Bathers*, 1908 (oil on canvas, 180 × 225 cm, private collection). Michel Kellermann, *Catalogue raisonné de l'oeuvre peint*, vol. 1 (Paris: Éditions Galerie Schmit, 1992), no. 387.

47 Leighten, chapter 5.

48 Lomas, chapter 6.

49 Mauss was a protégé of Emile Durkheim, who was his uncle. The *Esquisse* was one of the publications produced by Durkheim's 'L'Année sociologique'.

50 See note 35.

51 In particular, Picasso's friendship with Michel Leiris exposed him to the new anthropological ideas. Mauss himself contributed a short personal statement on Picasso, who he admired, to the special Picasso issue of *Documents*. *Documents*, 2nd Year, no. 3 (1930), 177.

52 The key study of Picasso's 1912 metal *Guitar* and the semiotic terms of his synthetic

cubism is Yve-Alain Bois, 'Kahnweiler's Lesson', *Representations*, no. 18 (Spring 1987). Republished in Bois, *Painting as Model* (Cambridge, Mass. and London, England, 1990), 65–97.

53 André Breton to Jacques Doucet, 6 November 1923. Cited here as translated in Cousins and Seckel in Cousins et al., as in note 17, 177.

54 This follows in particular from Freud's evolutionist adherence to the idea that a direct relationship exists between the development of the species and the development of the individual, which leads to the elaboration of parallels between the child and the 'primitive', and, most derogatively of all, between the European neurotic and the 'primitive'. See Sigmund Freud, *Totem and Taboo* (1913), translated into English in *The Origins of Religion*, vol. 13, The Pelican Freud Library (London, 1985), 43–224.

55 Cf. Rubin, in Cousins, et al., as in note 17, 14–17.

Select Bibliography

Baldassari, Anne. 'Grasping the Visible: An African Source for *Les Demoiselles d'Avignon*', in Anne Baldassari, *Picasso and Photography. The Dark Mirror*, translated from the French by Deke Dusinberre. Paris: Flammarion, 1997.

Barr, Alfred H., Jr. *Picasso: Fifty Years of His Art.* New York: Museum of Modern Art, 1946; reprinted 1974.

Bois, Yve-Alain, 'Painting as Trauma', *Art in America* 76, no. 6 (June 1988), 130–40, 172–3. Published in French as 'Le Trauma des Demoiselles', *Critique*, no. 497 (October 1988), 834–57.

Chave, Anna C. 'New Encounters with *Les Demoiselles d'Avignon*: Gender, Race, and the Origins of Cubism', *Art Bulletin* 76, no. 4 (December 1994), 596–611.

Cooper, Douglas. *The Cubist Epoch.* London: Phaidon; Los Angeles: Los Angeles County Museum of Art; New York: Metropolitan Museum of Art, 1971.

Cousins, Judith (with Hélène Seckel). See Seckel (1988).

Cousins, Judith (with Hélène Seckel). 'Chronology of *Les Demoiselles d'Avignon*', in *Les Demoiselles d'Avignon, Studies in Modern Art* 3 (New York: Museum of Modern Art, 1994).

Daix, Pierre. *Picasso créateur: La Vie intime et l'oeuvre* (Paris: Seuil, 1987); translated by Olivia Emmet as *Picasso: Life and Art.* New York: HarperCollins, Icon Editions, 1993.

Daix, Pierre. See Seckel (1988).

Daix, Pierre. 'Les Trois périodes de travail de Picasso sur *Les trois femmes* (automne 1907–automne 1908), les rapports avec Braque et les débuts du cubisme', *Gazette des Beaux-Arts*, series 6, vol. 3, nos. 1428–9 (January–February 1988), 141–54.

Donne, John. 'African Art and Paris Studios, 1905–1920', in Michael Greenhalgh and Vincent Megaw (eds.), *Art and Society: Studies in Style, Culture and Aesthetics*. London: Duckworth, 1978.

Duncan, Carol. 'Virility and Domination in Early Twentieth-Century Vanguard Painting', *Artforum* 12, no. 4 (December 1973), 30–9. Reprinted in Norma Broude and Mary D. Garrard (eds.), *Feminism and Art History: Questioning the Litany*. New York: Harper & Row; Toronto: Fitzhenry & Whiteside, 1982.

Foster, Hal. 'The 'Primitive' Unconscious of Modern Art', *October*, no. 34 (Autumn 1985), 45–70. Reprinted in Francis Frascina and Jonathan Harris (eds.), *Art in Modern Culture: An Anthology of Critical Texts*. New York: Harper-Collins, 1992).

Fraser-Jenkins, David. '*Baigneuses* and *Demoiselles*. 'Bathers' in Cézanne, Picasso and Matisse', *Apollo* 45, no. 421 (March 1997), pp. 39–44.

Fry, Edward F. *Cubism*. London: Thames and Hudson; New York: McGraw-Hill, 1966; republished, New York: Oxford University Press, 1978.

Gedo, Mary Matthews. 'Art as Exorcism: Picasso's *Demoiselles d'Avignon*', *Arts Magazine* 55, no. 2 (15 October 1980), 70–83.

Golding, John. 'The *Demoiselles d'Avignon*', *The Burlington Magazine* 100, no. 662 (May 1958), 155–63.

Golding, John. *Cubism: A History and an Analysis, 1907–1914*. Cambridge, Mass.: Harvard University Press, 1988 (3rd ed.); London: Faber & Faber, 1959 (1st ed.).

Golding, John. 'The Triumph of Picasso', *New York Review of Books* 30, no. 12 (21 July 1988), 19–26; reprinted in revised form in Golding, *Visions of the Modern* (London: Thames and Hudson, 1994), 101–18.

Gopnik, Adam. 'High and Low: Caricature, Primitivism, and the Cubist Portrait', *Art Journal* 43, no. 4 (Winter 1983), 371–6.

Green, Christopher. *Art in France, 1900–1940*. New Haven, Conn., and London: Yale University Press, 2000.

Hubert, Etienne-Alain. 'Appendix to Chronology', in *Les Demoiselles d'Avignon*, *Studies in Modern Art* 3 (New York: Museum of Modern Art, 1994).

Johnson, Ron. 'The *Demoiselles d'Avignon* and Dionysian Destruction', *Arts Magazine* 55, no. 2 (October 1980), 94–101.

Johnson, Ron. 'Picasso's *Demoiselles d'Avignon* and the Theater of the Absurd', *Arts Magazine* 55, no. 2 (October 1980), 102–13.

Kahnweiler, Daniel-Henry. *Der Weg zum Kubismus* (Munich: Delphin, 1920); translated by Henry Aronson as *The Rise of Cubism*. New York: Wittenborn, Schulz, 1949.

Laessøe, Rolf. 'A Source in El Greco for Picasso's *Les Demoiselles d'Avignon*', *Gazette des Beaux-Arts*, series 6, vol. 110, no. 1425 (October 1987), 131–6.

Laude, Jean. *La Peinture française (1905–1914) et "l'art nègre": Contribution à l'étude des sources du fauvisme et du cubisme*, 2 vols. Paris: Klincksieck, 1968.

Léal, Brigitte. See Seckel (1988).

Léal, Brigitte. *Musée Picasso. Carnets. Catalogue des dessins*. 2 vols (Paris: Musée Picasso, 1996).

Leighten, Patricia. *Re-Ordering the Universe: Picasso and Anarchism, 1897–1914.* Princeton, N.J.: Princeton University Press, 1989.

Leighten, Patricia. "The White Peril and *L'Art nègre*: Picasso, Primitism, and Anticolonialism', *The Art Bulletin* 72, no. 4 (December 1990), 609–30.

Leja, Michael. "'Vieux Marcheur" and "Les Deux Risques": Picasso, Prostitution, Venereal Disease and Maternity, 1899–1907', *Art History* 8, no. 1 (March 1985), 66–81.

Lomas, David. 'A Canon of Deformity: *Les Demoiselles d'Avignon* and Physical Anthropology', *Art History* 16, no. 3 (Oxford, U.K., and Cambridge, Mass., September 1993), 424–46.

Lubar, Robert S. 'Picasso, El Greco, and the Body of the Nation', in Jonathan Brown (ed.), *Picasso and the Spanish Tradition.* New Haven, Conn., and London: Yale University Press, 1996.

McCully, Marilyn (ed.). *A Picasso Anthology: Documents, Criticism, Reminiscences.* London: Arts Council of Great Britain, 1981; Princeton, N.J.: Princeton University Press, 1982.

Olivier, Fernande. *Picasso et ses amis* (Paris: Stock, 1933). Translated by Jane Miller as *Picasso and His Friends.* New York: Appleton-Century, 1965.

Penrose, Roland. *Picasso: His Life and Work.* New York: Harper & Row, 1973; first published, London: Victor Gollancz, 1958.

Richardson, John. 'Picasso's Apocalyptic Whorehouse', *New York Review of Books* 4, no. 7 (23 April 1987), 40–7.

Richardson, John (with the collaboration of Marilyn McCully). *A Life of Picasso,* vol. 11: 1907–1917. London: Jonathan cape, 1996.

Rosenblum, Robert. *Cubism and Twentieth-Century Art* (rev. ed.). New York: Abrams, 1976; London: Thames and Hudson, 1960 (1st ed.).

Rosenblum, Robert. 'The *Demoiselles:* Sketchbook No. 42, 1907', in Arnold Glimcher and Marc Glimcher (eds.), *Je suis le cahier: The Sketchbooks of Picasso.* New York: Pace Gallery, 1986.

Rubin, William. 'Cézannisme and the Beginnings of Cubism', in William Rubin (ed.), *Cézanne: The Late Work.* New York: Museum of Modern Art, 1977.

Rubin, William. 'Pablo and Georges and Bill', *Art in America* 67, no. 2 (March–April 1979).

Rubin, William. 'From Narrative to 'Iconic' in Picasso: The Buried Allegory in *Bread and Fruitdish on a Table* and the Role of *Les Demoiselles d'Avignon*', *The Art Bulletin* 65, no. 4 (December 1983), 615–49.

Rubin, William. 'Picasso', in William Rubin (ed.), *"Primitivism" in Twentieth-Century Art: Affinity of the Tribal and the Modern* (vol. 1). New York: Museum of Modern Art, 1984.

Rubin, William. See Seckel (1988).

Rubin, William. 'The Genesis of *Les Demoiselles d'Avignon*', in *Les Demoiselles d'Avignon, Studies in Modern Art* 3 (New York: Museum of Modern Art, 1994).

Salmon, André. 'Histoire anecdotique du cubisme', in André Salmon, *La Jeune*

Peinture française. Paris: Société des Trente, Albert Messein, 1912. Excerpts in English translation included in Fry (1966/78); see earlier.

Seckel, Hélène. *Les Demoiselles d'Avignon*, 2 vols. Paris: Réunion des musées nationaux, 1988. Includes Léal, Brigitte. 'Carnets'; de Couëssin, Charles, and Borel, Thierry. 'Images révélées'; Steinberg, Leo. 'Le Bordel philosophique'; Rubin, William. 'La Genèse des *Demoiselles d'Avignon*'; Daix, Pierre. 'L'historique des *Demoiselles d'Avignon* révisé à l'aide des carnets de Picasso'; Cousins, Judith, and Seckel, Hélène. 'Éléments pour une chronologie de l'histoire des *Demoiselles d'Avignon*'; Seckel, 'Anthologie', 'Parole de peintre', 'Témoins'.

Seckel, Hélène. 'Une Étude pour *Les Demoiselles d'Avignon*,' *Poésie*, no. 60 (Paris, 1992), 121–5.

Seckel, Hélène, *Max Jacob et Picasso*. Paris: Musée Picasso, 1994.

Steinberg, Leo. 'Resisting Cézanne: Picasso's *Three Women*', *Art in America* 66, no. 6 (November–December 1978), 114–33; 'The Polemical Part', *Art in America* 67, no. 2 (March–April 1979), 114–27.

Steinberg, Leo. 'The Philosophical Brothel', *October*, no. 44 (New York and Cambridge, Mass., Spring 1988), 7–74. Revised from the two-part piece published in *Art News* 71, no. 5, and 71, no. 6 (September 1972 and October 1972), 22–9, and 38–47. Translated into French in Seckel (1988).

Zervos, Christian. *Pablo Picasso*, vol. II*, VI–supplement to vols. 1–5; XXII–supplement to the years 1903–6; vol. XXVI–supplement to the years 1907–9. Paris: Cahiers d'Art, 1942, 1954, 1970, and 1973.

Index